THE WHALES' JOURNEY

THE WHALES' JOURNEY

Stephen Martin

ALLEN&UNWIN

First published in 2001

Allen & Unwin
83 Alexander Street
Crows Nest NSW 2065
Australia
Phone: (61 2) 8425 0100
Fax: (61 2) 9906 2218
Email: info@allenandunwin.com
Web: www.allenandunwin.com

National Library of Australia
Cataloguing-in-Publication entry:

Martin, Stephen, 1951–.
 The whales' journey.

 Bibliography.
 Includes index.
 ISBN 1 86508 232 5.

 1. Humpback whale—Behaviour. 2. Humpback whale—
 Migration. 3. Human–animal relationships—History.
 4. Wildlife conservation—History. 5. Whaling—History.
 I. Title.

599.525

Set in 11/15 pt Apollo by Midland Typesetters, Maryborough, Victoria
Printed by CMO Image Printing Enterprise, Singapore

10 9 8 7 6 5 4 3 2

Contents

Acknowledgements

A book such as this owes much to many people, and also in this case to two humpback whales, whose ritual dance in the Whitsunday Islands was the beginning point for the research.

At Allen & Unwin, John Iremonger and Ian Bowring added a heroic patience to their initial enthusiasm for the concept. Ian's advice was listened to and I hope incorporated into the final work. Ann Crabb pushed the project along and Colette Vella steered the resulting text through to publication. The close and perceptive attention of editor Karen Ward is particularly appreciated.

Cetacean expert Peter Gill answered my many questions and checked the manuscript. Renowned scientist William Dawbin also assisted the project until his death. His family kindly permitted access to his papers and granted permission to publish extracts from his work. The book is richer for their support. Any errors are, of course, mine alone.

Stan Knowles and Eddie May also granted permission to publish extracts from their work.

My colleagues and friends at the State Library of New South Wales were always helpful, steering me towards possible sources of information with unfailing generosity. The staff of other institutions in which I researched were equally supportive.

The support of family members was a source of inspiration, Pic Willoughby's thoughts on whaling regulations were informative. Valerie Thomas and Gabrielle Porteous helped in more ways than they could imagine. My son Tom showed me his whale books and pointed out material on television. My other son Max ate part of the first draft and liked it. As with all my work, the love and comments of Rebecca Thomas were invaluable.

A note on measures

Over the centuries, the unit for measuring volume of whale oil has changed according to nation or period. The measures are left in the text as indications and a guide to the relationships is produced below.

Gallon

Imperial:	277.4 in^3 = 9.0 lb
US:	231.0 in^3 = 7.5 lb

Barrel

International:	50 US gal = $\frac{1}{6}$ long ton (approx.)
US:	31.5 US gal (except as below)
	49.12 US gal (Antarctic and Australian waters)

Ton

British or long:	2240 lb = 298.7 US = 6 bbl
Metric:	1000 kg = 2204.6 lb = 293.9 US gal

Tun

An English liquid measure of seven colonial barrels, each holding about 30 gallons of oil.

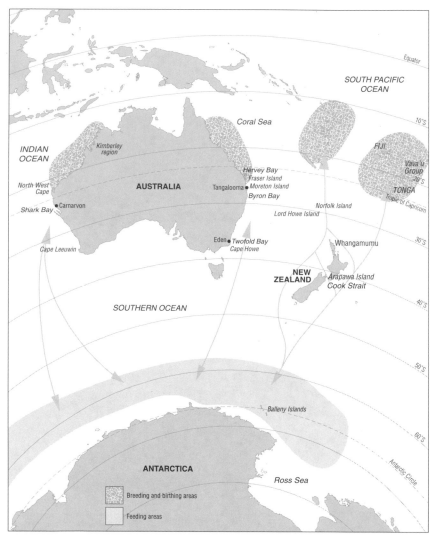

Migration routes of the humpback whales of Australia.

Introduction

The story of the humpback whale encompasses many journeys. Once humpbacks were sought out as prey by whalers, who set out in boats and ships into oceans and along the coasts of islands and continents. At the same time, naturalists, and later scientists, pursued a greater understanding of the whale and its behaviour. Their work contributed to the growing and now widely held perception of the whale as a creature deserving protection rather than slaughter. These human journeys, and the changes in their course, can be traced in the most significant humpback journey, the annual migration.

Like many of the great animal migrations, the rhythms and routes of the humpback whale's journeys embrace the globe. Prompted by seasonal change, the migration is a pattern of movement to which individuals are behaviourally adapted and physiologically bound. They travel in extended processions of small groups or individuals, swimming through oceanic surface currents and near the coasts of lands that guide their migration. Cliffs, gently sloping beaches, reefs and plumes of silt from rivers and lagoons mark this passage. After several months, as the season turns again the humpback whales begin their return. In this constant and cyclical pattern, humpbacks travel between feeding grounds in the polar regions to birthing and breeding areas in tropical seas.

This book is particularly concerned with the journey of the humpback whales that live in the seas and oceans of Australasia, Antarctica and the South-West Pacific. Although only two of the many humpback populations of the world, they stand as an example of the human impact on the world's whale populations and for the optimism which now surrounds their recovery from near extinction.

Over the centuries, humpback whales have been seen periodically in many locations within these parts of the Southern Hemisphere. Whaling captain Charles Scammon once described them as having a 'roving disposition'. In the nineteenth century, humpbacks were caught in seas as far apart as the Arafura Sea, just off the southern coast of the island of New Guinea in August and September and the Cook Strait between the two islands of New Zealand, between April and July. By the late nineteenth century, people knew that humpbacks existed near the Balleny Islands off the coast of Antarctica. During the Antarctic exploratory expeditions of the early twentieth century, humpback whales were seen during the southern summer months in the Ross Sea as far south as the Ross Ice Shelf and near the pack-ice edge which stretches out from the Antarctic coast.

These sightings were made before the impact of the twentieth-century slaughter, at a time when humpback whale populations were vigorous and many times larger than today. While researchers know that the limits of humpback roving are indistinct, they also know that the animals may not be as widespread as during the nineteenth and early twentieth century. However, during the last twenty years, humpback whales have been seen in seas off Tonga and close to the Antarctic coast. It may be that the slowly replenishing humpback population is travelling within the broad limits set by their ancestors.

Interlocked with this remarkable journey is the saga of whaling, which in the late nineteenth and the twentieth century involved periods of indiscriminate slaughter of humpback whales. Although humpbacks were not the first choice of prey for whalers until the late nineteenth century, this species was taken from time to time when other species were not available. The large-scale destruction of humpback stocks began in 1904 with the opening of the modern phase of Antarctic whaling. It was so comprehensive that stocks declined rapidly. Whaling based on Australasian and South-West Pacific stocks began in the nineteenth century and continued intermittently until humpbacks were protected in 1963, when many nations ceased the slaughter. Yet Soviet whalers continued illegally killing humpbacks from the Antarctic seas south of New Zealand and Australia. They finally stopped this killing in the 1970s.

In 1963, the International Whaling Commission banned the killing of humpback whales throughout the world. Humpbacks were killed after this, both legally or illegally as part of a wider indiscriminate whale catch, with records deliberately obscured or falsified. Fortunately, the killing of these animals ceased in time to save individual populations from extinction. Thirty-seven years after the ban, some of the populations are gaining rapidly in numbers. While this is encouraging, other populations remain precariously balanced, with numbers sustaining the population, but not growing as much as they could.

The prevailing human attitude towards humpback whales is now one of affection and respect. The whale is a symbol of human concern for the environments, plants and animals of the world. However people have not always been so protective and this perception has only recently emerged as a dominant view. It is in stark contrast to the prevailing view in the early twentieth century, when many saw the whale as an economic resource, one to be exploited.

This other journey, of changed human attitudes—the passage of human understanding from seeing the humpback as a beast for slaughter to viewing it with respect and even reverence, has come about with our increased understanding of the natural world of the humpback and of the animal itself. A body of knowledge has developed through the careful observation and tabulation of information by natural historians and scientists. It is both contradicted and enriched by the fables and folklore from centuries of human contact and supposition about humpback whales.

Politics, specifically the debates and conflicts of national territory, institutional control of whaling and animal welfare, have been an integral part of the human association with whales. The history of humpback whaling is no exception.

Throughout the history of human contact with the humpback whales, each of these courses has at times intertwined and then separated. Some have waned in importance, while others have strengthened. Despite changes in the attitudes and activities of humans, the humpback whales have continued their migrations, following the timeless paths between birth in the tropical regions to sustenance in the Southern Ocean.

CHAPTER 1

People and whales

In the early eighteenth century, sailors told Jesuit missionary Father Bourzes that the 'River of Milk' or luminous material that appeared in the wake of ships in the Indian 'seas' was the 'Spawn or Seed of Whales'. This fanciful explanation of phosphorescence was discussed more practically in one of the first modern scientific journals, the *Philosophical Transactions of the Royal Society of London* in 1713. Father Bourzes did not know what made these lights but explained 'that the Principle of this Light consists in the Motion of a subtle Matter, or Globules, caused by a violent agitation of different kinds of salts'.[1]

Over 200 years later, in September 1857, Governor Sir William Denison watched humpback whales play as he made his way ashore onto Norfolk Island, off the east coast of Australia. The whales were 'pretty close to the shore' he wrote in his description.

> Their antics were amusing; they would first swim quietly, keeping their tails out of the water, and giving an occasional blow; then all of a sudden, one would raise his fins, two large pectoral fins, at least ten feet [3 m] in length, till they nearly met over his back, and would bring them down upon the water with a crash which covered him with foam, and I almost fancied I could hear the blow at a distance of a mile; after that he would rear himself out of the water till little but his tail remained underneath, and then throw himself backwards into the air just like a rope dancer turning a summersault backwards.[2]

Since people first made contact with whales, descriptions and explanations of their traces and behaviour were incorporated into stories, philosophies and publications. Images of whales appeared in a wide range of books, magazines and pamphlets, the tone of which ranged from serious attempts to describe them and communicate understandings about their behaviour, to popular accounts of whaling. While the forms of publication and their distribution have varied over time, the themes remained remarkably constant.

In popular and scientific literature, whales have been depicted as gods, deliverers of success, failure or destruction, as sources of wisdom, prosperity, nutrition and health. In the early eighteenth century, for example, 'a stranger' told Dutch scientist Antony van Leeuwenhoek that whales' penises were 'used in Physik'. Leeuwenhoek's whaling friend 'presented me with some Slices of a Whale's Penis; adding, that a little of it grated, or cut into small pieces, and boil'd in Milk or Beer, was very good against the Bloody Flux, and that a Neighbour of his, who had been ill of that Distemper a whole Year, was cur'd by the same Medicine'.[3]

Another, more recent example of the believed beneficial effects of whale is the odd cure that was sometimes taken at the whaling community of Eden on the south-east coast of Australia. The heat and moisture retained in the rotting carcass of a whale was believed to be an effective cure for a range of ailments including rheumatism. During the whaling season in the summer, sufferers occasionally visited Eden for the 'cure'. A hole, $1\frac{1}{2}$ m wide and about 1 m deep, was dug in the whale carcass blubber with spades. Into this the sufferer lowered him or her self. Encased to the neck, they remained as long as they could stand the heat and smell. Despite the potential of such a treatment, there were side effects, as one commentator noted in 1908: 'The after effects are not so pleasant; the patient for a week or so gives off a horrible odour, and is abhorrent to man and beast, and a fit subject for prosecution under the "Diseased Animals and Meat Act".'[4]

People's fascination with whales extended to whaling stations and their dramatic operations. Stan Nolan, Whaling Inspector of the Byron Bay whaling station in New South Wales from 1954 to 1962, remembers tourists flocking around the station until the flensing deck, where the whale was cut up for processing, resembled 'the centre court at Wimbledon . . . At one stage crowds grew to such proportions that police officers were needed to control the traffic. Spectators taking photos sometimes got in the way of whaling operations, especially as the whales were being moved, which led to areas being fenced off.'[5]

While many whalers repressed any affection for the animals in sight of the greater goal of survival or profit, they retained a respect for their power and ability. The challenge of hunting one of the world's largest animals attracted some to whaling, but the hard work and disappointment tempered romantic longings. The lure of the great chase was the stuff of story rather than reality.

Unfortunately for those who sought accurate information about whales, the reliability of many popular accounts was questionable. This scepticism has a long history; as indicated by whaling writer Amaso Delano in 1817:

> I had frequent opportunities of being acquainted with many captains who are employed in the whale fishery on this coast. These men are possessed of great share of courage and intrepidity in the pursuit of their business; but are in the habit of boasting of their superiority, when in company, and of exaggerating their exploits.[6]

However, not all records of whaling voyages are such stories. Although many of the journeys were undoubtedly exciting and sometimes dangerous, numerous accounts recorded the details of catch and location, even the technique of whaling. Other accounts included more explicit explanations of the biology and habits of whales. These became the source of important information for natural historians.

During the 1840s, artist and observer Oswald Brierly worked for two and a half years at Twofold Bay, on the south-east coast of

A fanciful image from the dream ride of John Tabor, one of the many entertaining whaling stories of the nineteenth century. Tabor claimed to have ridden on the back of a sperm whale from the waters off southern Africa to his home in north America, and back again. (*Etchings of a whaling cruise,* 1846)

Australia. The whaling technique then practised was bay whaling. When a whale was seen from coastal vantage points, crews in whaling boats chased the whale, first making fast (catching) to it with harpoons, and when close enough to reach out of the boat, killing it with lances. The carcass was then towed back to a small station, where it was butchered and the blubber rendered into oil. Whalebone, the baleen, was cut from the jaws, dried and sent to Sydney for export. Brierly witnessed many whale kills and his writings include striking descriptions of the romance and skill of Australian whaling. Whaling was a form of hunt, and Brierly described the excitement, danger and pathos of the killing of a southern right whale, making reference also to the presence of killer whales, which for decades became a significant aspect of Twofold Bay whaling.

> Whales are often killed [quickly] but in some instances the Boats may be fast to one for many hours without being able to lance it mortally— the whale becomes 'cunning' and is both difficult and dangerous to approach. When dying, the whale frequently goes into what is termed

a 'flurry' when this . . . occurs—[the flurry] scarcely has its parallel in nature—up to a certain point the whale may take killing easily—he rises languidly bleeding copiously from numerous deep clear cut lance wounds, while columns of blood ejected from the blow hole shew that life is rapidly ebbing but in an instant he appears as if electrified with new life and with the possession of his fullest powers, a wild rush to the surface and the enormous tail is whirled high in the air and descends in a succession of rapid blows which beat the water into a wide spreading sheet of foam. In a fresh contortion of agony, the huge black head upheaves, with the lower jaw dropping and the mouth open—followed by a portion of the shoulder and back, the laminae of the whale bone suspended from the great white arch of gum that lines the mouth giving an expression peculiarly hideous. Barnacles encrust the snout and upper part of the head or burrow in groups upon the lips and cluster thickly round the eye—as though trying to put it out—giving a rugged character which adds to its monstrous appearance and the whole emits a peculiar rank odour which strongly pervades the air to leeward.

At this critical moment the Boats are exposed to great danger, for as the whale sometimes turns rapidly in its flurry, it is impossible to tell in what direction he may rush, the Headsman shouts hoarsely to their crews 'stern all' and keep clear of the dying fish, perhaps a boat gets stove or capsized and its crew struggling in the 'white water' amongst fragments of oars and planks and falling gear is in danger of instant destruction from the movement of the whale killers [killer whales] are plunging about in all directions rushing at the whale meeting and worrying it at every turn tearing off portions of the lip and tongue regardless of boats and men—flocks of gulls keep hovering and screaming incessantly overhead with the varying play of light upon everything, the wonderful colours, creamy froth resolving into deepest blue or taking varying tints of crimson and purple from the blood mingling with it, to the unceasing bewildering movement of everything—in some accidental turns the black skin of the whale flashes into excellent light the fluttering of the bright coloured wiffs [flags] which turn and follow and rush through the water with every movement of the whale—all these are scenes of the surroundings of the terrible death which under the glare of the tropic sun on the long swell of the South Pacific is something indescribably exciting and extraordinary . . . and no sport is [comparable] to this.[7]

Although whalers were hunters, and personally and commercially bound to pursue their occupation, they continually witnessed the cruelty of their work. Some, like Thomas Melville, surgeon of the whaling ships *Britannia* and *Speedy* from 1791 to 1796, recognised this and were moved to record their response.

> One cannot help admiring the wonderful contrivance of Nature in constructing the Organs of these monstrous Animals so as to render them incapable of noise. Were they favour'd with the powers of Voice, who could stand the dreadful yelling that must be uttered when labouring under such a weight of pain . . .[8]

The main business of this voyage was sperm whaling, and Melville's journal includes many observations on that species. His attitude to the practice of whaling was businesslike and stemmed from his overall belief in man's centrality in the order of things. It was representative of most European whalers: 'all things are ordered for the good, and for the advantage of Man. It is delegated with a supreme authority over the Animal Creation, and while he does not destroy them in wantoness, or in waste is at full liberty to convert them to his own purposes.'[9]

A related human attitude to the bounty of the world, including the large sized stocks of whales, is one cause for the depletion of so many whaling grounds. People could see the damage being done by overhunting, and yet continued to pursue a course of action in the knowledge that the commercial viability of the whaling ground would be ruined. Whaling on the high seas, in waters not claimed or controlled by any nation, was unrestrained. A whaling captain knew that if he did not take any available whales, another would. These attitudes and practices—principally the pursuit of commercial gain above all other considerations and the unregulated exploitation of a resource over which there is no clear ownership or control—have become known as the 'tragedy of the commons'. They are attitudes still held towards many of the earth's resources, and one of the best documented and oldest examples of their exposition is whaling, and humpback whaling in particular.

The frustration of those, including many scientists and some whalers, who witnessed the slow realisation of this tragedy found some release in twentieth-century international efforts to protect endangered species of whales. However, these efforts, most notably the establishment of the International Whaling Commission, proved inadequate. It was not until a more generalised worldwide concern for the earth and its resources arose in the second half of the twentieth century that effective cessation of whaling saved many species from extinction.

The history of European whaling

Patterns of whaling have changed over the centuries during which men have been killing whales for food and fuel. Initially, whaling was a subsistence form of hunting. When commercial whaling commenced the nature of the enterprise changed and patterns of exploitation began which continued into the twentieth century. Once the whales in a new whaling ground had been exploited beyond further commercial advantage whalers moved on to another region, or to exploit a different species. The development of new techniques and practices changed processes but not patterns and certainly not results. Many species were hunted to near extinction.

The first whaling away from the relatively sheltered coasts and bays was probably undertaken by Bronze Age Norwegians. An early reference to whaling was made in *The voyage of Octher made to the northeast parts beyond Norway, reported by himselfe unto Alfred the famous king of England, about the yere 890.* Octher sailed north as 'commonly the whale hunters used to travel'. He travelled to a land where 'Fynnes' and 'Biarmes' lived. Octher's principal purpose was to 'encrease the knowledge and discoverie of these coasts and countreys, for the more commoditie of fishing of horse-whales, which have in their teeth bones of great price and excellenie: whereof he brought some . . . their skinnes are also very good to make cables for shippes'. The whales, probably narwhales, were not big, and the account continued, 'And as for the common kind of whales, the place of most and best hunting of them is in his owne countrey . . . in the space of 3 days killed threescore'.[10]

[7]

The Basques began systematic commercial whaling from the eighth century when they hunted the Biscayan whale (northern right whale) as it gathered in the Bay of Biscay to breed. It was called the right whale because it was easily found near coasts; when killed the carcass floated and provided ample quantities of oil—it was the right whale to catch. The oil was sold for lighting, baleen (bony plates found in the mouths of filter-feeding whales) and bone were used for implements, and the meat may have been eaten. At first Basque whaling was intermittent. By 1372 the Basques had extended their whaling domain to Iceland, Greenland and Labrador, primarily hunting for whale oil.

The disruption and hunting may have been enough to drive away the whales. As whaling spread north, Basque skills and techniques were passed on to the whalers of Britain, Norway, Denmark and Hamburg (Germany) and the Netherlands. Captain Willem Barents discovered Jan Mayan Island and Spitsbergen archipelago in 1596. Soon after, the archipelago and its coastal seas became a famous whaling region. In 1598 Elizabeth I of England sent a whaling fleet to Greenland. By the late sixteenth century, Basque whalers were crossing the Atlantic to Newfoundland.

As whaling on Spitsbergen grew, conflicting interests of whaling vessels from different nations emerged. The English clashed with the Dutch. In 1618, the coast and bays of Spitsbergen were reserved for ships from particular regions—mainly English, Dutch, Danes, Hamburgers and Biscayans. In 1630 the Dutch established Smeerenberg (Blubbertown) in Spitsbergen. In its peak years, between the 1630s and 1640s, the settlement housed 150 men who serviced the ships that hunted the Greenland right whale (or bowhead). Smeerenberg was closed in the 1660s probably because of colder weather rather than a lack of whales. In a prelude to more widespread open sea whaling, Dutch and German vessels hunted away from the coasts. After a whale had been killed, the blubber was stripped from the carcass while beside the vessel, stored on board in barrels and returned to home port for processing. Putrefaction of the blubber was only a minor problem in these cold seas.

Other European nations established whaling enterprises. In 1768, Frederick of Prussia nominated the town of Emden as a trading centre for oil and baleen. In 1772 the Swedish king provided ships for whaling. The French government in 1784 fitted out six whalers. Russia established settlements on Spitsbergen to undertake whaling.

Americans were also bay whaling in the eighteenth century. The plentiful supply of whales, including humpback whales, off the coast of New England stimulated whaling near Cape Cod, Long Island and Rhode Island. But these stocks were hunted beyond commercial advantage and Cape Cod whaling declined. By 1750 it was practically abandoned.

In 1712, the crew of Nantucket-based Captain Christopher Hussey killed a sperm whale and rendered its carcass into oil. Once word passed around that the oil was better than that from right or humpback whales, whalers turned more readily to the new catch. The sperm whale was more free ranging than the coastal animals previously hunted and whalers went farther across the oceans to catch this species.

The sperm whale also provided ambergris, a substance which was used in the manufacture of perfumes and used by pharmacists, and spermaceti—a very fine oil, much sought after because it burned with a smokeless, odourless flame—taken from the cask or head case of the sperm whale. Ambergris was sometimes as valuable as gold. Sperm whale teeth became ornaments and trinkets for carving.

In the 1760s try works, the brick ovens used to render blubber into oil, were installed on board American vessels and the problems of blubber putrefaction on board a vessel were no longer a restraint on the extent or period of a whaling voyage. Often the voyages were long and the men hunted seals and other types of whale, especially the right whale, as well as the sperm. By 1770 the American whaling fleet had grown to 125 vessels and the localities visited included Brazil, the West Indies, the banks of Newfoundland and the

Cape Verde islands. From 1810 to about 1840, the migrating humpbacks and some fin whales were again the targets of the shore whalers, using bases along the American coast from Maine to South Carolina.

In 1788–90, the *Amelia* of London sailed around Cape Horn and into the Pacific in search of whales. She returned with 139 tons of good sperm oil and whalers quickly moved into the Pacific to exploit the newly found whaling grounds. In 1789 sperm whaling extended into the Indian Ocean. In 1820 an English ship found immense numbers of whales off the coast of Japan and by 1835 there were 100 whaling vessels in those waters.

The sperm whale catch in this period of whaling was high. United States vessels left from eastern seaboard ports such as New Haven and Mystic in Connecticut, Newport and Providence in Rhode Island, and Martha's Vineyard and Nantucket in Massachusetts and sailed to many parts of the world. Although the ships of other nations such as the British vessels also sought sperm whales, United States whaling was the most productive. In 1837, 5 329 138 gallons of sperm whale oil were sold. The success of that year led to an increase in ship numbers and, by 1846, the US fleet was at its highest level— 729 vessels. During the decade 1830–40, 41 241 310 gallons of sperm oil were sold. By the 1880s the catch declined markedly; in 1870–80, 12 819 493 gallons were sold. Even at this return, the known sperm whale grounds were considered overfished.

The whaling vessels of this period were purpose-built for long ocean voyages. They were sturdy vessels with crews of up to 50 men and eight lightweight whale boats. When a whale was sighted, boat crews gave chase, and a skilled harpooner threw a harpoon attached to a long rope into the animal. The whale usually dived and resurfaced, sometimes it fought or fled, dragging the whale boat behind it in what became know as a 'Nantucket sleigh ride'. When the whale was exhausted, a long steel lance was used finally to kill it. The carcass was lashed to the side of the ship, where the blubber was stripped away. This was hauled on board, cut into chunks and fed into trypots, large iron pots used for rendering the carcass into

Working the whale in the mid-nineteenth century. After being stripped from the carcass, the blubber was rendered into oil in large trypots set up on the decks. (Etchings of a whaling cruise, 1846)

oil. Once poured into barrels, the oil was stored below for later sale. Vessels could be at sea for years, returning home only when holds were full. There were many disasters and whaling was a hard and dangerous way to make a living.

This period was a high point in whaling romance and these voyages, of vessels as large as 300 tons, became the focus for the most commonly reported whaling stories. But the knowledge was not all fanciful and the information about whaling grounds and whale habits possessed by many whalers was a commercial asset as well as an enlargement of human understanding. Whaling captains such as William Scorseby and Charles Scammon became widely respected as experts on both whaling techniques and the habits and biology of whales.

During the middle years of the nineteenth century American whaling declined. Other nations' whaling fleets had earlier faltered. The Dutch fleet, so strong in the previous century, had virtually collapsed early in the nineteenth century. The British fleet in the Arctic declined after 1840, due mainly to overfishing of right whales, and the development of new technologies overtaking traditional markets. Known sperm whaling grounds became depleted and new products began to challenge the economic viability of whaling. In 1859 the petroleum industry was successfully developed in Pennsylvania. The new source of fuel for illumination began to affect the price received for whale oil, particularly sperm whale oil. Steel-boned corsets began to replace whalebone corsets, and vegetable oils and gas-fired lamps became commercially available.

Techniques of whaling remained essentially the same for centuries, although there were attempts to improve the tools and procedures. In 1831, Scottish whalers suggested the use of prussic acid on the harpoons to assist the kill. In 1852 the first successful explosive harpoon was invented in Connecticut, USA. The 'bomb lance' consisted of an explosive missile armed with a time-delay fuse which killed or mortally wounded the whale after it had been thrust into the animal's body.

European whaling develops in Australasia

The whaling techniques, traditions and commercial expectations of Europeans and Americans were introduced into Australasian coasts and waters soon after the British established a colony in Sydney in 1788. At this time, deep sea whalers hunting sperm whales were about to spread across the Pacific and Indian oceans, participating in a rapid and destructive growth of the industry. Whaling vessels were off the coasts of Australia and New Zealand in the 1790s. By 1801, when restrictions on trading, including whaling, placed on behalf of the British East India Company were lifted, whalers had fished off many of the Australasian coasts. By 1805, whaling captains were trading with Maori groups in New Zealand. Soon after, Maori became crew.

Australian bay whaling began in Ralph Bay, on the Derwent River, Van Diemen's Land in 1806. The practice spread along southern Australia, from Twofold Bay in south-east New South Wales to the Swan River in Western Australia and to New Zealand. The whalers took whales such as the southern right whale and the humpback whale which migrated along the coasts.

As with shore whaling elsewhere in newly settled territories, a small amount of capital, some basic equipment and luck were required to establish European whaling. Trypots, knives and barrels were essential shore items, and two or more longboats, with harpoons, lances and rope, for the hunt. Buildings were often rudimentary structures, built from local materials.

Inevitably shore and deep sea whaling was affected by the decline in right whale numbers and many stations closed in the 1840s. Other whalers continued to hunt the sperm whales, numbers of which had not declined so rapidly. A small New Zealand fleet operated from Dunedin. In Australia fleets were based in Sydney, Twofold Bay and Hobart. After 1850 the importance of whaling in New South Wales declined until the twentieth century. Hobart, Tasmania remained a whaling centre. In 1859 the port had 27 deep sea whalers employing 680 men.

The products of this whaling were vital for the growing colonies. For a few years, the colony of New South Wales relied heavily on whale products. In 1833 whale oil and bone still formed more than half the exports of New South Wales. The frequent visits of ocean-going whalers, to resupply their vessels, brought much-needed trade to the colonies and their settlements. The small yearly take of whales at those bay whaling operations which survived, helped support a stabilising colony and so develop what seemed to colonial administrators an open and undeveloped land.

Modern whaling

In the late nineteenth century two technological developments—the steam engine and the explosive harpoon—facilitated whaling, heralding the 'modern age'. Both enabled a marked increase in the whale catch.

In 1857, the first auxiliary steam engines were installed in whaling vessels. This enabled the ships to be more manoeuvrable and to go faster, catching faster swimming and previously unsought species such as the fin and blue whales. Two years later the first steam whaling ships were built. In 1863 Norwegian sealer Sven Foyn built a new 25 m steam-driven schooner *Spes et Fides* (Hope and Faith). Foyn's vessel was the first of the modern whale chasers. After many years Foyn perfected the development and use of the harpoon gun. In 1864 he mounted a battery of seven prototype cannon onto *Spes et Fides* and tested them off the county of Finmark. After modifications, in 1868, he killed 30 whales in quick succession.

Modern shore stations, with factories and equipment for processing the increased catch quickly developed. In 1870 the first factory for converting whale flesh into guano was opened at Kirkeö, Norway. By 1887 Norway had twenty companies and 35 ships operating in nearby seas. Shore whaling began in Newfoundland in 1897, and by 1905 there were eighteen stations on the island and nearby. In the late nineteenth century, whaling stations were opened in Japan and in Russia, along the coasts of Siberia. The first modern whaling station on the Pacific coast of America was completed in 1905, at Sechart in Barclay Sound, on the west coast of Vancouver Island. Norwegian Johann Bryde built the first whaling station in southern Africa at Durban opening for business in 1909, and another at Saldanha Bay, opening later that year. Stations were quickly established in the Antarctic and on the coasts of South America, in Brazil, Argentina and Chile, and others in Greenland, the Galapagos Islands, the Faroe Islands and Shetlands.

By 1910, shore-station whaling using modern techniques had become a world industry. Many of these stations were situated at locations known to be close to humpback whale migration routes.

Indigenous contact with humpback whales

Many indigenous peoples living near coastlines relied on the sea to provide additional nutrition. From time to time they feasted on the bodies of stranded whales of all species. Such feasts were an important part of their culture.

In and near Sydney, New South Wales, in sites within view of the sea, Aborigines recorded their relationship with whales in the carved images of whales and men and women. These rock carvings, which may date back thousands of years, were probably sites of religious significance, areas in which a ceremony might entice a whale to strand on nearby shores. In the early 1840s one Aboriginal told geologist Reverend W. B. Clarke that they would 'call the whales and sharks off the coast Uncle [,] and call to them not to go away'.[11]

The feasting from the carcass of a stranded whale was a social occasion. In 1790, two years after the establishment of the British penal colony, a whale carcass stranded at Manly Cove in Sydney Harbour attracted about 200 Aborigines. British military officer Watkin Tench described how the group used shells attached to the end of throwing sticks to cut the flesh from the carcass then 'broiling the flesh on different fires and feasting on it'. A small group of colonists approached them cautiously. The discussion was joined by the Aboriginal Bennelong, who knew them and who was acquainted with Governor Phillip. As the colonists left, the Aborigines brought three or four 'great junks of whale' as a gift, 'the largest of which Baneelon [Bennelong] expressly requested might be offered in his name to the Governor'.[12]

In 1931, journalist James Morgan wrote that the Aborigines of south-east Australia came to Twofold Bay each year for a 'blow out' on whale meat. They would scoop out a large hole in the ground, fill it full of flat stones, make a large fire in it, and then roast the whale meat. Morgan also noted the unverified story of Aborigines actually hunting whales. He quotes the whaler Alex Greig as the source.

An old Aboriginal named Cooper about 50 or 60 years of age who worked for Mr Grieg's grand father, 70 years ago when Mr Greig was a boy, told him that when he was [young], the killers [killer whales] used to round the Hump Back Whales up in the bay, that his people went out in their bark canoes, and filled the whales full of spears untill they were like porcupines, and they killed them and took them ashore, and ate the throat of the whale.[13]

[*15*]

The Aborigines of the district believed that the killer whales which frequented the seas off the coast were spirits of ancestors and called them Beowah. They also believed that the humpback whales were the spirits of old women and called them Jan-dah. Oswald Brierly notes that in one instance, when a humpback killed an Aboriginal whaler, other Aborigines refused to go out whaling for some time afterwards.[14]

Polynesians were familiar with the oceans of the South-West Pacific and included sea animals in their legends. Although they did not actively hunt humpback whales which migrated regularly to nearby seas before the arrival of European whalers, Tongans ate the flesh of stranded animals. They also sought the teeth of sperm whales, which they prized as ornaments and ceremonial objects.

One Tongan legend tells of Lo'au, a chief of ancient Tonga, who, with a group of men, set out on an ocean voyage to look for the limits of the horizon. After a series of adventures and disasters only two were left. One, Kae, landed on a small island and after lighting a fire suddenly found himself to be on a whale which moved away, leaving him floating in the sea. Kae swam to another island, where a large bird lived. When it landed nearby, he lashed himself to the bird's leg.

Soon after, the bird took off and flew far over the sea to a land which Kae recognised as Samoa. He undid the lashings and fell down to the island. Here, he talked with the chief Sinilau, who fed and sheltered Kae.

Sinilau was friendly with two large whales named Tununga and Tonga. Kae was surprised that a man could own and command whales, but he persuaded Sinilau to allow him to return home on the back of the whales.

Sinilau agreed and after a short journey, Kae reached his homeland. The whales asked him to swim ashore and return with Tongan tapa cloth and Tonga oil, as a message to Sinilau that the whales had completed their task. But Kae persuaded them to come closer to shore and the whales went aground. Kae then called on the people to come and kill and butcher the whales. The people killed Tununga, but Tonga escaped.

Tonga returned to Samoa and told Sinilau of the treachery. Sinilau and his men came to Tongatapu one night to capture Kae and seize the bones of Tununga. After returning to Samoa they killed Kae and laid out the bones of Tununga, which they had brought back. They covered the bones, but not the teeth of the whale, which they had left behind, with leaves and medicines. Soon the flesh and skin began to return to Tununga's bones and after nine days it was able to return to the sea.

Tonga's progeny became sperm whales. Those of Tununga, without teeth, humpback whales.[15]

In New Zealand, coastal Maori groups also fed from stranded whales and included them in their mythologies. Images of whales can be seen carved into the decorations of some Maori village storehouses.

The scientist's gaze

Scholars and philosophers have always attempted to describe and explain the natural world and to determine its laws. However, as whales and dolphins spend most of their lives under water, it was difficult for observers to gather reliable data. The only time they could get information was after fleeting glimpses of pods, or when whalers or fishermen sympathetic to their desires provided stories, descriptions or specimens. Sometimes anatomical studies were carried out on whale carcasses stranded on accessible coasts. Despite the difficulties some of the first references to whales and dolphins are illuminating.

The Greek philosopher Aristotle (384–322 BC) noted the lack of knowledge of whales but in his *Historia animalium* described dolphins and right whales and correctly classified them as 'mammals'. 'Thus', he wrote, 'the dolphin is viviparous, and accordingly we find it furnished with two breasts, not situated high up, but in the vicinity of the genitals . . . and its young have to follow after it to suckle'. He also noted that cetaceans, unlike fish, breathe with lungs. He marked the difference between odontocetes (toothed whales) and mysticetes (baleen whales). Mysticetes, he noted, have no teeth but have hairs which resemble 'hog bristles'. Aristotle was aware that dolphins communicated with each other, describing it as a 'murmuring sound'.[16]

With the renewed interest in explanations of the natural world that accompanied the Renaissance, knowledge of whales increased. As naturalists and philosophers continued their work, the informal groups and networks in which they shared knowledge and sought fresh information began to formalise their discussions in more institutionalised form. Scientific societies began to grow throughout Europe. In 1660 The Royal Society for the Improvement of Natural Knowledge was established in England. Now known as The Royal Society of London, it emerged from a complex of mercantile, scholarly and craft traditions and had its aims chartered and regally sealed in 1662 by Charles II. Distinguished men were appointed as Fellows of the Society (FRS), a recognition which signified great achievement in a scientist's chosen field.

John Wilkins and businessman Henry Oldenburg, who had extensive connections in continental Europe, were appointed as joint secretaries. Oldenburg collected information and published the first volumes of the *Philosophical Transactions giving some account of the present Undertakings, Studies, and Labours of the ingenious in many considerable parts of the world*. The coverage of the first volume, for 1665 and 1666, was broad. In his dedication to Charles II, the patron of the society, Oldenburg noted that 'these Glimpses of Light' were 'To spread abroad Encouragements, Inquiries, Directions, and Patterns, that may animate and draw on Universal Assistances'.[17]

The attitudes, assumptions and practices that now constitute scientific method were in their infancy and the process of gathering information about the natural world for these developing 'scientific' explanations and descriptions were not as rigorous as we would see today. Some of these first letters and notices appearing in the *Philosophical Transactions* were observations, straightforward reports of natural phenomena or animals. The first titles reveal the scope: *Optick Glasses; A Spot in the Belts of Jupiter; An Experimental History of Cold* and *Of the New American Whale-fishing about the Bermudas.*[18]

The report, an account of information passed to the author by an 'understanding and hardy Sea-man' is possibly the first account of humpback whales in a scientific journal. The author noted that:

> hitherto all Attempts of mastering the Whales of those Seas had been unsuccessful, by reason of the extraordinary fierceness and swiftness of these monstrous Animals; yet the enterprise being lately renewed, and such persons chosen and sent thither for the work, as were resolved not to be baffled by a Sea-monster, they did prosper so far in this undertaking, that, having been out at Sea, near the said Isle of Bermudas, seventeen times, and fastned their Weapons a dozen times, they killed in these expeditions 2 old Female Whales, and 3 Cubs, whereof one of the old ones, from the head to the extremity of the Tayl, was 88 Foot in length, by measure; its Tayl being 23 Foot broad, the swimming Finn 26 Foot long, and the Gills three Foot long: having great bends underneath from the Nose to the Navil; upon her after part, a Finn on the back; being within paved (this was the Seamans phrase) with fat, like the Cawl of a Hog . . .
>
> The shape of the Fish, he said, was very sharp behind, like the ridge of a house; the head pretty bluff, and full of bumps on both sides; the back perfectly black and the belly white.
>
> The celerity and force he affirmed to be wonderful, insomuch that one of those Creatures, which he struck himself, towed the boat wherein he was, after him, for the space of six or seven Leagues, in ¾ of an hours time. Being wounded, he saith, they make a hideous roaring, at which, all of that kind that are within hearing, come towards that place, where the Animal is, yet without striking, or doing any harm to the wary.
>
> As to the quantity and nature of the Oyl which they yield, he thought, that the largest sort of these Whales might afford seven or eight Tuns if well husbanded, although they had lost much this first time, for want of a good Cooper, having brought home eleven Tuns. The Cubbs, by his relation, do yield but little, and that is but a kind of a Jelly. That which the old ones render, doth candy like Porks Grease, yet burneth very well. He observed, that the Oyl of the Blubber is as

clear and fair as any Whey: but that which is boyled out of the Lean, interlarded, becomes as hard as Tallow, spattering in the burning and that which is made of the Cawl, resembleth Hoggs grease.

One, but scarcely credible, quality of this Oyl, he affirms to be, that though it be boiling, yet one may run ones hand into it without scalding; to which he adds, that it hath a very healing Virtue for cuttings, lameness Etc. the part affected being anointed therewith. One thing more he related, not to be omitted, which is, that having told, that the time of catching these Fishes was from the beginning of March, to the end of May, after which time they appeared no more in that part of the Sea: he did, when asked, whither they then retired, give this Answer, that it was thought, they went into the Weed-beds of the Gulf of Florida, it having been observed, that upon their Fins and Tails they have store of Clams or barnacles, upon which, he said, Rock weed, or Sea tangle did grow a hand long; many of them having been taken of them, of the bigness of great Oyster-shells.

In 1671, when he was 33 years old, the Dutch linen merchant Antony van Leeuwenhoek constructed his first simple microscopes or magnifying glasses. His work was an important contribution to the way in which naturalists of the late seventeenth century saw their world. He was made a Fellow of the Royal Society in 1680. Although he is now remembered for revealing a new world of organisms, some of his microscopic work was on the tissues and other specimens of whales, which he received from people associated with the Dutch whaling industry, including his friend Captain Isaac Van Krimpen.

Leeuwenhoek's published work gradually added to a more rational picture of whale anatomy. Whales' testicles were large, he noted, as big as a 'Firkin of Butter that weighs about a hundred Weight. The same Captain told me also, that the Female of a Whale (on the side of the Uterus, but a little nearer its Tail) has two Nipples, or Teats, which yield Milk, and that he had drank thereof; and he show'd me the Teats, the Diameter of one of which was no more than an Inch and a half, and it was two Inches long, but it was dried hard.'[19]

Using his microscope, Leeuwenhoek examined the flesh of a whale brought to him and:

I cut through the Flesh both cros and length ways, in order to discover the thicknes of its Particles; and after I had cut thin Scales a-cros, they appear'd of a bright red colour; but when I cut them thicker, they were of a dark Red; and when very thick, they were blackish. In this Operation I observ'd, that the small Fleshy Muscles were surrounded with very thin Fibrous Particles, that look'd like little Membranes torn to pieces: And upon several Parts of these little Membranes, there lay Fat, which, when there is a quantity of it together, they call the Train; and these train Particles lay pressed together . . . and many of these Particles were like melted Fat; insomuch, that when I squeez'd the Flesh, the Fat came out at the end of it.[20]

He continued his studies, gleaning from the captain that the whale had three layers to the skin, a thin uppermost layer, the next a layer 'as soft as velvet' and the third and 'undermost is a thick Skin, which we call the Sward'. This layer was whitish and strong—so strong, Leeuwenhoek concluded, that 'in case the Harpoon Iron was struck so deep into the Whale, that the Beard or Hooks thereof did penetrate into the aforesaid white or third skin, it would keep its hold'. Beneath the third layer he noted, was 10 to 15 inches [25 to 38 cm] 'thicknes of Fat'.[21]

In 1725, British naturalist Paul Dudley published a paper that described several species of whale, basing his work on a range of sources, including information from the men and women who owed their livelihood to the careful observation of whale behaviour. His work included one of the first descriptions of a humpback whale.

The bunch or humpback whale is distinguished from the right whale, by having a bunch in the place of the fin in the finback. This bunch is as large as a man's head, and a foot high, shaped like a plug pointing backwards. The bone of this whale is worth but little, though some-what better than the finback's. His fins are sometimes 18 feet long, and very white; his oil much as that of the finback. Both the finbacks and humpbacks are shaped in reeves lengthwise, from head to tail, on their bellies and their sides, as far as their fins, which are about half way up their sides.[22]

British naturalist John Hunter examined many whale carcasses, which he obtained from a variety of sources. In 1787 he published a long account of his research in the *Transactions* of the Royal Society. In this he explained the difficulties he and other naturalists encountered in their work. Once he hired a whaling ship's surgeon to make a trip to Greenland, then a rich whale hunting area. Unfortunately all he received in return was 'a piece of whale's skin, with some small animals sticking to it'. Hunter commented that from 'our unfitness to pursue our researches in unfathomable waters' it would be difficult to obtain information. Marine animals' bodies rot and opportunities to examine preserved carcasses were rare. Reliance on whalers also had its difficulties as he noted:

> Some of these aquatic animals yielding substances which have become articles of traffic, and in quantity sufficient to render them valuable as objects of profit, are sought after for that purpose; but gain being the primary view, the researches of the naturalist are only considered as secondary points, if considered at all. At the best, our opportunities of examining such animals do not often occur till the parts are in such a state as to defeat the purposes of accurate enquiry, and even these occasions are so rare as to prevent our being able to supply, by a 2nd dissection, what was deficient in a first. The parts of such animals being formed on so large a scale, is another cause which prevents any degree of accuracy in their examination; more especially when it is considered, how very inconvenient for accurate dissections are barges, open fields, and such places as are fit to receive animals or parts of such vast bulk.

Despite these difficulties, Hunter managed to examine specimens of porpoise, grampus [killer whales], bottle-nosed whales, 'balaena mysticetes or large whale bone whale', a sperm whale and the narwhale. His compilation of information into an 'order of animals which naturalists have subdivided into genera and species' represents a careful, anatomical and considered tabulation of data about the known cetaceans. It is one of the first and more accurate attempts at classifying cetaceans.[23]

In 1820 one of the most influential whaling books, *An Account of the Arctic Regions*, was published. It is an example of the knowledge and expertise that an experienced whaler could bring to whaling studies, and of the awareness of the destructive capacity of the industry. The writer, William Scoresby, was the son of a noted whaling captain, also named William Scoresby. Scoresby the younger was born in 1789, and by the age of ten had made his first whaling voyage on his father's ship. By 1809 Scoresby had completed studies at Cambridge, where he studied Chemistry, Natural Philosophy and Anatomy. In 1810 he returned to whaling, this time as captain of the *Resolution*. After a successful whaling career, Scoresby moved in 1823 to a career in the church but continued his scientific studies. In 1824 he was made a Fellow of the Royal Society. Scoresby's work concentrated on Arctic whaling and the Greenland whale (bowhead). He was well aware of the excesses of the industry which led to the drop in numbers of bowheads, calling the process 'a violent war of extermination, continued during more than a century'.[24]

Artist and natural observer Oswald Brierly's accounts of whaling also reveal mixed sentiments. Brierly was excited by whaling, despite seeing the practice as a 'terrible cruelty', and intrigued by the great whales hunted by the men with whom he lived.[25] His 'unscientific' yarns as he described them, were published in 1861 in *The Athenaeum, the Journal of Literature, Science and the Arts*, a popular journal which published notes and letters about scientific topics. They are another vivid example of the process by which information about whales from interested observers became more widely known:

> My own observations, extending over some years in the South Seas, lead me to think that different kinds of whales migrate at particular seasons, and that some species have a wider geographical range than is at present supposed. The Right whale taken off Twofold Bay generally makes its appearance on that part of the coast of Australia about the end of May or beginning of June; first one or two, the numbers increasing until the middle and end of September, after which they begin to leave, and finally disappear by the end of November. In some

seasons comparatively few Right Whales are seen; in 1847 they came in much greater numbers than in the three preceding years.[26]

Intriguingly, Brierly notes that the 'Humpback remains upon the coasts all the year round, but appears in greatest numbers during the Right whaling season'. Brierly's notes added to a slowly growing body of knowledge about southern humpback whales. The fact that he recorded the presence of humpback whales all year round may indicate the strength of numbers of these animals in the years before they were comprehensively killed.

In 1864 Dr John Edward Gray published *On the Cetacea which have been observed in the sea surrounding the British Isles*. This list was another of the attempts to gather together information about cetaceans. Gray delivered the paper to the Zoological Society in London, noting the difficulties of working with cetacea.

> There is no series of large animals more difficult to observe and to describe than the Whales and Dolphins; they are unwieldy to collect and compare. It is almost impossible to preserve their skins; and when preserved, they are difficult to keep without deterioration, and on account of their odour . . . They are seen at distant periods, and generally either isolated or each kind and age in the same school or herd. They are only seen alive at a distance from the observer, and generally in rapid motion and under favourable circumstances for study . . . The only chance that the zoologist has of examining fresh specimens of these animals is to watch for their occurrence and hasten to see them while they are in a more or less complete state.[27]

Despite these difficulties Gray and others managed to publish a number of works listing and describing cetaceans. Like many scientists Gray used the bones and skeletons of the whales to classify them into groups.

Scientist James Hector published the results of his work on whales in two papers given to the New Zealand Institute in 1872 and 1874. One of the papers included accounts of the humpback whales found near New Zealand:

The Humpback whales are well known to whalers, but are seldom
molested . . . they roam about the ocean in small herds, seldom at any
great distance from land. They are to be recognised by their having a
short robust form, broad flat-topped head, a low broad dorsal fin or
lump behind the middle of the body, very long pectoral fins, and the
skin of the throat and chest deeply plaited with longitudinal folds.[28]

In the early twentieth century, whale scientists began to see
whaling shore stations as a fresh opportunity to gather more
information about whales. No longer would information be derived
from fleeting examinations of carcasses at sea or washed up on
beaches. Scientists could, in cooperation with the staff of the whaling
station, take measurements of samples, make dissections and build
a large set of data concerning age, anatomy and diet.

Roy Chapman Andrews, Assistant Curator of Mammals at the
American Museum of Natural History was one of many scientists
who took up the new opportunity offered by the development of
shore stations. In 1911–12 he worked in Korea and Japan on different
types of whale and collected specimens for the museum. In 1916,
Andrews published a descriptive account of his work as *Whale
hunting with gun and camera; a naturalist's account of the modern
shore-whaling industry, of whales and their habits, and of hunting
experiences in various parts of the world.*

Andrews noted that this 'new era' of whaling gave

the scientist undreamed of opportunities for the study of cetaceans.
Until shore stations were established, few indeed were the naturalists
who had examined more than five or six whales during their entire
lives. A whale's body begins to generate gases at an astounding rate as
soon as the animal is dead, and within a very few hours becomes so
swelled and distorted that the true proportions are almost lost. Even
trained naturalists did not always take this fact into consideration, and
their descriptions and figures were consequently notable chiefly for
their inaccuracy.[29]

He continued his assessment, discussing the natural variation among
individuals of a particular species, such as skin colour and skeleton:

Quite naturally when these extremes came under the notice of a scientist who had, perhaps, seen but three or four whales in his entire life, they were at once judged to be representative of different species and were given new names. This course cannot be wholly condemned, for under existing conditions it was almost the only one to be followed. Although it did put on record many valuable facts concerning the history of the animals, it also resulted in multiplying nominal species to such an extent that the work of later investigators in separating the valid from the invalid has become a herculean task; quite false conclusions as to the distribution of the various whales were also drawn, which only a vast amount of labour and study can rectify. Whales are such enormous creatures that the ordinary methods used in the study of other animals cannot be applied to them. Instead of having actual specimens before one for comparison, a naturalist must depend almost entirely upon photographs, notes, measurements, and description.

By the establishment of shore stations these difficulties have been largely eliminated. The whales are usually drawn entirely out of the water upon the slip where, before the blubber is stripped off, they can be measured, photographed, and described. As they are being cut in it is possible to make a fairly detailed study of the fresh skeleton and other parts of the anatomy—if the investigator is not afraid of blood and grease. Moreover the great number of whales of a single species brought to the stations allows a study of individual variation, which evidently is greater among some of the large cetaceans than in other groups of mammals.

Andrews concluded that the international spread of shore stations would enable widespread study on the 'distribution, life history and relationships of whales'. He commented on the cooperation of company directors and station managers who 'generously extended the courtesies of ships and stations'.[30]

Andrews' comments and predictions proved to be accurate. With the establishment of scientists at shore stations and the cooperation of whalers a new body of knowledge about whales, and particularly humpback whales, was about to be created.

Until the nineteenth century, little was known of the worldwide migrations of the humpback populations and individuals were found in many of the world's seas. The different populations were often considered by observers to be different species and were classified as such. Not surprisingly, many names were used for these individuals and confusion continued until the turn of the twentieth century, when scientists began to suspect that the humpbacks of the world were one species.

The distinctive hump distinguished it from other whales and one of the first French names for the whale, 'gibbar', has the same Latin root as the French word for hump. In his *Regnum animale* (1756) Brisson, who created the order Cetacea, named the species 'baleine de la Nouvelle Angleteer' probably because of the appearance of the species off New England in North America. In 1871 the German naturalist Georg Borowski latinised the name as *Baleana novaeangliae*. Lacépède removed the humpback from the family Balaenidae, reclassifying it as a balaenopterid, and called it *Balaenoptera jubartes*. In 1846, J. E. Gray established the genus *Megaptera* (Greek for 'big wing') and added *longipinna*. In 1932, the United States biologist Remington Kellog used *Megaptera novaeangliae* (Borowski, 1781) and this name continues to be used for the species.

However, the winning of this knowledge came at a price. Scientists like Andrews were aware of the final cost and he published his concerns. While acknowledging the obvious benefits to science, Andrews added:

> It is deeply to be regretted that the wholesale slaughter of whales will inevitably result in their early commercial extinction, but meanwhile science is profiting by the golden opportunities given for the study of these strange and interesting animals. Thus, the old saying that 'it is an ill wind that blows good to no one' applies very decidedly to the whaling industry.[31]

A journey towards understanding

The humpback whales of Australasia are now less wary of people. Whale watching captains report a growing acceptance of tourist vessels among whales in Hervey Bay, Queensland. Filmmaker Ross Isaacs encountered whales that reached out their pectorals to touch him, and in early October 1996, during the southern migration, astonished and delighted whale watchers near Montague Island on the south coast of New South Wales looked on as a motionless humpback whale allowed a man onto its back while he untangled rope from the whale's body. Later that month a group of people at Coolum Beach, Queensland, freed a humpback whale calf from a shark net and directed it back out to sea towards its mother.

In 1970, a new musical work, *And God Created Great Whales*, was premiered at the Philharmonic Hall at the Lincoln Center for the Perfoming Arts, New York. The genesis of the concert was explained by Dr Roger Payne, who had done much to bring the songs of the humpback whale to public awareness. He had played humpback songs to musician Andre Kostelanetz, who immediately suggested that composer Alan Hovhaness compose a piece inspired by these sounds. Payne's passion for whales is famous. His program notes for the concert convey the sense of wonder and compassion which sums up much of the late-twentieth-century concern for whales. He concluded his piece with a passionate call for the protection of whales, then still being hunted throughout the world:

> In my mind the tragic quality of some of the humpback sounds is loosely bound to the sad fact that the industry is not only killing whales, but with them their songs. We who live on land deal with our world largely through vision, but in the sea, where sound is carried far better than light, hearing is more useful than vision. Thus it is perhaps not so surprising that some of the most beautiful sounds of the wild world come from the sea.[32]

In the centuries leading to this sympathy and understanding, the public perception of whales was determined from whaling stories and whatever reliable information, sketchy though it might be— filtered through to the public imagination from the published scientific and popular works. Understanding was won at a cost—the slaughter of many whales. But ironically, the slaughter was also to bring about a change in human attitudes to the humpback whale. Knowledge of the humpback's anatomy, its parasites, more accurate details of individuals, populations and seasonal migration were gathered through the work on animals caught in massive numbers.

Our knowledge of the characteristics and habits of the humpback whale is still growing, and it is growing on the base of information supplied during the whaling era.

CHAPTER 2

The life of humpback whales

Humpback whales are mammals. They breathe air, are warm-blooded, the females nourish their foetuses via the placenta and suckle their young. 'Hand' bones, remnants of an evolutionary phase when the ancestors of today's whales lived on land, can be seen within their long pectoral flippers.

Scientists today classify whales and dolphins into the mammalian order Cetacea. The word cetacean has its etymological roots in 'cetus', the Latin derivative of the ancient Greek word 'ketos', meaning 'big fish'. Cetaceans are further divided into two suborders: the Odonto-cetes, toothed whales such as sperm whales, dolphins and porpoises; and the Mysticetes, or baleen whales. Along with other members of this suborder, humpback whales have baleen, a set of plates or combs of keratin attached to their palates, which act as sieves for straining out food. Within the Mysticeti, taxonomists have devised three fam-ilies: humpbacks are placed in the family Balaenopteridae (rorquals—those whales with baleen and grooves along their throat). The rorquals have shorter baleen plates than other Mysticeti, such as the right whale, and range from the small, 10 m minke whale to the very large blue whale, at over 30 m long—the largest mammal thought to have ever lived. The humpback genus is *Megaptera* (big wings) and species *novaeangliae*, 'New Englander' a name that marks the place in North America where humpbacks were first commercially exploited.

The oceanic world

Humpback whales live in the dense, fluid environment of the world's oceans. The effects of gravity are greatly reduced by this density and the consequent buoyancy is an advantage to the large animals. They appear weightless as they move with grace and balance through the sea. The two main boundaries of the humpback's environment are the shallower sea floors with adjacent coastal landforms, and the surface of the water. The whales are familiar with the surface. They break it often, to breathe, to see and to play. As they play they may 'breach', rising almost clear out of the water before crashing back against its substance. Near beaches, swells rise and fall, and the whales must be careful to avoid being washed too far inshore.

Ocean currents and eddies also define the humpback's environment. Layers of sea water move in long currents and waves. Warm upflows and cold sinks of water rise and fall across these layers. Pushing, turning, mixing, eddying through undersea valleys, over mountain ranges or around peninsulas, currents change in intensity, temperature and flow strength.

Light passing into the sea also changes. Affected by weather and the cycle of day and night, it gradually loses its luminosity as it filters through to the depths. On clear days, the sunlight appears solid, emanating from a white gold ball at the surface. It splinters down, refracted through surface ripples and waves. As storms wash over the surface of the sea, the strength of the light diminishes to shades of grey and jade. At night, the light is silver, and changes in intensity in concert with the waxing and waning of the moon.

In the higher latitude feeding grounds, the summer daylight is constant, varying only with cloud cover and sea water density. As the season closes and the length of daylight shortens, the humpback whales begin their staged departure for the tropics, where daylength is more evenly divided into dark and light. The subtle but constant, and therefore reliable, changes in daylength are a natural system against which humpbacks—if unconsciously—judge when to continue the migratory movements.

Sound surrounds the whales. The songs and noises of other whales, chatter of dolphins, clicks of shrimp, the wash of undersea currents and crash of coastal waves are familiar characteristics of their environment. And increasingly, humpback whales accommodate the noise from the engines and propellers of large and small vessels that move across the surface of their world.

The migratory journey

The humpback whales of the east Indian Ocean migrate between a region of the Southern Ocean and the sea off the coast of north-western Australia. When whaling managers first divided maps of the seas around Antarctica into sections, this region, between longitudes 70°E and 130°E, became known as Area IV and the humpbacks of this sector Area IV whales. Area V humpbacks, those from the adjoining area between 130°E and 170°W, are thought to migrate in two or more streams. One travels to the east coast of Australia and north to the protected shallow waters of the Great Barrier Reef off the north-east of the continent. The other main stream swims to New Zealand, on to the islands of New Caledonia, Tonga and Fiji. The precise migratory routes of these whales is not known. In the past, before twentieth-century whaling destroyed most of the stocks of humpback whales of these areas, there was a limited intermingling of whale stocks. Area V whales were found in Area IV. Others may have crossed from New Zealand to the seas off Queensland. It was even suggested that individuals might cross the equator.

The migration of humpback whales is the longest yet documented of any mammal. The humpbacks of Area V, for example, may migrate from near the Balleny Islands off the coast of Antarctica to the tropical seas of the islands of Fiji, a journey of well over 5000 km. On the other side of the hemisphere, one humpback was observed at its feeding grounds near the Antarctic Peninsula and, less than five months later, was seen again at its breeding grounds off the coast of Columbia. The shortest swimming distance between these locations is 8334 km.

Humpback physiology

At first sight humpback whales appear large and thickset. At maturity, females can be 19 m long and males 17.5 m. A fully grown female is usually larger than the male and can weigh 45 tonnes. The head is large, taking up one-third of the body length. The body is thickest at the middle, with a fleshy 'hump' on the back, and tapers towards a large, broad tail. The humpback underjaw extends forward beyond the upper jaw.

One small dorsal fin sits on the fleshy hump. It is this hump, showing prominently as the whale curves in a dive, which gave rise to the name humpback. As the whale submerges slowly, the elegant tail is often the last part of the body to be seen. It remains visible momentarily, like a marker before the animal slips below the surface.

Among the world's humpback whale populations, pigmentation varies. In the Southern Hemisphere, the humpbacks are usually black or dark grey or brown, and white. The back and sides of the body and the back surface of the flippers and tail flukes (tail fins) are black or dark grey. White extends from the belly up the side of some individuals. The underside of the tail flukes is white with a wide range of individual markings such as spots or shapes. There are also variations within specific populations—an all-white male is seen periodically off the east coast of Australia.

Humpback whales have long pectoral flippers, about one-third of their body length. The flippers are shaped like aircraft wings, allowing for greater ease in swimming. Nine rounded callosites (hard bumps) are on the forward edge of the flippers. These knobs coincide with the digital joints of the 'fingers', now bony structures within the flesh of the flipper. The graceful 'arms' are rich in superficial blood vessels, suggesting that they are used in modifying heat exchange,

A signal and means of propulsion, the tail of the humpback carries unique markings: these are used by researchers to identify individuals within populations. (Brett Williams photograph)

a vital part of the whale's physiology as it moves between cold and warm seas. Once described as 'angels' wings', they are always moving; balancing, guiding, communicating whereabouts and emotions, protecting young and clasping.

The flexible and firm tail has many functions. It is a balance, a weapon, a turning aid and an agent of communication. There are no bones in the tail, which is composed of masses of connective tissue beneath a layer of flesh and blubber. The tendons that drive the base of the tail diverge into countless branches, which spread power and flexibility throughout the flukes. Using massive muscles connected to the spinal column, the animals sweep their tails up and down against the water, propelling themselves forward with a measured, flowing motion.

Humpbacks are 'surface' dwellers and rarely dive to depths below 100 m. Their ability to swim with a minimum of turbulence is facilitated by their streamlined shape. As they swim, water flows along their bodies almost without friction or drag. When swimming leisurely, the humpback whale moves at 3.5 knots to 5 knots. Females accompanied by calves swim at about 3 knots, while the average migration speed is between 1.3 knots and 3.6 knots. When chased, a humpback may accelerate up to 9 or 10 knots.

The small bumps on their large heads, and on their lips, chins and snout, are tubercules surrounding the base of the few hairs which remain as a vestige of the typical hairy covering of mammals. Arranged in a characteristic pattern, these fine hairs are about 38 mm long, although only 13 mm protrudes from the base.

Although the sexual organs of both male and female whales are tucked away in genital slits, it is easy to determine the gender of humpbacks by examining the genital areas. Females have a lobe known as the 'hemispherical lobe', shaped like half a melon, at the end of the genital area. The female has labia and a clitoris. They also have raised mammary slits either side of the genital area from which the nipples protrude when a calf is feeding. By contrast the male genital area is flat and has no lobe. The penis is enclosed within a sheath, and at rest is withdrawn within the body. The testes, also within the body, are large. On a mature male they can weigh 7–9 kg.

Sensitive skin covers the blubber of humpbacks. When the skin is exposed to the sun for prolonged periods it turns dark and peels. It is fast-growing, which may also assist the animal get rid of barnacles. The blubber is firm and is made up of clusters of tightly packed connective fibres with large oil-filled cells in the interstices. In living blubber, the networks of blood vessels which criss-cross the fatty matter allow a gradual heat loss. Blubber is a good insulator and thickness varies from season to season. Humpbacks lose about one-third of their body weight during the winter when they are not consuming vast quantities of food. Rarely more than one-third of total body weight, the blubber is thickest on a humpback around the middle and towards the tail. It is thinnest on the flippers and tail and near the head and mouth.

The buoyancy provided by the sea supports a whale's weight, reducing the importance of a firm skeleton to carry body weight. Whale bones are sturdy and light. They have a spongy, weblike structure, with an oil-rich marrow. The total weight of a whale skeleton is about 17 per cent of the body weight. The humpback has 53 vertebrae ranging in size from small bones near the tail to large, thick vertebrae at the neck. The skull, with the large upper jawbone that stretches out like a broad beak, is from 2 to 5 m long and may be 2 m wide. It is around this central, slightly arched frame that the remainder of the bones are attached. Fourteen ribs curve down as a protective cage for the internal organs. Measured along the curve, the largest ribs are from 3 to 4 m long.

The bones of the pectoral flippers, the 'forelimbs', are attached to a fan-like shoulder-blade. Although there is no external evidence of them, internal examination of the humpback skeleton reveals vestigial pelvic bones and hind limbs. Two curved bones about 45 cm long are the only traces of the pelvic girdle, and these bones are embedded in the body wall of the animal. Attached to each there is a small knob of cartilage which is described as a femur. This is the last remnant of a hind limb, which the animal must have used before it returned to the seas millions of years ago. External rudimentary hind limbs have been found in humpback embryos and sometimes a humpback whale has been found with the more developed hind limbs, a throwback to a previous age. One specimen, found by American scientist R. C. Andrews, had hind limbs which extended 1.3 m outside of the body, and which contained bones identified as tibia, tarsus and metatarsal, all bones of the mammalian lower leg and foot.[1]

The humpback brain is about 60 cm in circumference and 22 cm long. Its average weight is 5 kg although one was weighed at 6.8 kg. The important pituitary gland, 3 or 4 cm long, lies nestled in its own recess beneath the brain. The whales have well-developed sensory systems, to interpret and analyse their world. They see the life around them, they feel the force of the currents and the surge of the waves against their skin. They regulate migratory timing in response to the changes seen in daylength. A tactile sense is fundamental for their communication and socialisation.

In a sea alive with noise, humpbacks have good hearing. They do not have external ears, but a tiny opening near the eye leads to a system of sinuses and bones which are the inner ear, connected to auditory regions of the brain by a thick nerve. The narrow canal to the inner ear is blocked by an accumulation of wax and shedded skin cells. The ear plug builds up, layer upon layer, rather like the strata of sedimentary rocks; scientists use the 'laminations' in the ears as an indicator of age.

Unlike some other cetaceans such as dolphins and sperm whales, humpbacks are not generally thought to use echolocation, although some researchers believe that it is a possibility and that echolocation would enable humpbacks to assess the location of potential partners, antagonists, food and the shape of immediate topography.

Humpback whales make many sounds, both in the water and in the air: some are indistinct to human ears and as yet unexplained by researchers, others are thought to be social; blowing, wheezing, bellowing and groaning. Some sounds are made through the nostrils as the air is expelled. Muscles change the flow of air expelled, producing a variety of noises from the commonly heard whoosh as the whale breathes to a whistling sound. Male humpback whales create a 'song', the purpose of which is probably a mating signal, but which may also serve as a territorial or migratory call.

A Tongan whaler recalled hearing a calf making noises described as a 'mournful lowing' as it followed the carcass of its mother being towed into the Tongan island of Vava'u. Feeding humpbacks have been described as grunting, yelping and snorting. On a moonlit night in July 1993, scientist R. Paterson heard a sound like a 'subdued foghorn' from whales migrating north past Cape Moreton in southern Queensland. In September 1992 he heard sounds from humpbacks migrating south. He described these as 'similar to those made by lowing cattle'. Much earlier, in October 1980, he watched as a south-bound humpback 'raised its head from the sea on a number of occasions and made a barking noise'. This noise, also described as a 'yap', is made when singing whales surface to breathe.[2]

Underwater vision is important for humpbacks which live an important part of their lives in relatively shallow, well-lit waters, near a variety of reefs and landforms. They can probably also see through air and often 'spyhop'—hang vertically in the water with their heads exposed—watching people in boats or landforms. The eyes, about 102 mm in diameter, are near the corner of the mouth in the middle of the head. A film of thick mucus protects the eyes from the water. They have elastic lenses and strong surrounding muscles that can be moved to adjust the lens to function in either air or water. The enlarged pupils collect large amounts of light in the dark ocean depths.

Like other cetaceans, humpbacks have only a rudimentary sense of taste. Mysticetes may have retained a sense of smell and some researchers claim that they use this to find concentrations of the tiny shrimp-like crustaceans commonly called krill.

Humpbacks may be guided in their migrations by use of the sun's position, a combination of changes in landforms and the sensation induced by reactions to changes in terrestrial magnetism—a vast network of magnetic lines which encompass the earth—and crystals of magnetic iron oxide, or magnetite, stored in their brains. As they are guided along their migratory paths by their mothers, humpback calves may learn the routes, memorising the geomagnetic patterns and the shape of coastal and undersea landforms as reference points.

Usually the first people see of a humpback is the distinctive 'blow' as the whale surfaces to breathe. The blow, expelled from two nostrils on the back of the head, extends for 2 to 4 m into the air and appears as a bushy, misty column. The whale has strong muscles attached to its diaphragm to propel as much exhaled air out of its lungs as possible. When a humpback blows, it forces a full column of pulmonary gases, such as oxygen, nitrogen and carbon dioxide mixed with water vapour into the air. The mixture also contains tiny particles of oily mucus from the animal's breathing passages and air sinuses, an ingredient that may account for the fishy smell sometimes attributed to whale blows. Immediately after exhalation, the whale refills its lungs before submerging. Depending upon the strength of the wind, the blow may hang briefly before dissipating, providing the onlooker with a beautiful trace.

When storms arise at sea and the swells grow, breathing becomes more of an effort and at times can be hazardous. Cetacean expert Roger Payne watched a humpback swim through 10 m seas, worked up by a 60 knot wind. The storm was so intense that he could see only a continuous spray at what normally would be the surface. To avoid inhaling this mixture of sea and air, the humpback waited until the steepest face of a large swell formed and then took a breath while emerging from the wave and before crashing into the trough. Then it expelled the air and took the next breath. Payne wrote that the sound of the forceful inhalation could be heard above the scream of the wind.[3]

When resting or sleeping, especially in the warmth of tropical waters, humpbacks breathe about once every 30 seconds. They sleep in short bursts, lying at the surface, stretched out, with the broad tail flat, flippers moving slightly to maintain balance. However, while asleep they remain alert. As humpback breathing is thought to be voluntary, the animals may need to be wakeful, monitoring and controlling this action as they rest.

Whale lungs are not lobed but have an abundance of elastic tissue, thick pleurae and alveoli. There are more alveoli in whale lungs than in other mammals and two layers of capillaries, an arrangement that increases the efficiency of the gaseous exchange which is the fundamental process of breathing. Each breath taken is more efficient in that more of the residual air—that air which is not expired on exhalation—is pushed out of the lungs than in other mammals. In this way more fresh air can be drawn into the lungs and this enables a deeper and longer dive. A humpback can remain submerged for 3 to 10 minutes, or in extreme circumstances up to 30 minutes.

Whales, including humpback whales, have other mechanisms for maintaining oxygen reserves while diving. While underwater whales retain oxygen in the muscle tissue and blood as well as in the lungs. They have a greater number of red blood cells per unit of blood than humans—it is therefore richer in haemoglobin. Whale muscle contains myoglobin, which stores oxygen. During a long dive, oxygen supplies are cut off to all organs except the brain and heart. The circulation is cut off from muscles used in swimming. These muscles then tap into the oxygen reserves stored in the myoglobin.

While diving, the heart beat slows, which also restricts the flow of blood and it has been suggested that the blood flow can be directed to the brain. In whales, selective circulation is enhanced by the retia mirablia ('wonderful network'). This tangled network of blood vessels, located between the ribs and near the spine, acts as a reservoir of oxygen. When a whale dives for an extended period the oxygen stored in the network re-enters the circulation and thus keeps alive areas which would otherwise fail.

The heart of a 12 m humpback is 1.2 to 1.5 m long, and the dorsal aorta is over 60 cm in diameter at the connection with the heart. A small child could crawl through the aorta and into the heart.

Humpback whales are predators, consuming enormous quantities of krill during powerful and lengthy bouts of feeding. While most of this feeding takes place in the Southern Ocean, Southern Hemisphere humpbacks are known to 'snack' feed or opportunistically feed off the east coast of Australia at Eden, off the south-east coast of Tasmania and at Foveaux Straits, New Zealand, and may do so at other locations. There are recent reports of whales feeding off Fraser Island, Queensland.

The world's humpback whales are not restricted to eating krill and other forms of zooplankton. Northern Hemisphere humpbacks have been known to eat capelin, anchovy, cod, herring and mackerel. In the Southern Hemisphere humpback whales have been reported feeding on pilchards and small shrimp as well as the massive consumption of Southern Ocean krill. The feeding is persistent. The whales lunge into the mass of krill or fish with a forceful determination. Any small animal in the way will probably be swallowed. One humpback examined in the North Atlantic was found to have six cormorants in its stomach and a seventh stuck in its throat.

It has been estimated that when feeding on adequate supplies of krill in the Southern Ocean, a humpback whale will consume about 2000 kg of food a day. About 2 per cent of this will be used to build blubber reserves.

Like all rorquals, humpback whales are filter feeders, sieving food from the sea through triangular fibrous plates of keratin, called baleen. An average of 330 pairs of plates hang—from 1 to 2 cm apart—from the upper palate on either side of the humpback's enormous mouth. The plates vary in length but the largest may be 63 cm long and 4 cm wide. The smallest side of the triangular section is attached to the upper palate. The longest, which face the inside of the mouth, is frayed out into bristles. These become entangled with those of adjacent plates, resulting in a coarse matted inner surface. This mat of bristles is an effective sieve.

The skin under the lower jaw of the humpback is ribbed or corrugated, about 24 pleats extending down past the chin and well behind the flippers to the middle of the body, an adaptation that allows for the stretching and ballooning of the throat. When feeding they take in large mouthfuls of water and plankton and by pressing their tongues against the roof of their mouths expel the water, straining the food through the baleen. Once the water is strained the food is swallowed.

The humpback throat is narrow. The mass of krill and other plankton is swallowed without any form of chewing down into the first of a four-chambered stomach, where it is probably ground down into a more digestible form. In the second chamber peptic glands provide acids, before the food is passed into a third and large chamber, a pyloric chamber and then into a bulge in the intestine, where the food receives the pancreatic fluid and bile. The humpback intestine is over 60 m long, with a caecum and colon as in land mammals.

A whale's kidneys are large, to assist with the processing of salt water and food and to filter wastes. They are compound, each section being composed of a large number of smaller kidneys, which are joined by connective tissue and collecting ducts. Whales do not drink but obtain water from their food and from the water that passes into their body through osmosis. They secrete a highly concentrated urine.

In common with all species of whales, humpbacks have parasites. Often barnacles grow on their bodies, and clusters can be seen near the point of the lower jaw, where more than a hundred may be attached, or smaller clusters near the genital slit. The commonest barnacle found on humpback skin is *Coronula diadema*, which is about 5 cm across and 3.8 cm high. They are also found on the forward edge of the flippers and on the tail flukes. The barnacles are firmly attached to the skin. The bond is so strong that at the Perano whaling station in New Zealand, they were levered off with triangular-headed iron bars before the carcasses were flensed (stripped of blubber), in order to avoid any chance of damage to the flensing knives. Attached to the *Coronula* are *Conchoderma auritum* (stalked barnacles). Growing to 101 mm long, these animals hang like tassels from the *Coronula*, those under the whale's chin sometimes giving the appearance of a scraggy beard. The barnacles feed on the micro-plankton which passes by as the whales swim through the water. Some are seasonal infestations, and drop off as the whales move north into warmer seas.

Sometimes the load of barnacles is heavy. One unfortunate humpback examined by a scientist was carrying over 450 kg of barnacles. Humpbacks have been observed scratching themselves against rocks or outcrops of coral, and it is thought that this behaviour is to rid themselves of the infestations of barnacles. One casual observer at the rock-enclosed lagoon at Shelly, Port Stephens on the east coast of Australia described hearing the satisfied noises of humpbacks scratching themselves as 'splashing noises and gurgles and grunts, like a big contented dog rubbing an itchy spot'. This lasted for an hour before the whales swam off.[4]

There are other parasites, both on and within the humpback whale's body. Small crustaceans such as *Cyamis boopis*, about 7 mm long, gather among the barnacles. They have adapted well to the slow pace of the humpback swimming and hang on with feet so sharp they leave a tiny prick on a human hand. They feed mainly on the dead skin of the whale. Remora, or sucker fish, sometimes attach themselves to humpbacks. Often individual humpbacks are seen with small round white circles on their flesh, usually on the tail or flippers. These are the tooth marks of the 'cookie cutter' shark, a shark which takes a small bite out of the whale. The whales have internal parasites. One researcher found roundworm reaching to 1.2 m in length in the kidneys, other species of worm in the stomachs and even in the baleen, and numerous hookworm in the intestines of whales he dissected at Cook Strait, New Zealand.[5]

Behaviour and social life

On 21 October 1955 off the east coast of Australia, two officers aboard the cargo ship *Sibajak*, W. Bannan and T. J. Hermans, watched in amazement as humpbacks turned a series of somersaults, involving a bellyup roll out of the water, dive, circle and roll again. The motive for this behaviour remains a mystery but it may have been sheer exuberance.[6]

The explanation of animal behaviour is fraught with the confusions of attributing human-like motivations and emotions to animals. In the case of whales the realistic explanation of whale behaviour is obscured by centuries of myth and story. However, despite these difficulties and those of observing creatures that live underwater, a coherent, if generalised picture of many aspects of humpback whale behaviour and social life is emerging.

Swimming both night and day, humpback whales migrate in small groups or pods, and their relationships and movements north or south are dictated by sex, age, maturity and state of pregnancy. The migration is not a simple movement; the behaviour of individuals and pods is complex. Bonds between individuals appear to be loose and it seems

A breach, such as this one off the coast of Queensland, is one of the most dramatic forms of humpback behaviour. (Mark Simmons photograph)

that the strongest bond is that between cow and calf. Although courtship rituals have been observed, humpback whales do not mate for life. However loose these bonds may be, there is evidence of a form of 'companionship'. The whales have been observed supporting injured animals under the surface for up to 40 minutes. While being hunted both sexes came to each other's assistance. In feeding grounds, where groups of twenty have been observed, the imperative of food draws them into forms of social behaviour and cooperative feeding.[7]

Although researchers do not understand all aspects of humpback communication, they are aware that the whales communicate aurally, physically and visually. The whales hear the splashes and crashes of pectoral and tail slapping and the booming sound of other whales as they crash back into the water after a breach. Tail slapping is sometimes a defensive warning: the noise is clearly heard by others and the broken water is also a sign. Males defending themselves against an attack will sometimes blow a network of bubbles which acts like a smokescreen to confuse the attacker. The screen is also used as a threat to competitors for a female. They use their bodies and long sensitive flippers to protect calves, to feel and in the case of fighting males, to barge and hit opponents. Humpbacks may give their partner a playful slap with a pectoral fin.

Play is an accepted term for animal behaviour which brings no material benefit, and is not concerned either with the capture of food or sex relations. Many mammals such as dogs and monkeys play and it is reasonable to attribute no further motive to some humpback behaviour than play or enjoyment. Humpbacks are known to be curious. Young whales may play to learn. They act out behaviours mimicked from adults in particular situations as a means of becoming familiar with the 'rules' of a particular group.

Most animal species display some form of body language and that of the humpback whales seems to be complex. Every position or every gesture may have a meaning. After many hours of patient observation, researchers are beginning to classify and understand some of this communication.

Of the many behaviours of the humpback whale, breaching is the most spectacular. It seems effortless for the whale, which, after a few powerful sweeps of its tail flukes, bursts out of the water, hangs in the air momentarily, and flops backwards or sidewards onto the surface. A whale may only emerge half out of the water in a breach but on rare occasions will it leave the water completely. At the top of a breach, the whale's head could be 15 m above the surface. A breach may be repeated several times and humpbacks have been seen to breach over 100 times.[8] The reason for breaching is not completely understood and it may have several purposes. It could be a way of looking around, or a method of scaring or intimidating enemies or male competitors. It may also be a way of dislodging barnacles. A humpback calf will breach many times, part practice and part simple enjoyment of power and freedom, like a human child enjoying a slippery slide into cool water.

The tail and long pectoral fins of the humpback whale are significant indicators of mood or presence. Humpbacks 'lobtail' when diving steeply, displaying the uniquely marked tail for a while before slipping completely underwater. The tail is used as a warning or sign of location. In a full tail slap, often interpreted as a warning, almost one-third of the body is raised out of the water and brought forcefully down against the surface with a loud slap and splash. Humpbacks swim on their sides with the long pectoral fin extended in the air. While this behaviour may be associated with heat regulation, it is also a sign. They slap their pectoral fins against the surface, another action which creates noise and splash, making their presence known.

'Spyhopping', a behaviour wherein the humpback puts its head out of the water and leaves it there for up to 30 seconds, is interpreted as investigative behaviour. With the head out of the water, the animal may turn around in a full circle. Humpbacks spyhop near tourist vessels and near obstructions like reefs.

These behaviours occur at the surface. But a humpback spends more than 70 per cent of its life under the water and much of its behaviour is acted out in this other world. The glimpses and sightings of these animals underwater reveal consummate swimmers, balanced and buoyed by their medium, twisting and arching through the seas, using subtle changes and flicks of the tail and fins to balance, touch and glide. They will swim slowly to the surface, head first, the flat beak-like head looming out of the depths. They will swim together, calf at the back of its mother, another sometimes on top in a sort of aquatic triad. Researchers have only recently begun to closely observe these underwater behaviours and to analyse their meanings.

Despite their size and the mysteries of their underwater lives, humpbacks have charmed observers for years—as much as they did whaling captain Captain Charles Scammon in the years before 1874, when he wrote:

> Even when beneath the sea, we have observed them just 'under the rim of the sea', alternately turning from side to side, or deviating in their course with as little apparent effort, and as gracefully as a swallow in flight.[9]

CHAPTER 3

Preparing for the journey

T he Southern Ocean surrounds the continent of Antarctica.
Uninterrupted, it sweeps west, building sometimes into wild
storms with large swells, and north into the large oceans of the
Southern Hemisphere. At times it is calm and sunlit, at other times
blanketed with fog. In some places, close to the Antarctic coast, it is
covered with sheets of pack-ice or ice shelves that extend out from
the continent's glaciers. Each winter, the sea surface freezes and great
plains of ice extend far from the Antarctic continent out over the
ocean. The months of maximum sea ice coverage are between
September and October, the later months of winter. There is variation
in the extent of the winter pack-ice but its northerly limits are
between 65°S and 60°S.

The Southern Ocean feeding grounds

Despite the seemingly hostile environment, the Southern Ocean
supports a profusion of wildlife, ranging from microscopic plankton
to seals, sea elephants and penguins. Seabirds such as petrels and
albatross feed upon the life in the Southern Ocean, from small droplets
of fat or refuse on the water or the large krill swarms, to the abundant
quantities of squid and fish. Whales, like the humpback whale,
migrate south into the Southern Ocean to feed, some swimming close
to the ice edges. Blue whales migrate and single male sperm whales
travel south. Others, such as the minke whale, may remain close to

Antarctica throughout the year. They are adapted to the icy conditions of winter, living out the season in the gloomy light, cold and pack-ice. Killer whales live in the Southern Ocean capturing mainly penguins and seals for food. Fin whales are also common, and are often seen in association with humpback whales.

The pattern of life in the Southern Ocean is affected by the seasonal rhythm of advancing and retreating ice. The pack is rarely static, it is broken by storms, and winds may blow pieces farther out to sea. Long leads, channels of open sea in the pack, open and close. Polynas, open spaces inside the pack-ice, often occur and persist throughout the year. Icebergs, some of them enormous, calve from the ice shelves and glaciers of Antarctica into the Southern Ocean. Driven by currents and winds, they float around the continent till they run aground, or north till they melt and break up.

During spring and early summer, the daylight lengthens and intensifies. As temperatures slowly rise the pack-ice melts and the plains of ice retreat to their minimum range between February and March. The combination of increased light and the high level of nutrients such as phosphates and nitrates in the Southern Ocean, constantly mixed and stirred by currents and storms, make a rich environment. Phytoplankton, tiny plants which have spent the winter in the hollows, tunnels and cracks in the underside of the sea ice are released into the water and begin to grow and reproduce, utilising the sun's energy through photosynthesis. The phytoplankton blooms are dense and can cover thousands of square kilometres. They are a source of food for zooplankton; tiny animals, especially krill, which in turn is food for fish, seals, penguins and whales. Krill live in all of the world's oceans, but two main species inhabit the Southern Ocean—the most common species *Euphausia superba* and *Euphausia vallentini*.

The mass of summer krill has been estimated at between 400 to 650 million tonnes. Concentrations can be kilometres across and reach depths of 100 m. Vast swarms gather, often close to the pack-ice edge. The krill may be in thick concentrations, as closely packed as

35 kg per cubic metre. They are so dense that the sea in which the swarm exists may have a reddish hue that can be seen for kilometres.

Krill spawn from January to March. The females lay up to 10 000 eggs at a time, and they sometimes lay several times a season. Once laid, the eggs sink to a depth of about 2 km, where they hatch. As the larvae develop through several stages, they move closer to the surface. Krill can live to five years or more and grow to 6 cm in length, to a top weight of about one gram. Large concentrations of krill have been found near the ice edge from about 90°E along the coast towards the Ross Sea, near the eastern section of the Ross Ice Shelf and in the seas near the Balleny Islands. However, as they are fast swimmers and their swarms are affected by currents, they are not fixed in a specific location.

The Ross Sea lies between 160°E and 150°W, the western region within Area V. It is a distinct oceanographic entity within the Southern Ocean, and is the summer location for many species of whale, including the humpback whale. A large belt of pack-ice which sometimes stretches across the entrance to the Ross Sea acts as a barrier, but once this has been crossed, a whale or vessel moves into relatively clear waters. The Ross Ice Shelf, an enormous ice shelf up to 60 m high, extends out from the continent, covering large areas of the Ross Sea.

Humpback location in the Southern Ocean is initially determined by the extent of pack-ice coverage, the whale's stage of maturation and, for females, their state of pregnancy. The first to arrive in Antarctica and begin feeding are the pregnant females. They need to build up the blubber reserves for themselves and for the foetus growing within their wombs. These females will remain at the ice edge and move south as the pack ice retreats and the plankton blooms, providing food for the krill. The second phase to arrive in the Southern Ocean are the immature animals, the adolescents. Behind these are the mature humpbacks and resting females. The final pods to arrive in the Southern Ocean are the cow/calf pods. As these humpbacks have swum south, their calves will have begun to learn patterns of social and migratory behaviour. These pods arrive in December, though some possibly later as cow/calf pairs are sometimes seen off south-east Australia in late November.

As spring and summer develops, humpback whales congregate in loose groups wherever the krill swarm. Although the whales are not usually restricted to one location in the Southern Ocean, researchers have identified loosely bound regions of higher concentrations of humpback whales than others. Within the two southern areas, IV and V, further congregations occur. But these locations are not fixed for all humpback whales. One individual from Area V was later found in the seas off Western Australia, an exchange that may have occurred while it was in the Southern Ocean. These areas of humpback whale concentration are divided roughly at 120°E to 140°E. Krill rarely occurs here and there are fewer humpbacks than either east or west. Although humpback whales have been found in this region, it appears to mark the extent of the two populations.

Sightings indicate that humpback whales will swim in all conditions of the Southern Ocean. Twentieth-century sightings of humpbacks show that they are found along sections of the east Antarctic coast. They may frequent seas away from the ice edge but will at times swim within loose pack-ice and around icebergs, and have often been seen close to the ice edge. Japanese whalers working in Areas IV and V noted that 'herds' of humpbacks move in relation to the retreating ice.[1]

Surviving in an icy environment

Humpback whales are careful and deliberate swimmers, and can manoeuvre to within centimetres of other creatures and objects near them in the water. If necessary they will 'touch' these things with flippers or tail. However, swimming in the Southern Ocean brings a new element, ice, to their lives. Icebergs and broken pieces of ice, directed by current and wind may float downwind for kilometres. Plates and collections of pack-ice, also affected by the winds and currents, float continually in differing places on the ocean. The whales will hear, see and feel the presence of ice in the water. For experienced humpback whales, ice is familiar and they will use sensory skills to locate and to work their way around the obstacles. They hear the bumps and groans of the pack-ice as it grinds and breaks, and the surge and crash of the swell as it makes contact with the pack and crashes into icebergs. Although their eyesight may not be as effective, they see and will avoid the rough underside of the pack-ice fragments and the curves and edges of the icebergs underwater. The water temperature near icebergs is noticeably lower than in surrounding seas and the humpback whale feels this as it swims through ice-strewn seas.

On reaching Antarctic seas, weaning begins for the young calves born in the previous winter in the tropics. The powerful bonds between mother and calf, which have lasted for five to six months, now begin to change. Although the calf will remain with its mother for several more months, continuing to feed from her milk and making the return journey north in her company, the arrival in the Southern Ocean marks a definite stage in its development and independence. Calves in the south for the first time will need to pay careful attention to the ice. The early months of swimming in shallow northern waters, with other whales and near coastlines, rocks and reefs have taught them the skills required for detection and manoeuvring in icy seas. Although they remain close to their mothers the calves will move into the larger, looser-knit feeding congregations of humpbacks while their mothers feed.

Despite the cold waters of the Southern Ocean, maintaining body heat is not a problem for whales. The humpback whale is eury-thermal (it is able to live in a wide range of temperatures); capable of life in both polar seas and in the warmth of tropical seas with temperatures up to 30°C. Its system of thermoregulation is so efficient that overheating may be an occasional problem. All mammals generate heat in their body mass and lose it through their skin The surface area of a whale, compared to its enormous bulk, is small and it loses heat at a much lesser rate than would, for example, a mouse. Whale blubber, a good insulator, is interlaced with blood vessels. The flow of blood through this network allows for efficient heat transfer as it is carried from warmer to cooler parts of the animal's body. Heat loss is effected through the tail, flippers and dorsal fin. These appendages have no blubber and allow heat to pass into the water if the animal's internal temperature begins to rise too far.

Feeding behaviours

Humpback whales are predators. When they find their prey they feed voraciously, sometimes for hours, taking massive quantities of krill each session. Despite living in small, loose-knit pods or even at times individually, humpbacks gather in larger numbers at krill swarms. The feeding is noisy and excited; the frenzied jumping and twisting of the krill breaking away from the surface as they attempt to escape make a hissing, rasping sound. The whales' lunging movements through the krill make a rushing, splashing noise as their heads break through the surface. They snort and wheeze as they breathe and make social noises as they feed. Attracted by the noise, other whales join the feeding.

Different feeding methods are used. The lunge is used sometimes to catch krill near the surface. Usually acting individually, the whales swim quickly up from below the krill with mouths agape. As they move through the swarm they take large mouthfuls of krill and seawater. The whale pushes its huge tongue up against its palate, and the excess water pours out through the baleen which catches the krill. The food is passed to the back of the throat and swallowed. A variation of the lunge is a sideways movement through a surface swarm. Southern Hemisphere humpbacks have been observed feeding in circular sweeps in what has been described as a 'washing machine' feeding behaviour.

The most spectacular feeding method is bubble netting. While this method is observed more frequently in the Northern Hemisphere, bubble netting has been observed in the Southern Hemisphere humpbacks. Diving below the krill swarm, humpbacks circle, blowing large bubbles about the size of a dinner plate. A glittering circle of bubbles ascends, acting as a trap, herding the krill into a smaller, denser mass. Two or even more animals may work this method, slowly spiralling upwards, creating the net of bubbles as they go. When the bubbles break the surface, completing the trap, the whales surge upwards through the krill, mouths wide open, jaws stretched to a stupendous size with water and krill. Once the lunge is completed, the whale closes its mouth, the large pleated throat remains expanded like a bellows, an enormous balloon of flesh extending from the top of the mouth down and out to nearly one-third of the animal's length. The process is repeated again and again, the whale taking tonnes of krill at a time.

Although the Southern Ocean can be wild and cold, the humpback whales are at home in this feeding ground and they are familiar with its conditions. If the krill is plentiful, the whales will be well fed and they will build up substantial reserves of blubber. The reserves need to be large. There will be no feeding like that of the Southern Ocean on the migration north, in the breeding grounds or during the return migration.

In late February or March, the whales know when to begin their orchestrated departure as the dark returns to the southern regions. The first to leave are the cows weaning their young. These animals usually leave when there are only eight and a half hours of daylight over a 24-hour period. The second group to leave, about twelve days after the first, are the immature males and females, the sub-adults. About two weeks later, the migration peaks. This next group to leave includes mature males, and 'resting' females—those that are neither pregnant nor nursing. Finally, the females in late pregnancy leave the feeding grounds, making the most of the late summer to feed, preparing for the journey north, birth and milk production. They begin their northern journey when the length of daylight is no more than six and a half hours.

The birth of southern whaling

While the first sightings of whales in the south were made by the early explorers who sailed near Antarctica and its islands, whaling in earnest did not begin until the late nineteenth century. The first successes came in the early twentieth century, and whaling in these rich seas has continued with few interruptions ever since. One species after another has been exploited, usually with devastating results, until in 1984, when most whaling, with the exception of whaling for scientific purposes, was effectively banned.

One of the first to record the presence of humpback whales in the south was J. G. Forster, naturalist aboard Captain Cook's ship *Resolution*. In December 1774 Forster wrote of the humpback whales in Success Bay, near Tierra del Fuego.

> Lieutenant Pickersgill was sent into Success Bay, and on this occasion it was remarked that no less than thirty whales played about them in the water. Whenever they were seen, blowing to windward, the whole ship was infected with a most detestable rank and poisonous stench, which went off in the space of two or three minutes. Sometimes these huge animals lay on their backs, and with their long pectoral fins beat the surface of the sea, which always caused a great noise . . . Here we had an opportunity of observing the same exercise many times repeated, and discovered that all the belly and underside of the fins and tail are of a white colour, whereas the rest is black. As we happened to be only sixty yards from one of these animals, we perceived a number of longitudinal furrows on its belly. Besides flapping with their fins in the water, these unwieldy animals, of forty feet in length, sometimes fairly lept into the air, and dropt down again with a heavy fall. The prodigious quantity of power required to raise such a vast creature out of the water is astonishing, and their peculiar economy cannot but give room to much reflection.[2]

Soon after Cook's crew reported these events, with the additional news of the rich fur and elephant sealing grounds on nearby islands, sealers quickly moved into the region to exploit the stocks for both oil and skins. They came first to the subantarctic islands near the continent and probably landed on and worked regions of the Antarctic

Peninsula, that long tail of Antarctica beneath the subcontinent of South America. Whalers did not come south until the late nineteenth century. Many Europeans saw whales in the Southern Ocean in the mid to late nineteenth century and reports of these sightings stimulated interests in the whaling potential of the south. British explorer Captain James Clark Ross noted the presence of whales in the Southern Ocean. He saw many in the Ross Sea, which he discovered, in 1840. Ross identified 'common black whales, resembling the Greenland whale, sperm whales and finners'. He also saw whales he described as hunchback. Ross saw the economic potential of these regions, writing in his published narrative for 1 March: 'We saw a great many whales whenever we came near the pack edge, chiefly of a very large size; and I have no doubt that before long this place will be the frequent resort of our whaling ships, being at so convenient a distance from Van Diemen's Land.'[3]

During the last decade of the nineteenth century, several attempts were made to locate and exploit the reported whale stocks of the south, stimulated by declining numbers of whales in traditional whaling grounds of the northern seas and in the Pacific Ocean. In the main these expeditions sought the familiar right whale, and although noting the presence of other species, did not attempt to catch them.

In 1891, the Tay Whale Fishing Company of Dundee sent four steamers to the Falkland Islands, and thence to the Antarctic, where they remained from December 1892 to February 1893. The *Jason*, captained by Carl Anton Larsen, left Sandefjord on 4 September 1892 and sailed south reaching the Antarctic Peninsula region late that year. They sought right whales but saw that 'blue whale frolicked in countless shoals, as well as humpback'.[4] The Dundee whalers were met and whalers from both expeditions noted the absence of right whales. The men caught seals and the expedition returned a large loss to investors. In an ominous pointer to the future these expeditions returned with news of the presence of other whales. Despite further expeditions and further losses, Larsen remained optimistic about the potential for whaling in the south. He was later to have a great impact on the development of whaling in the Southern Ocean.

Others saw the potential of southern whaling. Australian businessman Henrik Johan Bull organised a whaling expedition primarily to search for right whales. His vessel, the *Antarctic*, set out in the summer of 1893. This voyage proved to be as fruitless as the previous whaling expeditions; the men saw humpbacks and blue whales and watched as whales fed from krill, but saw no right whales. They returned to Melbourne with seal oil. The *Antarctic* set out again and in January 1895 entered the Ross Sea. It sailed along the western coasts of the Ross Sea, naming geographical features of what was then new land, but doing little whaling. On 24 January, men from the vessel landed at Cape Adare. On their return to Australia, they claimed to have been the first to land on the Antarctic continent, perhaps unaware of the 70 years of human activity in the peninsula region or making the geographical assumption that east Antarctica was not connected to the peninsula. The voyage was significant in that it proved again that the Ross Sea was navigable and in doing so stimulated attention towards an area which was to later become both a whaling ground and one of the main means of access to the heart of the Antarctic continent. Despite not seeing right whales, the crew reported seeing fin whales. This time they knew that with the right equipment, these whales could be successfully hunted.

In 1903, the first humpback whale was 'commercially' killed in the south. Using 'modern' equipment Norwegian whaler Adolf Andresen, then based at Punta Arenes at the southern tip of Chile, killed a humpback whale in the Straits of Magellan. Andresen subsequently purchased two whale catcher vessels and established the Sociedad Ballenera de Magallanes near Punta Arenes. The whale catchers of this company operated in the seas near the South Shetlands and Deception Island, off the Antarctic Peninsula.

In 1902 the Swedish Antarctic explorer Otto Nordenskjöld took the *Antarctic* south to explore lands near the tip of the peninsula. The experienced Carl Anton Larsen returned to the region as captain.

After a series of mishaps, the expedition was stuck in the south, and the vessel crushed in the ice. It was not until rescued by an Argentinian vessel that the expedition was ensured of survival.

While recuperating in Buenos Aries, Larsen suggested to Argentinian businessmen that they organise and pursue the many whales seen in Antarctic waters. Acting on his advice, the businessmen formed the Compania Argentinia de Pesca. In 1904, the first Southern Ocean whaling station began operations from Grytviken, King Edward Harbour, on South Georgia. The expertise and personnel were mostly Norwegian, men who were willing to leave Norway after a decline in nearby whale stocks, and a ban on coastal whaling, instituted by the Norwegian Parliament after representations from local fishermen who claimed that whaling adversely affected fish stocks.

Whaling in this part of the Antarctic was immediately successful. The humpbacks in the seas near South Georgia were plentiful, they were slower moving and therefore easier to catch than the fin whales and blue whales also known to be in the area. From 1904 to 1918, 22 825 humpback whales were killed off South Georgia. In one season, 1910–11, 6175 humpbacks were killed, an average of 326 animals per whaling boat. But the supply of humpbacks was exhausted after seven years. The whalers turned to the fin whale for prey.

Whaling politics

The growth of interest in whaling in the south followed similar patterns to the sealing days of the nineteenth century. The slaughter of the stocks of animals was relatively unrestrained and despite the certain knowledge of the ruination of the resource through overkilling (and in the case of seals, calls for the regulation of the industry as early as 1788) continued to near extinction of a species. The commercial interest in the region was accompanied by political interest, from people and nations keen to gain influence over a resourceful region.

In July 1908, the British Government issued letters patent proclaiming that specified islands in the South Atlantic—South Georgia, the South Orkneys, the South Shetlands and the South Sandwich Islands, together with portions of the Antarctic continent known as Graham Land, would be regarded as dependencies of the Falkland Islands.

The Governor of the Falklands, William Allardyce, a supporter of conservation, introduced legislation in 1906 to restrain the slaughter of whales within his area of responsibility. Factory ships—large vessels that processed the carcass and stored the products, thereby eliminating the need for shore stations—and their attendant chasers, small ships designed specifically for the purpose of chasing and killing whales, began to be used in the area with devastating effect. From 1906 to 1911, the number of shore-based whaling stations, whale chasers and factory ships was restricted and whales with calves protected. Whaling operations were licensed and royalties collected.

In 1910–11, there were reports that Falkland Island Dependency seas were being overexploited. The catch was too large for efficient processing and many carcasses were wasted, left to rot in the harbours near whaling stations. In 1911, a further ban on the issue of whaling licences, and regulations enforcing the full utilisation of whale carcasses were introduced. Although there were moves to protect the whales for scientific reasons, these measures were essentially aimed at the conservation of an economic resource, as Allardyce noted in his Budget speech of 1911: 'The policy of this Government will continue to be that of endeavouring to establish a permanent industry rather than the rapid collection of a large revenue.'[5]

In October 1911, Norwegian whalers applied to the British Government for a licence to whale in waters off Enderby Land, Victoria Land and Wilkes Land—areas later to be placed into Areas IV and V. Although it was not fully comprehended at the time, these regions contained humpback whale feeding grounds. The application implied recognition of British sovereignty. These enquiries, and those of the Australian Douglas Mawson concerning territoriality in 1911, prompted the British Government to consider policy concerning Antarctic claims.

Scientists in the south

The first methodical studies of whales in the Southern Ocean were carried out by the zoologist Emile Racovitza, who was a member of the Belgian Antarctic expedition of 1898–99. While near the Antarctic Peninsula he observed whales, including humpbacks, and later began collating references to Antarctic whale sightings. He provided excellent and scientifically trained comments on the value of the existing data and his work was the first of many attempts to establish a considered and verified picture of the distribution of whales in the then-known parts of the Southern Ocean. It also provided information for the whaling industry.[6]

By the time Racovitza was compiling his lists, humpback whales from Areas IV and V had been already taken by whalers. American ships had taken humpbacks off the Western Australian coast in the mid-nineteenth century, Eden whaling on the east coast of Australia was about 70 years old and in New Zealand, migrating humpbacks had been taken in small numbers from the seas off the North Island and a new form of catching humpbacks, by large nets, was about to begin at Whangamumu in the Bay of Islands region in the North Island.

Many scientists became involved in whaling and whaling techniques. They were keen to know more of the natural history of whales, and to further the commercial success of an important industry. In 1908, innovative Norwegian whaling engineer Jan Andreas Mörch wrote to the editors of *Scientific American*, pointing out the waste in not processing whale carcasses in the Antarctic shore stations, noting that 'about 1600' carcasses a season had been left to rot in the seas, due in part to poor processing facilities. One solution to this, he wrote, was to link licence approval to the complete utilisation of the whale carcass. The next year Mörch published a longer letter in the *Scientific American*, explaining the processes whereby the whole whale carcass could be used productively.[7]

In 1911, Sir Sydney Harmer presented a paper by Mörch, 'On the whalebone whales', to the Zoological Society of London. In this Mörch put forward propositions about the movements of humpback whales. He suggested that the humpbacks of South Georgia might migrate from Africa. More significantly, he noted that whales might use the ocean currents as 'highways' during their migrations, that 'along the border layers of the great polar currents where these meet and intermingle with warmer currents or waters that, given a sufficient activity of light for the production of vegetable plankton, we may expect to find the most favourable conditions for the subsistence of the plankton Whales'. Discussing the decline in whale stocks near Newfoundland, he suggested that 'if the catches had been proportional to the approximate natural increase, the industry might most probably have been carried on to the same extent for some time to come'. Mörch suggested that 'the geographical positions of the various whaling grounds in the Southern Hemisphere should offer special opportunities for observations upon the migrations, breeding-season, food, and other questions of biological and economical interest relating to these Whales'.[8]

Others agreed. Sydney Harmer approached the British Government, and the Interdepartmental Committee on Whaling and the Protection of Whales was established. In 1913, G. E. H. Barrett-Hamilton was sent to South Georgia to 'make enquiries into the whale fisheries'. Barrett-Hamilton worked at the shore station at Leith Harbour on behalf of the Government of the Falkland Islands, the British Colonial Office and the Trustees of the British Museum until his death on 17 January 1914. His work was invaluable and one of the first sets of scientific work to be drawn from the opportunity presented by the newly established Antarctic shore stations.[9]

At this time and slightly earlier, other scientific assessments were being made of humpbacks caught and processed at Southern Hemisphere shore stations. In 1912, just before Barrett-Hamilton was sent south, Norwegian Sigurd Risting published information about the Southern Hemisphere humpback whales that migrated up from the Antarctic and along the coasts of Africa. Risting's work was based in part on that of a Norwegian whaler, Morten Ingebrigtsen, and on whalers' logbooks which recorded catch statistics and locations.[10]

Risting's is a key paper in the study of humpbacks. It summed up much of the general knowledge then known about these animals. Commenting on the pigmentation of humpbacks, he noted the possible mixing of different populations—marked by different pigmentations—in the seas off South Georgia. The humpback, Risting continued:

> undertakes great and extensive migrations, and its course appears to be more regular and more constant than that of the other large Cetacea. Therefore if the whalers have found a station from which it can be hunted on its course it is easier to shoot down and exterminate than any of the other species to be thinned out upon a particular field. This is the same phenomenon which we today have occasion to observe, especially at South Georgia and South Shetland. Since whaling began in the South Seas one has, on the whole, acquired a better notion of the migrations of the whales and of their whole course of life besides; this is especially the case with regard to the humpback.

Risting also discussed the similarity of feeding behaviour and migratory patterns of southern humpback whales with those of the north, noting that: 'all the there occurring forms of humpback are very nearly allied to, if not identical with, our northern form'. He, like many others, was aware of the importance of krill, remarking that each Antarctic spring, 'great quantities of whalefood sprout up' along the ice edge and that this food is swept along by currents. He added that from November each season, the humpbacks 'find food in all luxuriance', and that the whales feed and grow 'fatter and fatter' till they leave on the northerly migration, from February to April.

Risting knew that the northwards migration was towards the great continents and that by mid-May humpbacks were to be found, for example, along the coasts of South America. The migration continued until the end of July by when they were in tropical waters. He cited one case of humpback whales being found just south of the equator. By the end of August, after the pregnant females have given birth and after mating, the southward migration had begun. Although they had not been studied to the same extent as the populations south of South America, the timing and migratory routes of the Pacific populations were known to researchers such as Risting.

Generally, Risting noted, the humpback had good hearing and was thought to have learnt to recognise and swim away from the noise of whaling boat engines. He added that: 'there are, namely, two things which make it almost senseless: these are courting and the presence of food. A humpback in the midst of krill appears to have no thought for anything but provisions, and an enamoured humpback forgets all regard to caution.'

While the increased access to the humpback carcasses provided much-needed scientific information, some scientists continued to show concern, even if qualified, such as that expressed by Risting. 'The humpback has in recent years been caught in disturbingly large numbers at our southern whaling stations . . . The heavy toll levied [on the east coasts of East Africa] has here already noticeably affected the stock.' However that may be, Risting concluded optimistically: 'the humpback still exists in very large numbers, and it will certainly contribute for a further series of years to make the Norwegian whaling industry a profitable business'.

Conserving stocks and making whaling a profitable business required a basic knowledge of whales and in 1911, the first issue of the *Norwegian Whaling Gazette* (*Norsk Hvalfangst-Tidende*), a publication which disseminated information and articles about whales and whaling was published. During 1914–15, scientists such as D. Lillie, Ørjan Olsen, W. Kükenthal and Professor Collett contributed further to the understanding of Southern Hemisphere humpback whales and their movements. From this body of work came a growing realisation that the humpback whale populations of the world were one species with localised variations. Not as scientific, but equally as revealing, was the 1915 government investigation into whaling off the coast of Western Australia, an investigation which when published summarised, collated and made known information about this population of humpback whales.[11]

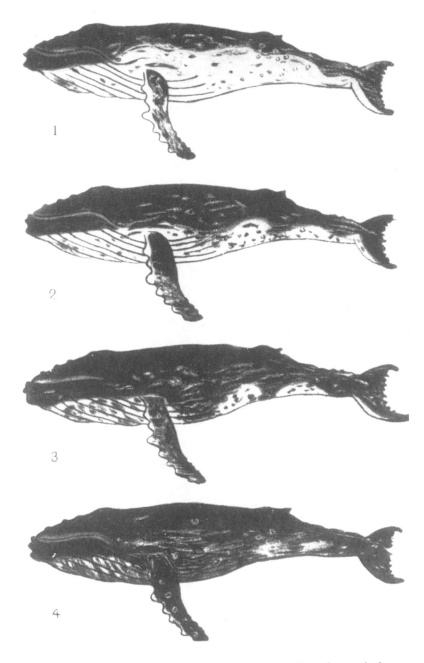

Pigmentation variation as described by zoologist D. Lillie, who worked on Area V humpbacks caught near New Zealand in 1912. (D. Lillie, *Cetacea*)

The coloration of humpback whales is a continual theme in the history of the assessment of the species and its separate populations. At Port Alexander in Africa, Risting's informant, the whaler Ingebrigtsen, noted that pairs occurred in mixed variations, which he divided into 'blue or grey-black belly', 'white spotted or striped belly' and 'quite white belly'. He also wrote that 'males and females of all these varieties were present in regular number throughout the whole season. These varieties do not keep apart in small lots but mingle together. Thus of a pair one could often be black, the other light bellied'. In 1925, biologist Martin Hinton later added to this, 'A special feature of the southern humpback is that the flipper is nearly always dark-coloured above. Of the above mentioned 115 [humpbacks in Ingebrigtsen's sample] only six had quite white flippers but this in the northern humpback is the rule; but having regard to the extraordinary variability of the humpback in the matter of colour, one can scarcely attribute much systematic importance to this character.'[12]

While Lillie commented on the colour variations in humpback whales he examined in New Zealand, he also published information about the migratory paths of the humpbacks of Area V. According to Lillie, the humpbacks of the far south migrated northwards at the beginning of winter into the warmer seas in the neighbourhood of Norfolk Island. They passed New Zealand on their northward run from the middle of April to the end of August, but principally during May and the early part of June. About mid-September they were to be seen in the same locality migrating south, on their way back to the Antarctic Ocean, most of them passing during October, while by the middle of December they were all to the south of New Zealand. Lillie believed that the northerly migration was a breeding migration.

In 1912, Professor Collett also published information about the migration of southern humpbacks:

The bulk of these southern humpbacks appear during the summer months (December to March) at a larger or smaller number of great feeding places in the south polar sea, in order to feed on the plentiful plankton-food which at this time of the year develops in the neighbourhood of the ice. Thence in the spring . . . they undertake extensive breeding migrations towards the north, along the South American and African coasts to the warmer regions of the ocean near the Equator; everywhere at present they are the object of an intense whaling. Other tribes of southern humpbacks wander about between the south polar sea and the South Sea islands, and can press up towards the Indian Ocean or around Australia.[13]

All this work relied heavily on the work of whalers in the newly developed whaling stations. In 1909, whaling pioneer Johann Bryde sent the whaler *Neptune* and the factory ship *Vale* to Saldanha Bay, a popular whaling ground in Southern Africa. In 1910 he and Lars Iversen built a station at Durban and another at Saldanha Bay. About the same time Ingebrigtsen, who also provided data to Risting, built a station at Benguela, Port Alexandra. Whaling stations quickly developed and by 1912 there were 25 companies, mostly Norwegian, taking whales in an area from the Congo round the coast up to Angoche in East Africa. In the words of a later commentator, biologist Martin Hinton: 'Foreigners joined in; the interest became a fever and foolish competition began.'[14] The catch was primarily humpback and information on the whales was sent back to Europe.

In 1912, at the time Risting and others were publishing groundbreaking work on humpbacks, the humpback whale catch began to falter. In 1912 notes attached to a report of the South Georgia stipendiary magistrate noted that humpback whales remained the preferred catch in South Georgia;

The generally recognised whaling season in the Dependency is from October to March, as it is between those months that the humpback whale comes and goes in large numbers, and it is from this whale that the whale-hunter relies to make his 'catch'. Finback and blue whales are to be found round this island at all times, but are very seldom hunted during the season when humpbacks can be obtained, this is owing to the fact that humpbacks are ever so much easier to kill and in every way give considerable less trouble.[15]

However, this ease was not to continue. The season of 1912–13 was the beginning of the end of the reliance on humpback whales. There had been earlier intimations of the change. In 1911, whalers noted that humpback whales had left South Georgia and that they had not returned. The figures of whales killed near South Georgia show that from 1909–10 to 1911–12 humpbacks whales formed between 97.5 per cent and 91 per cent of the total. But in 1912–13, 2251 humpback whales were caught and processed, representing only 53.8 per cent of the total. (By 1925 the percentage had dropped further, to about 20 per cent.)[16]

The destruction was not confined to those humpbacks in the Southern Ocean. Modern whalers were operating off the coasts of Africa and were about to begin hunting off the coasts of Western Australia. The concern for the known populations of humpback whales was worldwide. British naval officer Lieutenant Strong, reporting on whaling on the west coast of Africa, wrote to the Admiralty on 1 December 1912:

It was calculated that last year [1911] about 14 000 whales passed up the coast, of which about 4000 were killed. This year [1912] there have been about 12 000 of which about 4250 have been killed. Probably a far greater number will be killed next year. It is calculated that at this rate of wholesale butchery, in six years time practically all the whales on this coast will have been exterminated.[17]

On 11 January 1914 Barrett-Hamilton at Leith Harbour in South Georgia wrote:

A lot of whales are being killed and the season looks like being a good one. But the catch is of finners and blue whales chiefly, not as formerly, of humpbacks. Unless these latter arrive in greater numbers later on, it will be difficult to avoid the conclusion that the whalers, having killed off the humpbacks, are now doing the same thing to the other whales. But that is a conclusion that I am trying to avoid, as long as any other explanation can be found.[18]

Whaling station work

The work at the Antarctic whaling stations was grim in both task and environment. Visitors commented on the isolation and hard work of whaling in what were hostile but often strikingly beautiful surrounds. The whaling stations were large slaughter houses, with the size of the whale being butchered and rendered inevitably making the location appear a vast and gory site. Australian photographer James Francis (Frank) Hurley visited Grytviken, South Georgia in 1914, while a member of Sir Ernest Shackleton's Imperial Trans Antarctic Expedition (1914–17). He described the process of modern whaling, including his thoughts and reactions in his diaries:

> Our inquisitive dispositions induced us to explore the whaling factory, an examination only possible by holding the nose tightly and viewing from a respectable distance. The company owns a flotilla of four whalers, which scout seven days a week for whales patrolling a circuit of 50 miles [80km] from land. On the sighting of a whale the lookout in the crow's nest of the vessel starts in pursuit and by judicious manoeuvring approaches to within 30 or 40 yards of the quarry. The skipper on the bows stands alert by the harpoon . . . and when within range sights the piece and fires. One can follow the flight of the harpoon and the whizzing, coiling rope which immediately tautens and runs out at great speed as the huge fish, with a bloody spout sounds. The harpoon is filled with a concussion head, which on entering the whale explodes.
>
> The harpoon line passes over a brake winch in such a way that the harpooner can gauge to a nicety the strain on the line. When the brake is applied the line is slowly hauled in. When the whale is alongside, it is despatched with a lance. A tubular lance to which is attached a pneumatic hose is then inserted through the blubber and by means of an air compressor, the huge bulk is inflated, thus preventing the fish from sinking. The whale is towed into the station, where it is not uncommon to observe the vessels arriving with two fish towing over either bow. The whales are then hauled by powerful winches up an inclined jetty called the flensing plan. Here great strips of blubber are torn off longitudinally by winches, assisted by heavy knives secured to poles—a process known as flensing. The blubber then passes through a cutting machine, after which convenient sized pieces are transferred to steam heated digesters. The oil is drawn off by valves

*The whaling station at King Edward Cove, nestled against the South Georgia
mountains, Grytviken, when men from Sir Ernest Shackleton's Imperial
Trans-Antarctic Expedition visited in 1914. The first assaults on Southern
Ocean humpback whales set out from this station.*
(Frank Hurley photograph, Mitchell Library)

from time to time and graded, the residue being converted into
manures. At Grytviken the carcasses are allowed to go to waste. So
polluted are the foreshores of King Edward Cove with grease and
decaying carcasses that it is impossible to view the trade with other
than loathing.[19]

By the 1917–18 season, six shore stations were operating on South
Georgia, and the harbour on Deception Island, off the western
peninsula of Antarctica, was an important shelter for whaling vessels.
The increasing activity in this part of the Antarctic prompted further
political action. In March 1917, more letters patent were issued in
relation to the Falkland Islands Dependency region. Britain now
claimed responsibility for all the islands and territories in the sector
between 20°W and 80°W.

The Discovery Committee

In 1915 Martin Hinton drew together many of Barrett-Hamilton's observations for the use of the British Interdepartmental Committee on Whaling and the Protection of Whales. His work stressed the information then known and being readily produced on humpback and other whales and he included many references to the concerns about viability in unprotected situations. Hinton summarised the contributions of Barrett-Hamilton who made an

> accumulation of statistics concerning the size, relative proportions, sexes, and zoological characters of the whales landed at Leith Harbour. He devoted special care to the study of the female organs of generation and lactation and of their foetuses, with a view to acquiring information upon the little known breeding habits of the whales—a matter of which accurate knowledge is of vital importance if the whaling industry is to continue on modern lines without resulting in what appears at present to be the inevitable and speedy extinction of all the larger Cetacea.[20]

This committee was suspended during the First World War. In 1917 E. Darnley of the British Colonial Office drew the question of the development of the Falkland Islands to others in government. The Colonial Office had proposed a research vessel for the study of whales and whaling. During discussions it was pointed out that excessive hunting had resulted in the collapse of whaling in Greenland and Spitsbergen waters and that a similar threat for the Southern Hemisphere, although not fully confirmed, warranted further investigations. Towards the end of the First World War, the Interdepartmental Committee on Research and Development in the Dependencies was established. This committee drew together men from a number of sources, including E. Darnley, Sydney Harmer from the British Museum (Natural History), P. Lyon from the Department of Scientific and Industrial Research and Captain C. Smith of the Admiralty. The new committee was to consider what could be done to facilitate the preservation of the whaling industry and to develop other industries in the Falkland Islands, and to examine economic questions related to these considerations. Significantly, it was to consider both a proposal to purchase a research vessel and appropriate scientific investigations to support the proposed developments.

The committee met 21 times and submitted its report in 1919. During their deliberations, committee members consulted widely and received many submissions.

One theme that runs continually throughout the history of modern whaling is the debate concerning the real impact of whaling. Whalers and their supporters argued that the extermination of a species was not possible as whalers will not kill species that have reached commercial extinction. The remainder, they argued, breed back to sizeable populations. One of the proponents of this view, whaler Captain C. A. Larsen, talked to the committee:

> It may be argued that all kinds of whales can be exterminated by too intense hunting; I agree that the stock of certain species, such as the Greenland whale, can become very thin in that way . . . There is no reason to fear extermination, especially of the larger whales, as unlike some other kinds, for instance the humpback whales, they do not seek the coasts as breeding grounds. Even the humpback whale is protected by the fact that thousands of them seek coasts where no whaling is done. Thus a large contingent of this species is safeguarded for the future and the ocean. Should however the number of humpbacks be diminished decisively, then attention should be given to the breeding grounds. One might prohibit the shooting, catching, or killing of the species it is desired to protect. It might be decided to do this for a period, or merely during the season when pairing takes place, and when the young ones are born.
> I am absolutely of the opinion that no danger threatens, as the humpback has his undisturbed haunts in the ocean; we have many proofs that he is a migratory animal going from ocean to ocean.

Larsen also commented on the question of humpbacks crossing the Equator, noting that 'I can testify that I have seen both the humpback and the bottlenose cross the equator, both going south and north'. His experience told him that there were many whales to be taken in the Antarctic, particularly the 'hundreds of thousands which live along the edge of the ice and along the land. There are two oceans in those ice regions which protect the whales, viz., Weddell Sea and Ross Sea. In the latter there are immense masses of whales, and it will probably be long before anybody takes to hunting them.'

He continued, talking about 'the habits of whales'. The humpback:

hardly ever appears alone, but prefers company. They generally appear in small or large schools. If disturbed when feeding and the disturbance is repeated they go farther and farther away. The chief food of the humpback is 'krill' but he also eats fish. I have met with humpbacks which have lived exclusively on fish up to eighteen inches long. Apparently when he has started eating fish he prefers it, as I have found their stomachs filled to the utmost capacity with fish and no 'krill' although others in the same school have been full of 'krill' and no fish.[21]

Larsen's optimism was not shared by others who commented to the commmittee. T. E. Salvesen, of the Chr. Salvesen whaling company based at Leith, South Georgia, expressed the view that the

rate at which whales are being taken in South Georgia . . . has been in excess of the rate of production, with the result that the stock has been depleted. There is no doubt that excessive killing is taking place . . . As regards the . . . humpback, which comes closer to land, is the easiest to catch. Speaking from a purely commercial, and not from a scientific, point of view, this animal has for all practical purposes been exterminated, since it is no longer a paying proposition to hunt the humpback alone. This has been shown by experience on the coast of Africa.[22]

In his Memorandum to the Committee on the present position of the southern whaling industry, scientist Sydney Harmer was quite clear about his understanding of the causes of the reduction in whale stocks:

It may be stated in general terms that, prior to the commencement of intensive sub-Antarctic whaling, whaling operations have followed one invariable course, in whatever part of the world they have been carried out:—a period of great plenty, followed sooner or later by a diminution, usually coming on quickly (as in the case of the southern humpbacks), and culminating in a total cessation of whaling operations. Particular attention may be directed to the well known cases of the Greenland right whale (*Balaena mysticetis*) and the Pacific grey whale (*Rhachianectes glaucus*). It must be remembered that the destructive power of the older whaling vessels was far inferior to that of modern whalers fitted with guns and harpoons carrying explosive charges. If the older type of vessel could accomplish something nearly approaching extermination, it must be obvious that modern whaling is likely to produce the same results in a far shorter period of time.[23]

Besides these questions, the committee examined the commercial potential of increased whaling and other activities in the Falkland Dependencies and the possibility of a more formal scientific examination of the regions, an examination that would provide extremely useful information for both science and commerce. A central purpose of the committee was to place the whaling industry on a scientific basis. To do this, whale species had to be located, observed and tracked through their habitats during the southern seasons. Information, particularly statistics, about feeding and breeding, and growth rates had to be secured and analysed.

The committee surmised that of all the variables in the ocean habitats, whale movements (migration patterns were even less well known then than they are today) were determined by the sea temperature and the presence of food—krill. The presence of krill in turn was dependent upon currents and the seas' chemical constituents. Therefore one of the fundamental investigations was to examine the temperature, salinity, air content, biological content and current direction of water at various depths; to make this investigation methodically and over several millions of square kilometres of ocean; to do this repeatedly at all seasons of the year and for a sufficient number of years to establish a reliable statistical pattern. Many of these statistics could be obtained from the whaling stations. In association with this, a systematic examination of the nutritive and generative parts of whales was to be made. The knowledge of whalers was also to be considered, as a form of 'field craft' rather than as scientific evidence. It was a pattern of cetological studies which set the framework for studies throughout the twentieth century and which, in part, continues today.

To pursue the knowledge of whale movements the committee decided to improve a system of whale marking. Throughout the history of whaling, harpoons from attempted kills remained in whales, sometimes for many years. When the remains were recovered sometimes many years later, any identifiable parts or marks on the harpoon could be used to ascertain the movements of that whale. The systematic marking of whales probably began in 1908 when Japanese whaling captain Tasuke Amano of the large whaling company Toyo Hogei first experimented with whale marking as a way to examine whale movements. Its usefulness was recognised by the committee members who wished to institute a formal and long-term program of whale marking. The committee also addressed the problems of over fishing of certain whale species and suggested that factory ships not be permitted and that only annual licences be granted rather than long-term whaling rights.

The committee engaged staff and built a small laboratory at Grytviken, South Georgia. They purchased the *Discovery*, the Antarctic Expedition vessel used by Robert Scott, and became known as the Discovery Committee. The many calls and efforts to establish further information about whales which became manifest in the Discovery Committee also saw the establishment in 1929 of the International Bureau of Whaling Statistics in Norway.

At the same time as the men of the Discovery Committee were planning for their work, a more coherent British policy towards claiming the Antarctic and its seas began to develop. These political moves coincided with increased interest from other nations in Antarctic whaling. In mid-1919, another request for a whaling licence was received by the British from Norway. In administrative circles a suggestion was made that Britain 'ought quietly to assert her claim to the whole continent'.[24] Further discussions led to a proposal for a gradual extension of the British claim over Antarctica. Such a claim would begin with the Falkland Islands Dependency and then extend to other areas such as the Ross Sea. It was recognised that the Dominions, Australia and New Zealand, could become partners in this enterprise. The Australian scientist and explorer Sir Douglas Mawson had not only claimed parts of the continent for Britain but was also active in promoting those claims at political levels. One of Mawson's motives—one which was at the same time used as an argument supporting his desire for increased political influence— was the possibility for the successful and beneficial exploitation of the large whale stocks in the Southern Ocean.

The Australian and New Zealand governments were informed of British policy in 1920, and both governments agreed with the policy direction. In 1921 it was agreed that the Australian and New Zealand governments should have separate spheres of control over portions of the continent, which might conveniently be divided by the meridian 160°E. The Ross Sea would be the responsibility of New Zealand, the regions to the west of that, of Australia.

In 1922 an application for a whaling licence for the Ross Sea was received from a Norwegian company and this was used as an opportunity to advance the New Zealand claim of that part of Antarctica. The licence was issued on 21 December and the order in council declaring New Zealand control over the Ross Sea region was issued in July 1923. The New Zealand Government was responsible for 'all the islands and territories between the 160th degree east longitude and 150th degree west longitude south of 60°S'.[25]

Factory ships in the Southern Ocean

The advent of factory ships was to be a significant development in Southern Ocean whaling. Factory ships were large vessels that acted as supply for chasers and as base for both processing whale carcasses and storing the products until it was time to return to home port.

With a factory ship as a 'mother ship', whaling fleets could operate independently from costly shore stations and could move more readily than previously, from region to region. The large stores of oil and other products could also be taken directly to the most profitable market, if necessary without stops at home or processing ports. Such potential also placed strains on the licensing system. Fleets could now operate outside national areas of responsibility. Whaling had returned to unregulated seas and with it came the attendant issue of the tragic destruction of the 'common' resource. This issue was only seriously (albeit impotently) addressed by the later growth of international controls, in the 1930s.

Carl Anton Larsen's firm Larsen and Konow obtained a 21-year lease from the New Zealand Government to whale in the regulated region. The licence contained some conditions; two floating factories were permitted, with a restriction of five chasers to each and transport vessels. There was a charge of £200 per annum for each factory and 2s 6d for each barrel of oil produced over 20 000 barrels. Inspection was to be permitted at any time. No right whales were to be taken and no females with calves could be killed.

Larsen had the idea of hauling the whale carcasses onto the decks of the vessel to process them, rather than while they floated on the sea. The 13 000-ton *Sir James Clark Ross* was the first whaler into the Ross Sea in 1923–24, but it had difficulties hauling the large carcasses onto the decks. The carcasses had to be processed as the men stood on the whales in icy waters or worked from small boats. The season was not fruitful but during the next season 427 whales were processed. Despite the difficulties of ice conditions and storms, Larsen had demonstrated that whale carcasses could be processed on the decks of large ships in the Southern Ocean. It was the beginning of pelagic, or deep sea whaling in the Antarctic. Ships with oil-producing capacity had been used before this, but they had remained near the coasts or in bays.

The factory ships that followed were very large and the procedure for processing a carcass became an efficient operation. Huge winches pulled the carcass up onto a flensing deck. The blubber was cut and winched off the body and minced in mechanical mincers before being placed into steam pressure cookers or 'digesters'. Oil was also extracted from the meat and bone. Machines treated the whale meat, converting it with the remaining bone and residue to fertiliser. There was very little waste. Usually a fleet of six or seven chasers accompanied the factory ship to the Southern Ocean. These vessels sought out the whales, killed them and towed the carcasses back to the factory ship.

In 1926 the Larsen company's second factory ship, the *C. A. Larsen* was reconstructed with a large bow port leading to a slipway up which carcasses could be winched for processing. This technique was later changed, and by 1929–30, a stern slipway became the norm for factory ships.

For the next six seasons the Larsen company converted 4760 whales into oil. Whaling in the south became very popular and other fleets went south, some not bothering to obtain whaling licences. In 1926, for example, the Norwegian vessel *Nielsen Alonso* avoided paying New Zealand fees by using Hobart as a port for its operations into the Ross Sea.

In 1928 whaling fleets began to hunt closer to the ice edges. It was dangerous work. During the 1929–30 season the factory ship *Southern Princess* and her fleet of chasers sailed south. When confronted with the pack-ice that lay before the open waters of the Ross Sea, Commander Bernstern decided to crash through the ice to the whale-rich waters. As the author of the tale, Henry Ferguson, later wrote, 'We attacked the pack ice with superb confidence'. It was not enough, however, and as the chasers followed the *Southern Princess* through the channel made by the factory ship, the *Southern Sea* was holed by a large triangular piece of ice. She rolled over on her beam ends and the small crew escaped onto the surrounding pack ice. 'At a quarter past three in the morning, ten minutes after the collision, the mortally wounded *Sea* dipped her bows deep and, with a stern thrust high, crawled slowly to a frozen doom. A flag, a barrel and a man's cap whirled around in the swirling water until the slashed floe pressed together over the grave.'[26] The whaling fleet continued its work and returned to New Zealand with 60 000 barrels of oil, including some from humpback whales.

Whaling in the Ross Sea region increased steadily until the 1930–31 season during which more than 5000 whales were taken. It was a season in which 43 floating factories were in the Southern Ocean. With these vessels were 232 chasers, manned by about 11 000 whalers. Also during that season, Sir Douglas Mawson led an expedition south using the *Discovery*. The British Australian New Zealand Antarctic Research Expedition (BANZARE) was geographic, oceanographic and political in intent and was used to not only make scientific studies but to confirm a British and Australasian presence in Antarctica south of the Australian coast. The *Discovery* met the factory ship *Sir James Clark Ross*, with six chasers, to the west of the Balleny Islands near the mouth of the Ross Sea. It was a scheduled meeting arranged so the *Discovery* could take on coal from the whaler. As the coal was transferred, a whale carcass was used as a buffer between the two ships. Photographer Frank Hurley was sent onto one of the chasers, *Star X*, to get cinematic and still film of whaling, and scientist Harvey Johnston onto the *Sir James Clark Ross* to examine whales being cut up and to obtain specimens of whale parasites.

Mawson, a supporter of controlled whaling, was impressed by the operations he saw. He described some of the operations of the factory ship in his diary:

. . . it was a revelation, holds 20 000 tons whale oil when loaded. Diesel engines . . . A great flensing deck below which is the factory—an immense affair. The engine room also is a great sight. They can flense 4 whales at once, but 2 whales is more regular business. They are pulled up from the stern in great channel by winches on overhead gantries. One of these winches was recently pulled clean out and broken up—this was when trying to pull a large whale up the channel during a heavy swell. They were catching abundant whales at the time of our visit.[27]

Ninety per cent of the catch was blue and fin whales, but when humpbacks were seen they were killed.

Frank Hurley's account was published several years later. It remains as one of the more graphic and realistic descriptions of modern whaling in the Southern Ocean. Once again, Hurley was repelled by the business of whaling. His attack was explicit:

> As these huge units work in the open seas or in calm waters in the lee of the ice-packs, they are unmolested by licence, royalty, controlling law, and even the law of common sense. Already the massacre inflicted on the unfortunate prey, even at this early stage, to use a poultry metaphor, is 'killing the goose that lays the golden eggs'. Not content with the prodigious harvest of full cargoes, subsidiary tankers were filled as well: even crude fuel-oil was discharged into the sea to create further storage capacity. Such greed was scarcely excelled by early sealers, who completely exterminated fur seals from sub-Antarctic waters.

As the *Discovery* approached the *Sir James Clark Ross*, Hurley noticed

> the details of a monster abattoir, with blood cascading from its scuppers down into a red sea, scummed over with oil and grease, turn interest into revulsion. The dissection of carcasses and oil-extraction on an unrestricted scale is too colourful for description. We cannot, however, avoid contact with it as I transfer my paraphernalia from the exploring ship *Discovery*, to the chaser moored alongside, across steel decks awash with blood, and littered with blankets of blubber and hunks of flesh.
>
> The scene and the smell are nauseating, and the work of the flensers is a laborious routine. Bad enough in good weather, but when blizzards sheath decks with driving snow and freezing spray and carcasses become frozen hard, then the Antarctic adds stern revenge. The men who spend the entire season afloat amid these gory scenes are powerful, healthy good-humoured fellows who take the good with the bad and work in admirable harmony.

Hurley boarded the *Star X*. It was 27 m long and had a 6400-km range. Its harpoon gun was a short, muzzle-loading cannon 55 cm long, with a 76 mm bore, and 'pivoted to train in any direction by means of a small, wooden handle-grip at the butt end. The trigger is conveniently placed beneath the handle.' The harpoon weighed 52.6 kg and was about 106 cm long with four 30.5 cm flukes. When it entered the whale the flukes opened out and caught in the flesh so the harpoon could not be pulled out as the whale swam away. A bomb was screwed into the tip of the harpoon, and was usually charged to explode a few seconds after it entered the whale. A line was secured to the shaft of the harpoon. A mile (1.6 km) of line, ready to be played out was attached to a braking device on the winch, and then led down into the hold. The chaser was in effect a large fishing instrument.

Soon after, the chaser pursued some 'playful humpbacks' that were breaching nearby. When the chaser was within half a kilometre of the whales, they dived. The ship stopped engines and waited. Fifteen minutes later the whales resurfaced and the chaser followed, engines roaring. 'It seemed', wrote Hurley, 'as if the big fellows knew our striking distance—they would hump their backs in a graceful arch', dive and swim away. As the chaser closed distance, one humpback breached, '. . . the surface of the ocean seemed to split just before our bows, and from it an enormous body shot high into the air above our heads, poised for a moment, and then fell back amid a mighty upheaval of foam and crashing waters . . . We were so surprised that we just stared, speechless at the convulsion of waters, as if it had been a volcanic eruption. Twenty yards closer and we would have received the full weight of that 50 ton flop.' A whale was targeted. Hurley 'saw a quick dip of the gun, heard a deafening roar, and when the mist cleared, a mighty form was smiting the water violently with its flukes. Then stillness. It was a magnificent shot and the whale had been killed almost instantly.'

As the carcass was made fast to the side of the ship, 'the capricious Antarctic weather suddenly changed, and heavy mists rolled down over the sea. Then the wind began to pipe and with it came whirling snow flurries. The *Star X* deeply laden with a prize on either side, plugged valiantly into the rising blizzard and driving spray. Vision ahead was limited to twenty yards.' The chaser continued through the storm, with men on the bridge keeping a sharp eye out for drifting ice and keeping in touch with the mother ship through wireless signals. From these the men took bearings and eventually, through the fog and snow the watch saw the *Sir James Clark Ross* 'like a gargantuan monster from which blood caught in the snow flurries rained down on our decks'.

Never lost for colour in his writings Hurley used the following evaluation to end his story of the humpback hunt, making a final attack on whaling.

> I had marvelled at the devices that enabled man's ingenuity to triumph over Nature's moods and most powerful creatures, but their ruthless application to such unrestricted devastation provoked sad disillusionment. The absurdly mad scramble for quick money seems a deplorably short-sighted policy. The impossibility of securing international protection means that whaling must succumb in the near future to unreasonable greed.[28]

Many nations, such as Britain, Norway and Australia, had in fact developed a range of legislation and licence agreements in an attempt to manage or exert some form of control over whaling within their territorial seas or on vessels that used their ports. But these had no effect in international waters. The establishment of international controls over whaling, however ineffective initially, was a response to the pattern of exploitation of the world's whale resources. This pattern, one of stock location, stock depletion and commercial extinction was known to observers and whalers alike. The humpback whale of the South Georgia region, commercially ruined by 1913–14, was but the latest example of the fate of a number of species of whale, including the right whale, the bowhead and the grey whale.

International whaling agreements

During the period 1904–25, when most whaling in the Antarctic was within British territory, Great Britain alone was in a position to control southern whaling. As whaling developed around the world, other attempts were made to regulate whaling with international instruments. In 1911, the idea of international agreements was raised by staff of the Natural History Museum, London. Further suggestions can be traced back to a French proposal in 1913, by French concerned at whale hunting off Congo, then a French territory.

By and large these attempts were not fruitful, but they mark the beginning of work which continued throughout the period of modern whaling. In 1931, the year Frank Hurley criticised the lack of control over Southern Ocean whaling, the Convention for the Regulation of Whaling (CRW), an agreement supported by the League of Nations, was opened for signature. The International Convention came into force in 1935.

The 'main object' of the convention, a 1931 League report stated:

> is to secure the adoption by the greatest possible number of countries of certain rules intended to prevent the destruction of wealth available to all. The steady growth of the whaling industry in the last few years, thanks to improvements in equipment and technique, has resulted in an ever larger annual increase in the number of whales killed. Estimates from various sources show that the number taken varies from twenty five thousand to thirty thousand each season.[29]

The convention was the outcome of an inquiry initiated by the 1924 League Assembly into the subjects of international law. Among the questions recommended for discussion was the 'exploitation of the riches of the sea, with special references to the danger of extermination' to which whales were exposed. The discussion led to a draft based on regulations established for Norwegian whalers by the Norwegian Government. The convention covered all the waters of the world, including the high seas and territorial waters. It applied to all baleen whales (including humpback whales) and forbade 'absolutely . . . the taking or killing of species which have become very rare, calves or immature whales, and females accompanied by sucklings'.[30] Article 4 prohibited the killing of right whales, 'which shall be deemed to include North-Cape whales, Greenland whales, southern right whales, Pacific right whales, and southern pigmy right whales'. The fullest possible use was to be made of the carcass. In a move designed to build the knowledge of whales and whaling around the world, statistics of the catch were to be sent to the International Bureau of Whaling Statistics in Norway. Aboriginal whaling, the taking of a small number of whales by Indigenous peoples, was permitted.[31]

The people who drafted the convention saw its potential ineffectiveness and suggested that it should apply to all nations 'since it may be feared that, under the protection of States not parties to the convention, vessels may engage in operations contrary to the rules therein laid down'.[32]

It was an another fruitless attempt, almost impossible to police, but it marks a point in the long struggle to exert some form of management over whale stocks. The measures outlined within the convention were becoming established in international discussions as fundamental goals for whaling management. It was a small and idealistic step towards whale conservation.

Whaling fleets continued to go to the Southern Ocean. British and Norwegian based whalers dominated southern whaling until 1936–37, when Japanese whalers, backed by a long and successful tradition of whaling in Japanese waters, sent fleets to the Antarctic. In 1937–38, they were joined by German vessels. The world's humpbacks had continued to be killed during the 1930s: for example, between 1935 and 1939, at least 12 673 humpback whales (6804 males and 5869 females) were taken from the Area IV population.

As the impact of the Japanese and German whaling fleets became apparent it was clear to many that a new agreement was required, and in 1937 whaling nations signed the International Agreement for the Regulation of Whaling. In 1938 additional regulations were adopted. The main points of these measures were the total protection of right and grey whales, and the formal introduction of minimum lengths for blue, fin, humpback and sperm whales, and the prohibition of the catching of females with calves. The length of the pelagic season was limited to three months from 8 December to 7 March.

A sanctuary was established in the Pacific sector between 70°W longitude and 160°W. The Southern Ocean humpbacks remained protected until 1949, except for 883 individuals killed by Japanese whalers who refused to sign the agreement.

A decisive season

The 1937–38 season was one of the most productive in the history of Antarctic whaling. The worldwide total of whales killed during 1937–38 was 54 664 animals. Of these, 46 039 were killed in the Southern Ocean. In 1937 the 10 780-ton factory ship, *Ulysses*, with eight chasers and financed by interests in Britain, Norway, France, Denmark and the United States, completed a successful season off the West Australian coast. It processed 2036 humpbacks, some as little as 30 ft long despite the recent minimum lengths having just been set at 35 ft (10.6 m). In 1938, the *Ulysses* left New York for a season's whaling in the Antarctic. This season, a bigger catch was expected. The headlines of an article in *The Polar Times* read 'Journey of the Ulysses to Antarctic revives the glamour of fictional Moby Dick'. The author spoke enthusiastically about the voyage:

> This year, sure of its power, it sails to compete from Dec. 8 to the middle of March with the largest number of whaling vessels assembled at the farthest tip of the globe. Amid floating bergs, at the rim of the earth, there will gather one factory boat from Panama, nine from Norway, ten from England, five from Germany and four from Japan. Like the Ulysses, each will command, also, from eight to ten chaser boats.

The author discussed the catch regulations and the need for accountability as exemplified by the presence of an inspector on the ship, and then, with a more romantic eye continued:

> None but the most experienced are allowed to do the actual chasing . . . The most highly paid of all the crew is the gunner. Gunners, it is said, are born, not made. They must be possessed of a kind of cold fury, ignited at the sight of a whale, a relentlessness that

can outmatch the brute strength of the sea mammal and which can keep them riveted to the harpoon, their eyes unwavering from the sea for hours.[33]

Efforts to understand more about the whales of the Southern Ocean also continued in this devastating season. In 1937 L. Harrison Matthews of the Discovery investigations published the results of work to date on the humpback whale. His paper is over 80 pages of careful analyses and discussion of 62 humpback whales, collected over seven years. It was a summation, a picture of scientific knowledge of the southern humpback whale and therefore a significant step towards a more complete understanding of the species and its migrations. While it was written in a tone of considered examination, Matthews added words of caution: humpback stocks had been so seriously depleted that carcasses were not often available for examination at southern whaling stations.

In the paper, Matthews tabulated and compared body measurements, colouration, ventral grooves, baleen characteristics, food and blubber and noted that although there appeared to be differences in the pigmentation of a specific population, there were no structural differences between Northern Hemisphere and Southern Hemisphere populations of humpbacks. He discussed other aspects including parasites, reproduction, growth rates and the migrations of the humpback whales. Although the segregated nature of humpback migration was not fully realised until later in the twentieth century, the general pattern and timing of the migrations was becoming clearer, based on the analysis of catch data from the shore stations, and work by other scientists, including Australian zoologist and historian William Dakin. Matthews concluded that humpbacks may cross the equator and mingle with Northern Hemisphere stocks, possibly remaining with them and joining their migratory cycles. On the migrations he wrote:

The migration of the humpback whale can, then, be summarised as a southern feeding migration, as far south as there is open water in southern summer, followed by a migration towards the north which is pursued mainly in the coastal waters of the continents. The northward migration reaches the neighbourhood of the equator in August, when most of the females give birth to their calves, and the return migration begins at once; pairing takes place during its course and is, for the most part, over by the end of the year when the whales are on their southern feeding grounds. Some humpbacks are present on the South Georgia whaling grounds during the winter and may be non-migrating individuals which have spent the summer farther to the south. The migration is not restricted only to breeding whales, but includes immature as well as mature whales, pregnant as well as non-pregnant females.[34]

By the eve of the Second World War it was becoming clearer to scientists that humpback whales were one species, but with differences in pigmentation according to population.

G. Rayner, also a Discovery scientist, had told Matthews about the 'large schools of humpback whales' in Area IV. Matthews repeated his concern about humpback whale stocks, writing: 'The great destruction of the stock of Humpback whales during the last thirty years is attributable solely to the excessive slaughter during both the feeding and breeding migrations. The stock can only return to its former abundance, on which modern whaling in the south was founded, if the Humpback whale is afforded complete and world-wide protection for a long period of years.'[35] It was another in a long sequence of warnings about whale stock viability and it too went largely unheeded.

In 1938 the Discovery Committee research ship *William Scoresby* returned to port after having marked 800 whales, including many in the Southern Ocean below Australia. This latest voyage made the total of whales marked over the previous four years 3000. The scope and extent of whale marking, and the number of returned marks had an impact on knowledge of humpback whales. It was confirmed that humpbacks from Area IV migrated from the Antarctic to Western Australia and that another population swam up to the coasts of Africa. It began to appear to scientists that although there was some

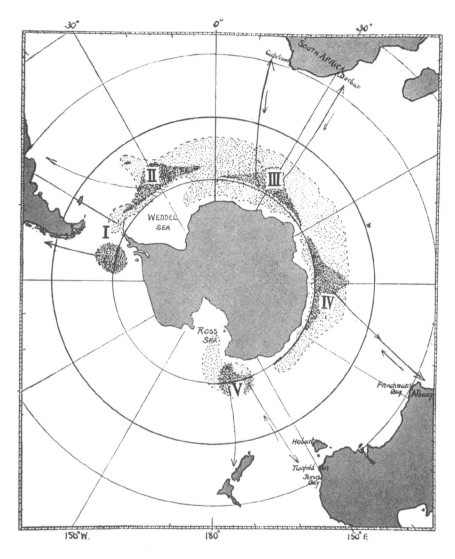

Areas of humpback whale concentration near Antarctica as known in 1946.
The five areas shown are numbered according to regions chosen as an aid to
understanding whale distribution in the Southern Ocean.
(William Dakin map, *Walkabout*)

intermingling of Southern Hemisphere humpback populations, they
were distinct populations that migrated north–south from Antarctica
to continents, rather than around the Southern Ocean.

United States biologist and conservationist Robert Cushman Murphy summed up the reactions of many to the destructive season of 1937–38 when he wrote a passionate article, 'Slaughter threatens the end of whales', for the *New York Herald Tribune*. The first sign of the 'unmistakable danger' to whales, he wrote, 'showed itself in a shift in species of whales that made up the preponderant part of the catch at South Georgia . . . Originally more than 95 percent of the whales captured were humpbacks, but as these became rapidly decimated the trend was progressively toward the finback and blue whales which have become the mainstay of the industry.' Despite some attempts to regulate the industry, as exemplified by the 1937–38 agreements, Murphy concluded: 'The number of whales being slain is at least fourfold what the oceans can endure on a long-term basis, yet the goal of reasonable, and hence perpetual, utilization seems farther off then ever'.[36]

International attempts at regulation

The Second World War (1939–45) drew whaling vessels away from the Southern Ocean. Many were sunk in the conflict, but some returned to whaling. Norwegian whalers returned south for the 1943–44 season and other nations' fleets were back at work in the south for the 1945–46 season. In 1944, delegates from allied nations that had signed the 1937 agreement met and limited total production. For the first two post-war seasons, the Antarctic pelagic catch was set at 16 000 BWU. (The Blue Whale Unit was a unit of measure based on the approximate yield of oil that the baleen whales yielded, that is 1 Blue whale = 2 Fin whales or $2\frac{1}{2}$ Humpbacks or 6 Sei whales. Its use was an attempt to simplify and regulate catch quotas.) The International Bureau of Whaling Statistics was given the task of collecting weekly catch reports from the whaling fleets, calculating when the catch was likely to be reached and therefore determining the date of closure for that season.

Whaling vessels from Norway, Britain and Japan quickly returned to whaling in the Southern Ocean. The presence of the Japanese fleets aroused a great deal of concern, particularly from nations that had suffered greatly through Japanese occupations or opposition during the war. However, there was a serious need for protein in war-ravaged Japan and the whaling enterprises would not only supply this but also establish a viable industry that would enable the Japanese economy to recover. The whaling fleets hunted in similar fashion to pre-war enterprises, with a system of factory ships and whale chasers. The whalers took all species of 'legal' whales and an unknown number of illegal whales. Mistakes and minor infractions of the regulations means that the full picture of the effect of this final period of whaling may never be known. However, despite a measure of protection, humpback whale populations from Area IV and V continued to be attacked both in the seas near New Zealand and Australia and in the Southern Ocean.

The next important step in the international management of whale stocks came with the establishment of the International Whaling Commission (IWC). In November 1946, delegates at an International Whaling Conference drafted a new convention, the International Convention for the Regulation of Whaling (ICRW) which was subsequently ratified and went into force in 1948. The 1946 convention established the IWC, comprising one commissioner nominated by each contracting government. A scientific committee of the commission was established to supply the IWC with reliable information concerning whale stocks and other relevant information.

The Preamble of the new convention reaffirmed earlier idealistic sentiments in support of whale conservation and many of the ideals of the convention were carried over into IWC decisions. The BWU was set at 16 000, and a pelagic season set from 22 December to 7 April. One of the decisions made at the conference had implications for Antarctica's humpback whales. The humpback slaughter of the late 1930s was recalled and hunting of this species was prohibited below 40°S.

The IWC was developed at a time of the regrowth of whaling in the Southern Ocean. There were many arguments for and against this whaling, in the midst of which were calls for sense to prevail. In 1947 William Dakin, then Director of the Zoological Department of the University of Sydney, published an article in the *Australian Quarterly*, arguing for regulation based on reliable scientific information. Dakin, a known advocate for wildlife conservation, had made submissions on these matters to the earlier League of Nations discussions on behalf of the Australian Government and was well aware of the economic and political currents in the discussions. In the article Dakin commented on the contribution made to whale research and conservation:

> I want to make it clear at this point that most, if not all, of the initiation and planning of whaling research came from scientists and others who realised the imperative necessity for protecting wild life. Such efforts in the first instance have often failed to arouse anything but antagonism in the minds of those engaged in industry. But in both fishing and whaling . . . it has now been fully recognised that uncontrolled slaughter is not profitable and that if you can't breed sea-fish and whales as the farmer breeds sheep, you can at least conserve them at the highest level of productivity by properly organised control.[37]

In 1949 permission was given (from the IWC) for a total catch of 1250 humpbacks. In a reaffirmation of the 1938 agreement, the South Pacific sanctuary was extended from 40°W to 160°W and now included the Ross Sea and the Balleny Islands, a known humpback region. (It was reopened to whaling in 1955–56.) The whaling season start was reduced from 15 December to 26 December. Expeditions were to submit to the IWC a weekly report of the catch. At four days' notice the IWC would instruct the whalers to cease hunting humpbacks when the total was met. The last day of hunting was to be 3 January 1950. The four-day grace period proved fruitful as an extra 867 humpbacks were recorded as killed before the season closed, giving a final total for the short season of 2117. This attempt at controlling humpback killing was abandoned and in 1950–51, one-day reporting was introduced, with the season reduced further, to begin from 1 February. This decision was made to avoid catching humpbacks which had returned from the northerly migration in poor condition and therefore returning less oil to the whaler. In 1953–54 the season was closed further to cover only three days each summer. However yields proved variable and from 1957 the catch declined rapidly, by 50 per cent a season down to 270 in 1962–63 when legal whaling of humpbacks ceased.

Meanwhile another major whaling nation entered the Southern Ocean. In 1947 the Soviet Union sent the first of its fleets (Slava fleets) south. They were to have a devastating impact on the stocks of humpback whales.

While many scientists were concerned about the impact of whaling and marshalled their arguments to protect species threatened with near-extinction, there were others convinced that the information provided was best used as a management tool. For example, in 1957 three Norwegian scientists published a paper analysing catch figures and making the determination that as humpbacks had not been taken (a false assumption given the extent of illegal whaling) and that as the catch figures for blue and fin whales were indicating a decline in numbers of these species, whalers should be able to return to taking humpback whales. It was arguments such as these that delayed crucial decisions to stop the whaling of species such as the humpback, blue and fin whales.[38]

By the 1950s humpback whales from Areas IV and V were being taken from their Southern Ocean feeding grounds, along the coasts of Australasia and in small numbers from the tropical waters near the Pacific islands of Tonga. Japanese whaling vessels, particularly, took humpback whales from Areas IV and V. From 1935–36 to 1951–52 at least 3578 humpbacks were taken by Japanese whalers from this region. Exact figures are not available as some records were destroyed during the Second World War. They are however minimum figures and serve as an example of the extent of Japanese whaling in these seas.

In 1963, the IWC officially banned the hunting of humpback whales in the Southern Ocean. The IWC had in the case of the humpback whale failed to live up to its stated aim of whale conservation. The 1963 prohibition on whaling humpbacks was a response to the simple fact of stock exhaustion. The Scientific Committee reported to the IWC that it would take sixteen years before it would again be possible to take only 100 humpbacks from Area V stocks, 26 years for a take of 200 and 32 years for 300.

Another major factor in the drop of humpback whale numbers was the extent of illegal and 'pirate' killing. Exact numbers are difficult to assess, but some cases have been documented. One of these is that of the factory ship *Olympic Challenger*, owned by Aristotle Onassis and registered in Panama, a nation which ratified the ICRW in 1953. The owner and crew of this vessel were responsible for persistent and continued deliberate infractions of the IWC regulations. The *Olympic Challenger* began pelagic whaling in the south during the 1950–51 season.

Soon after, rumours of infringements began circulating among whaling crews of British, Japanese and Norwegian whalers. The *Olympic Challenger* was observed infringing on a number of occasions, but on 13 January 1955, people aboard the Japanese chaser *Koyo Maru 2* found and photographed a humpback whale carcass. The killing of humpback whales at that time of year was forbidden by the IWC, the season running from 20 to 23 January. As the *Olympic Challenger* was the only factory ship in that area at that time, it was clear who was responsible. On 18 January, the crew of *Koyu Maru 2* saw and photographed the *Olympic Challenger* as it cast adrift another five humpback carcasses.

Finally, in 1955–56, seven men who had worked on the *Olympic Challenger* went to the Norwegian Consulate in Hamburg and listed the illegal whaling practices they had witnessed on the vessel. Their testimony was supported by diaries and photographs of logs that showed false reports of catches. Other infractions included hunting whales in the Antarctic outside seasonal limits during the 1954–55 season and killing whales regardless of size. During this season, the whalers of the *Olympic Challenger* had illegally taken humpbacks, many from Areas IV and V. For example, between 5 January and 7 March 1955, they killed a total 1125 humpbacks in these areas, reporting a catch of only 170.

The Olympic Whaling Company, which ran the *Olympic Challenger* was finally forced out of business by Norwegian whaling interests in 1956. Their management reasoned that unfair competition flowed from the processing of illegitimate catches.

The sudden decline in the numbers of humpback whales in the Southern Ocean perplexed some members of the Scientific Committee of the IWC. Others knew it was overfishing. A report addressed to the Scientific Committee of the IWC made it clear that illegal hunting for humpback whales was continuing. The author of the report based his information on a report on the activities of the *Olympic Challenger* circulated by the Norwegian Ministry of Foreign Affairs.[39]

The killing by the crew of the *Olympic Challenger* was not the only hidden attack on Southern Ocean humpback stocks. In 1994 the Special Adviser to the President of Russia for Ecology and Health, Dr Alexey Yablokov, told cetacean specialists attending a conference in Texas that much, if not all the Soviet Union catch data submitted to the IWC in the 1960s and 1970s was false. He advised that 'in order better to understand how various species had been over exploited, it would be highly desirable to investigate all whaling records now available'.[40] Yablokov provided some examples. Of four Soviet vessels working in the Antarctic in the 1960s, one alone killed 717 right whales, 7207 humpbacks and 1433 blue whales. The reported catch for this period was 152 humpbacks and 156 blue whales. In June 2000, further figures relating to the extent of Russian misreporting were announced to the Scientific Committee of the IWC meeting in Adelaide, Australia. The figures reveal how much worse was the attack on the humpback whale populations. Many of these were whales from the population which migrated north past New Zealand and on to Tonga and Fiji. The figures are astonishing. From the 1957–58 season to that of 1967–68, well after the ban on killing humpbacks, 44 795 humpbacks were killed. The fleets reported a take of 2035 to the IWC. After the 1963 ban 4615 were taken.[41]

Modern whaling, the most devastating period in the history of whaling, was extensively undertaken in the Southern Ocean and off the icy coasts of the subantarctic and Antarctica. Between 1904, when the first subantarctic whaling station was established and 1994, when the Southern Ocean whale sanctuary was established, hundreds of thousands of whales were killed by ships and men from many nations. 'Pirate' whaling, undertaken by vessels not bound by international regulation or convention, accounted for many more. As catch figures for pirate whalers are not completely known, the full extent of their impact is only guesswork. The total kill is higher than the published figures.

The story of humpback whaling in the Southern Ocean is a clear example of the failure of efforts to control international whaling— to somehow confront and ease the tragedy of the commons. During this period, scientists continued their work of observation, description and analysis, drawing much information from the carcasses of the whales pulled into shore stations and onto whaling ships for processing. Among the many stories and writings of whalers, scientists and observers can be found a variety of calls for caution in whaling to halt or slow the decline in populations. Most of these calls were ignored until whaling stocks of a particular species had been exhausted.

As modern whaling grew in the Southern Ocean, fresh enterprises developed along the coasts of Australasia and New Zealand. Their whalers took more humpback whales from the populations so seriously depleted in the south. This time the whales were killed as they migrated north towards their breeding grounds.

CHAPTER 4

The northerly migration

T he Antarctic pack-ice cover is at its minimum in February. Soon after, the southern summer changes into a brief autumn. As the weather gets colder, the sea surface near the continent begins to freeze. It looks 'greasy' as very small ice crystals gather. Temperatures continue to fall and the surface ice coagulates and thickens. Swells and storms break this layer into plates which, as they rub and bump together, form round shapes that look like pancakes. The pancake ice freezes and breaks up again until eventually it solidifies for the season. Water freezes to the bottom of the thickening pack and snow may accumulate on the surface. By late March the pack ice has formed around the coast. During the following months it thickens and extends north.

The long sunlit days begin to shorten and those animals that receive their migratory cues from changing periods of daylight begin to go north. In small groups, the humpback whales leave the feeding grounds and swim towards the landmasses of New Zealand and Australia. They are at their heaviest, with thick blubber reserves accumulated from months of eating. In mid to late March, the first humpback whales to leave are lactating females, with their calves. These calves have spent their first summer in the feeding grounds. Although still feeding on the extremely rich milk of their mothers the calves have learnt the rudiments of survival in the icy Southern Ocean. They are now about 6 to 7 m long. By the time they reach the breeding grounds, they are yearlings.

About twelve days later the immature humpbacks, the 'adolescents' leave in small groups. They are followed two to three weeks later by the mature humpbacks and 'resting' females, which are neither weaning calves nor pregnant. This is the largest group and its passage north represents the peak of the migration. The pregnant females are the last to leave about two weeks later. They have carried their young since conception the previous August/September and have been feeding for five months. They are now ready for the long trip north, and for giving birth and suckling.

As the migration continues, a procession of humpbacks extends north from the Southern Ocean. The rate of migration varies slightly and is affected by water conditions, currents and the weather. Individuals may swim at a different pace, but when migrating together they appear to swim in a rhythm, rising to breathe and then passing under the surface almost in unison. Although there may be a lingering at certain locations the migration is steady and the whales move north passing across an average of 15° of latitude a month. This is over 850 nautical miles a month.

Navigation

The exact means of navigating while migrating is not yet known. Navigation may be a reaction to a number of influences. Some researchers suggest that the whales simply swim north and find themselves at New Zealand or Australia after a period of swimming. Current flow is no longer thought to be a significant aid or hindrance to migration and no definitive link has yet been drawn between sea floor topography and humpback whale migration routes. However, there are undersea ridges that link parts of the Antarctic to New Zealand and Australia. If the whales use shallower waters, or the changes in sea swell and flow caused by sea floor topography as migratory guides, these ridges may assist them to locate or guide themselves as they migrate.

However, there is little undersea topography to lead the Area IV humpbacks north and it is reasonable to suggest that other means are used to direct humpback whales north. Researchers know that humpback whales have extensive aural communication, including a 'song' and it is possible that the sounds made by experienced whales travelling north may guide others in the population.

An interesting suggestion has been put forward by other researchers who suggest that whales navigate using the earth's magnetic field as a guide. The earth is encompassed by a web of magnetism. This web has many local variations and it is affected by the magnetic characteristics of the local geology. This can be mapped. Lines can be drawn to depict areas of magnetic intensity, like a contour map or a meteorological chart. These lines form a sort of magnetic topography with hills and valleys peculiar to a particular region. Whales may use these as guides or reference points.

The total magnetic field fluctuates in a fairly regular manner each day. These fluctuations reflect lunar, seasonal and sunspot cycles. However, there are also irregular fluctuations, caused by solar activity. It has been suggested that anomalies and changes in this magnetic pattern are one cause of whale strandings.

Dr Margaret Klinowska of Cambridge University has proposed that the whales may use the general shape of and changes within the magnetic field as a simple map and timer that allows them to monitor progress. The timer is the fairly regular daily fluctuation in the total magnetic field. If a whale perceives the changes as it passes through the magnetic fields, it may be able to determine location.

Although very sensitive receptors are required to 'read' the changes in the earth's magnetic field and researchers have little idea about how such reading takes place, small amounts of magnetic iron oxide have been found in the tissue and brain of whales. These may play a role in the detection of changes in the earth's magnetic field.[1]

As the humpback whales swim north, they experience changes in their environment. The length of daylight alters into more marked periods of day and night. There is less and less ice in the water as the remnants of the pack-ice are left behind. The frequency of large icebergs and their ice trails gradually diminishes. As the whales pass 60°S, they are in warmer, open water. They pass through the Antarctic Convergence, a shifting oceanic zone of variable width, which marks the northern boundary of Antarctic waters. Here, around 58°S the cool southern seas meet those of the warmer north. The convergence is characterised by a change in sea temperature and a slightly more saline density to the north.

During the northerly migration the vanguard of the procession, the females with calves, may pass the first newly pregnant females as they migrate south to begin feeding. This usually occurs south of 30°S. In the nineteenth century observers recorded that humpbacks were seen in southern locations throughout the year. These observations may reflect this link in the migratory passage.

When the whales reach the southern parts of New Zealand, most swim north along the south-eastern coast of South Island and after moving along the length of the island, turn north-west into Cook Strait.

The North and South islands of New Zealand are separated by Cook Strait. The Bay of Islands, on the north-east coast of the North Island contains shallow and protected waters. It is a haven for many whales: southern right whales, sperm whales and humpback whales. These two areas were sites for early New Zealand whaling. Two of the most interesting whaling operations, the Perano family business of Tory Channel (1911–64) and the Cook station at Whangamumu (1890–1931) relied almost exclusively on the migrating humpback whales for their catch.

Tory Channel whaling

The coastline of the north-west section of South Island is broken and twisted into a profusion of headlands and bays. Some of the bays are narrow and the land by their shores drops steeply to the water. A large inlet, Queen Charlotte Sound runs south-west into South Island, and contains on its southern side Arapawa Island. The clear and beautiful waters of Tory Channel flow between Arapawa Island and the coast of South Island, from Queen Charlotte Sound to Cook Strait.

Tory Channel is less than a kilometre wide. Nineteenth-century whaling ships chose not to hunt whales in the narrow channel. Instead, whaling was left to the bay whalers who settled on the coasts of Tory Channel and who hunted the whales from small open boats. The earliest, at Te-Awaiti, was set up by Captain John Guard in 1827. He built a home for himself and when seals, his first choice for the hunt, became scarce he turned to right whales, selling only the baleen as he was unable to keep for long any oil he made. Guard was succeeded by Messrs Barrett and Thoms who also only hunted for baleen. Speculators from Sydney joined the whaling here and with the equipment they brought, began to produce whale oil. From time to time Maoris caught whales and sold the carcasses to whalers for £20.

In the winter of 1911, Joe Perano began whaling from Te Rua Bay (also known as Yellerton Bay), on the north coast of South Island, facing Tory Channel. It was a change for the Perano family business, which had experience in fishing and small boat haulage. The family continued whaling from stations in the Tory Channel until 22 December 1964, when shore-based whaling ceased in New Zealand.

The first whale Joe Perano killed was a humpback whale. According to family legend, Perano was unnerved when a humpback rose close to his fishing boat in 1904. He determined to take revenge and, using a crude form of bomb lance, killed the next humpback he encountered. Soon after this experience Perano decided to begin commercial whaling.

The Te Rua Bay operation was rudimentary. Buildings left from the earlier whaling operations of the Heberley family at the western end of the small beach were used. A crude open-roofed structure served as a factory for processing the carcass. The Peranos set up a boiler to render the blubber into oil. Water was taken from a small nearby stream. At night during the season, the men slept on the wooden decks of their launches.

They used three motor launches, *Cresent*, *Mahau* and *Louisa*, to chase the whales in Cook Strait and, when close to a humpback, to throw a harpoon to catch it. A bomb fired from a hand-held gun usually killed the whale. Then the carcass was towed through Tory Channel back to Te Rua Bay. There was no ramp or lift to bring the carcass out of the water, and it was cut up in the water where it lay. The men cut to the waterline and, at the next high tide, rolled the carcass over to cut away the bottom blubber.

If the catch was a right whale, the head was removed and taken ashore, where the baleen was taken out and put into the stream to be washed. The constant flow of water softened the flesh surrounding the baleen roots making them easier to extract and clean. It was then dried and bundled for sale. The whale blubber was cut into pieces about 45 cm long and 15 cm wide, as thin as possible, and placed into small steam-boilers. When the pressure was adequate, it would be held for four or five hours. Water was then pumped in to raise the oil from the residue. Once the oil was taken, the residue was tipped into the channel. Treated in this way, a humpback whale would provide 4.5 to 5 tonnes of oil, most of which was sold to rope manufacturers in New Zealand and Australia.

It was a long first season, lasting from May to September, 1911. There was some whaling opposition to the Peranos at this time, from businesses like that of pioneer Tory Channel whaler, James Jackson. In the event of a chase between two whalers, the first fast harpoon in a whale was seen as a mark of ownership. The Peranos killed six humpbacks that season and hauled them back through Tory Channel to Te Rua Bay, a task that proved to be long and arduous. The trip back demonstrated the need for a station closer to Cook Strait. Despite the disadvantages of this effort, the Perano whaling that year proved that their launches outpaced both the whales and the open rowing boats used by other whalers in the locality.

The next season Joe Perano moved base to Tipi Bay on the coast of South Island over the channel from Arapawa Island. Here the land dropped steeply to the shores of the small bay. There was not much space for buildings and most of the level ground available was used for storing oil casks. At first their equipment was primitive; the whalers used knives to cut away the blubber. The whale oil was boiled down in drums. Later, purpose-built flensing knives, very sharp, curved blades on poles and spades were introduced. The whalers built small shelters near the bay and came to work in small boats. Most of the whales were not caught in Tory Channel, but in Cook Strait. When alerted by men on lookouts, the whalers took the fast launches out after the whales.

In 1916, there were three whale-chasing launches and a harpoon gun on a tripod was installed on the 12 m launch *Crescent I*. This was the first time a harpoon gun was used in Cook Strait whaling. By July that year, 62 whales had been seen and sixteen caught, three lost.

In 1919 the other whaling families withdrew, leaving the Perano men as the only whalers in Tory Channel. In 1924, Joe Perano used an explosive harpoon, the first use of this technology in New Zealand. From 1923 to 1928, Joe Perano and his brother E. C. Perano competed for the humpback catch. Both parties used speed launches and the intense competition for whales often produced spectacular chases. The Joe Perano party used a 'mother ship', the *Waitobi*, to tow the launches from Tory Channel out into the Cook Strait and to bring whale carcasses back to Fishing Bay. The E. C. Perano party had no such vessel and their fuel costs proved to be a significant factor in their eventual closure in 1927. Over the next two years, the equipment from Tipi Bay was transferred over the channel to the Fishing Bay Whaling Station at Arapawa Island.

In 1923, the Fishing Bay station had a small processing plant, a large digester (pressure boiler that assisted in the rendering of blubber to oil), a steam boiler, and a winch and six 1818-litre tanks for storing oil. The whale blubber was cut into small pieces by hand and fed into the digester. For the first few years the buildings were crude and life was rough. Whalers lived in nearby shacks. They made their own beer and liquor. Other everyday stores were brought to the station by a small boat and a 'pedlar'. Calling twice a year, 'Peter the Syrian' stocked a wide range of goods that he sold to the whalers and other isolated people in the region. From time to time the men ate whale meat, often stewed, whale liver, called 'lambs fry', and bacon.

The whaling was thrilling but required hard and skilful work and inevitably it was gory. Blood, fat, bones and organs of the whale were spread across the area as the carcass was cut up. After the whale had been stripped of all fat, the carcass was pushed back into the sea to rot or float away.

Despite the gore—possibly because of it—whaling operations such as the Peranos' drew tourists, and journalists seeking a good story. Their accounts are often sensational but sometimes accurate descriptions of the activities of the 'host' station. In the 1930s Stephen Gerard from the *Dominion* newspaper visited the Perano's farm at Whekenui, beside Fishing Bay. At this time there were three launches, *Miss Whekenui*, *Cachalot* and *Sea Raider* and the steam tender *Tuatea*. His story, 'Speed boat whalers', was published in 1938.

During the whaling season, a group of men kept watch 100 m up a hill overlooking the mouth of Tory Channel and from this observation point the whales could be seen as they migrated through Cook Strait. When Gerard visited, the lookout was a low iron-roofed structure, dug into the hillside. The view, stretching to North Island, 64 km away, was commanding. From this vantage point, fortified by tea and sandwiches, the watchers used binoculars to search for the blow. Once it was sighted the men rushed down the hill, leaving two at the lookout to raise a flag and send a wireless message explaining the location and number of whales seen to the *Tuatea*.

Two vessels put out immediately on hearing the message and the third waited for the lookout men. Gerard was on the 12 m *Miss Whekenui*. It was purpose-built and Gerard perhaps unkindly described the boat as 'little more than a modified sea-sled, drawing about 30 inches of water'.

While speeding out to the whales, the gunner placed a brass

cartridge filled with gunpowder into the breech of the gun and then inserted a harpoon down the muzzle. The harpoon had a sharp triangular head, packed with explosives and fired by a timefuse set to detonate eight seconds after the gun was fired. Three 15 cm barbed hooks behind the head of the harpoon opened out after impact and prevented the harpoon from tearing out of the whale. The maximum range of the system was about 18 m.

About 22 m of line was attached to the harpoon and this was coiled loosely on the bow. It led back around a loggerhead at the cabin to the main rope coil in the after hatch. The helmsman's duty was to both steer the boat after making fast to the whale and to watch as the line uncoiled if the whale swam away or dived. A 'bomb', containing three plugs of gelignite, at the head of a heavy iron spear was also kept near the helmsman who threw it into the whale after he had manoeuvred the boat close enough to have a go. Insulated wire led from the bomb to a secure fastening in the cockpit.

When spotted, the whales were chased, the launch engines roaring, which must have been frightening for the prey. On this day, the chase continued like 'greyhounds after a hare. The two whales double and dodge, blowing now ahead, now astern, with the relentless hunters never far behind. [The whales] keep together, the two humps showing always side by side.' As the hunters closed on the animals 'a huge flat head, warty and knobbed and hideous, like that of some uncouth prehistoric monster' broke out of the water.

The harpooner shot and the harpoon, followed by coils of rope flying in the air hit the side of the whale. Diving, it took the launch in tow. When it next rose the harpooner on the *Cachalot* threw his dart into the animal. Immediately the helmsman touched the end of the wire to electric points on the launch and the bomb was fired. A muffled thud was heard and the whale rose again, blowing blood. An air-spear was thrust deep into the animal and air pumped through a hose connected to the engine into the carcass. A dead humpback whale quickly sinks and this method was devised to keep the carcass afloat. Usually the whale was still alive when the air was pumped in.

Both whales were killed and wire strops passed through a hole cut in their flukes. As the *Tuatea* towed the carcasses and the launches home, the crews relaxed in the small cockpits. Gerard dramatically described the processing of the carcass, a procedure that took about three hours:

> The colossal carcass with the flensers slashing at it with their knives, the racket of the noisy chopper slicing up the blubber, the figures of the digester-men moving in the glare of the furnaces, through an atmosphere of steam, made an impressive sight. Over the factory circled screaming multitudes of gluttonous sea-fowl. The whole locality was pervaded by an overpowering aroma of whale. No doubt at all, it was a picturesque industry.[2]

During the Second World War, the Perano business was classifed as an essential industry and whaling continued. They were sometimes assisted by Royal New Zealand Air Force planes as they flew across the Cook Strait. Pilots who saw whales would sometimes fly in circles over the animals when they saw them, alerting the whalers. Two new radio transmitters were made available to the whalers to assist in their work and no doubt to alert authorities of any unusual events they saw.

In September 1940 Joe Perano went to Australia to advise the Australian Government on the potential of renewed whaling in Australia. His investigations indicated that a successful venture could be set up at Eden on the south-eastern coast of Australia, producing 500 whales a year taken from the flow of migrating humpbacks which regularly passed by. During his work, Joe Perano met George Davidson, a central figure in the Twofold Bay whaling which had ceased in 1930. Despite substantial planning and some investment—a whaling site near Eden wharf chosen, a plant costing £35 850 planned and test piles for the station sunk—Perano's plans eventually came to nothing.

While he was in Australia, the first major changes were made to the establishment at Fishing Bay. Perano's sons Gil and Joe rebuilt the flensing floor; rearranged the blubber floor, realigned the mincing engine and replaced a steam engine which drove the mincer with one powered by diesel. The moves were essential to speed the processing of whale carcasses which in busy periods lay in the water beside the ramp. Whale blubber goes 'off' as it deteriorates, and the resultant oil is of poorer quality; leaving carcasses to deteriorate in the water while awaiting processing was a wasteful procedure.

A few years later, in the 1948–49 season, a new technique was introduced to make the killing more efficient and more humane. Rather than kill whales with bombs, electricity was used. Once the whale had been harpooned, and when the launch was close, an electrical current was carried through a thick cable connecting the harpoon to generating equipment on the launch. Only one charge was required. Death was said to be instantaneous.

The system appeared to work. Joe Perano was quoted as saying 'It all seems so strange. The whale just rolled over without a struggle.' However, there were problems. The electric cable broke occasionally. Mild electric shocks had been received by whalers handling the equipment, a large generator had to be placed on the launches. For best results, the electric harpoon had to be fully embedded in the carcass. If not and the electric charge initiated, the current served only to infuriate the animal and in the consequent threshing around, endanger the whalers. But the main problem was that the electric current broke down blood tissue, causing blood to congeal and thereby spoiling the meat for freezing. Electrical methods were abandoned.[3]

At this time Perano whale steak was being marketed, the taste being compared to 'salmon-beef'. It was claimed to be nutritious, with the best cuts from the centre back the preferred cut of whalers. Much of the whale meat was exported to relieve a food shortage in some areas of the world still recovering from the devastation of the Second World War and a batch was sent to the United Kingdom in 1946. Whale meat was 'off ration' at that time and requests for the meat increased. A change in packing methods led to a high percentage of tainted cans, and to the collapse of the export trade after 1949.

In June 1950, fishmonger V. A. Barnao of Palmerston North, New Zealand began to advertise and sell Perano 'whale meat fillets'. His leaflet exhorted potential customers to:

Try it, taste it. It's delicious. It's fresh. Tender, appetising and economical. It has no fat, no bone, and therefore no waste. Cook it like ordinary meat. A recipe will be supplied with every purchase. Take home a pound on Thursday and try it. We guarantee that you will be back for more.

A recipe supplied by Barnao in a newspaper advertisement was basic:

Take 3 or 4 medium sized onions, cut up and brown in pot. Cut 1 lb of WHALE STEAK into cubes, place in pot with browned onions. Add water to cover. Simmer slowly for one and a half hours. Thicken and serve.

There were other ways of cooking it: 'You can cook it like any other meats; you may also fry or grill it, but because it is so tender it is not recommended for roasting. Whale steak is nutritious and full of proteins.'[4]

Despite hopes, predictions and enthusiastic marketing, whale steak did not become a popular meat for a population used to mutton, lamb and beef and the trade dwindled.

Joe Perano died in 1951 and his sons Joe and Gil took over the business, modernising the factory and forming in 1957 Whekenui By-Products, a family business that marketed the by-products of whales such as fertiliser, medical products, and blood and bone. The process ensured the complete use of the whale carcass.

The 1959 season was good for the whalers and 207 whales were killed and processed. The best year, however, was 1960, in which 472 whales were seen from the lookouts and 226 killed. During one successful 16-day period, the men took 78 whales. The processing backlog was such that they suspended hunting and went out marking whales for research, rather than continue the kill.

By this season the processing of the carcass had become more modernised and efficient than the days of the first Perano operations. A carcass brought in to the factory was winched up the slipway by a wire strop tied around its tail. It was then raised about 5 m to a flensing deck. Once on the deck, flensers marked off sections of blubber, after which it was torn off in three large sections called 'blanket pieces'. These were taken to and slowly fed into a Kvernar pressure digester. Body fat—between 7.6 to 7 cm thick, depending upon the condition of the humpback—lying between the blubber and the meat was cut away and also fed into the digester. Enormous 'steaks' from 2 to 3 tonnes each were cut away from the carcass and taken by winch to the meat processing section of the factory where they were processed and frozen. A humpback whale usually provided four of these large steaks. The rib cage was next removed. This was usually by steam winch pulling while a flenser cut the sinews away from their connections with the backbone. The entrails, heart, liver and stomach were now winched out of the carcass and placed in the digester. The head was then removed and then the carcass turned over to allow the flensers to remove the blubber, fat and meat from the underside of the whale. This revealed the bones, including backbone, all of which were cut up with either a steam- or petrol-powered saw. These were also placed in the digester where their movement in the blubber, fat and bones kept the mixture moving. Steam was used to cook and reduce the solids. The oil was periodically taken off to another pressure digester and further refined and the oil blown into a tank. Cooking time for a 25-tonne whale was about three and a half hours. After one more refining the oil was pumped into one of three large tanks near the factory.

In the latter years of the Perano's operation, from 1957, they abandoned the explosive harpoon fired by a harpoon gun in favour of a technique whereby a harpoon was shot into a whale and a launch immediately brought alongside. A hand-bomb was then used to kill or stun the whale. After this, an air tube was thrust into the animal and air pumped into it. If the whale was merely stunned, another hand-bomb was used to kill it.

Only thirteen months after the peak season of 1960, men had to be paid off due to the scarcity of whales. On 26 July 1962 the Peranos hunted and killed three killer whales. It was an act of desperation. The total humpback catch at the Peranos during 1962 was 24, the lowest in 30 years.

In 1963 the International Whaling Commission prohibited the taking of humpback whales throughout the Southern Hemisphere. In 1962 whaling from the Whangapara Harbour station, Great Barrier Harbour Island, ceased. In January 1965 it was announced that the Tory Island whaling station would be shut down after attempting to continue whaling sperm whales. Despite a government subsidy of £NZ45 a ton for whale oil, the company had been running at a loss. The closure of the Tory Channel station marked the end of New Zealand shore whaling.[5]

Scientists visit Tory Channel

The shore stations which developed around the coasts of Australia, New Zealand and Africa and the floating factories which sailed into the whaling grounds offered new opportunities for scientists to examine whale carcasses more closely. Several whaling scientists worked at the station in the 53 years of Perano Tory Channel whaling. In the 1930s English scientist Dr F. D. Ommaney visited the operations as part of the Discovery Committee work. Dr Robert Alexander Falla of the Dominion Museum, Wellington worked with the Perano operation, gaining information on humpback whale catches for 1947–48.

In 1948, biologist William Dawbin from Victoria University, Wellington, began a long association with the Perano whalers, when necessary sharing their hut accommodation at Fishing Bay. His work at the station involved dissecting and examining the carcasses and organs of the whales as they were cut up. By examining the contents of the stomachs of whales, for example, Dawbin could get a clear idea of what, and how often, the whales ate. For two years Dawbin worked on the flensing platform, dissecting and assessing, slowly building data, before going with the whaling crew on the boats. Initially he observed from the *Tuatea*, before taking to the chase in a launch. Dawbin's work resulted in many papers and laid the foundations of his later whale studies in other whaling areas, including Tonga, Japan, Durban in South Africa, Antarctica and the Australian whaling stations at Frenchman's Bay, Albany, Byron Bay, Norfolk Island and Tangalooma.

Dawbin's initiation to the Fishing Bay world was symbolic. As he bent to work near the distended stomach of a humpback whale, and as the whaling station crew watched silently, a whaler suddenly slashed the stomach open and a wave of foul-smelling, partly digested shrimp, krill and stomach fluids splattered over him. Determined not to be put off, Dawbin carried on as best he could. His quiet toleration of the trial proved his fitness for group membership. There was little trouble afterwards and throughout his research at the Peranos, Dawbin was liked, and assisted.

Often strong working relationships developed between scientist and whaler. During his work at Fishing Bay, Dawbin formed a friendship with whaler Cairo Huntley, who later became an interested and informed assistant. Huntley, an experienced whale cutter, knew the anatomy of the humpback and could be relied upon to provide certain information. One of Huntley's most interesting and valuable finds was a rare embryo hind leg 12.7 cm long, within the flesh of a whale.

In November 1955, the Perano administration made available the whale chaser, *Sea Raider*, for the specific purpose of tagging humpback whales in Foveaux Strait, at the southern tip of South Island. Here, in six days Dawbin and the crew tagged 106 humpbacks, using methods similar to those developed by the Discovery Committee. On 8 November 1955 they saw a group of humpbacks 'grazing', taking the food as they rolled over on their sides.

As he worked at Fishing Bay, and discussed his work with others, Dawbin began to discern more about the patterns and rhythms of the humpback migration as the whales passed through Tory Channel on their northerly migration. His studies confirmed that the path of the migrating humpbacks was usually fixed and seasonally regular and that the migration occurred in pulses of different sexes, small groups which moved north at different periods during the season.

That year, after six years of research, Dawbin published some of his findings. In his reports he noted that the Cook Strait whaling was dependent upon one species—the humpback whale, 'almost certainly' part of the same population 'killed off eastern Australia' and in the Ross Sea area. This dependence on the migrating humpback whale meant that the industry was open to variable supply as well as variations according to weather, craft suitability and price competition from vegetable oils. Dawbin repeated what must have seemed an unresponsive litany to the many scientists concerned with whale research.

> Whaling by Messrs Perano is on too small a scale to be likely to have an adverse effect on the whale stocks, but an increasing killing of the same humpback stocks by whalers in other areas over which New Zealand has no control could very easily so deplete the stocks that Messrs Perano would be profoundly affected.
>
> Discovery investigations and other research has shown that humpbacks congregate each summer into five groups in the Antarctic feeding grounds and there is practically no intermixing between the groups. Therefore if any group is depleted it is not restocked from other Antarctic groups. Humpbacks passing New Zealand are almost certainly from the group known as Area V, which is the Ross sea region; those passing up East Antarctica and others passing Norfolk Island, Tonga, the New Hebrides, etc, are all presumed to be part of the same stock. Catching in any of these areas will affect any other areas dependent on the same stock.[6]

In the same report, Dawbin noted that although the total Perano whaling season lasted from mid-May to mid-August, 71 per cent of the humpbacks had passed through Cook Strait in seven weeks and half the overall total had passed through in four and a half weeks.

To amplify his work at the Perano station, Dawbin obtained records of whale sightings in New Zealand and the Pacific from a wide variety of sources, including lighthouse keepers, fisheries inspectors, Royal New Zealand Navy, Royal New Zealand Air Force, Department of Island Territories, Department of External Affairs, Department of Agriculture, Tonga and individual fishmen. From the IWC he obtained and analysed all the day-by-day whaling returns, giving particulars of every humpback caught in the Southern Hemisphere.

In 1956 Dawbin transferred to Sydney University, from where he continued his research, maintaining contact with the Peranos. His work and friendship with the whalers was recognised in his life membership of the Whekenui Whalers' Association, an honour normally reserved for the paid whalers.

Whangamumu whaling

Whaling on the coasts and in the bays of the Bay of Islands in New Zealand has a long history. Whalers took southern right whales, sperm whales and humpback whales as they passed along the coast and into the islands. Sometimes the operations were small, involving only a few people and small amounts of money. They were little more than temporary camps.

In the late 1870s, whaler/journalist Frank Bullen took a seven-oared 10 m boat to the Bay of Islands to chase humpbacks. He based himself and small crew at Russell. Four of the men were experienced whalers, the others untried—'yet to be initiated' in Bullen's words. After some discussion with available crew he used only one boat, whereas the normal practice was usually to take two; one to hunt, the other to rescue any whalers in difficulty. With eight men, the base moved to the next bay north, Whangamumu where there were 'two try pots . . . These old souvenirs of bygone whalers had at one time served their purpose at Deep Water Cove, one of the first whaling stations set up at the Bay of Islands'.

The next few days were spent establishing a base. A shanty was built, and a rudimentary camp was established. Meals were basic, 'a billy of tea and a pot of potatoes and fish were what we usually sat down to at night. For lunch, when out on the look-out, we had a couple of biscuits, and the run of the rocks. Meat was hunted for when opportunity offered.'

One day two humpback whales came close inshore, swimming too fast to be overtaken by whaleboats. The decision was made to 'ambush' the whales and as they came close, the helmsman managed to get one harpoon into a fair sized bull. It began to roll and thrash about on the surface. The boatheader decided to get closer to the animal in hopes of a quick kill.

The first lance went wide of 'a vital spot' but the second went 'into the hitches'. The whale died but unfortunately the carcass began to sink. Two lines forward and two lines aft secured the whale's body under the boat, but the carcass was too heavy and the boat began to settle. A cleat broke and the boat turned. Someone quickly cut the line and in saving the boat lost the carcass, which sank to the bottom.

After 36 hours the whale had bloated with gases from putrefaction enough to be hauled up. 'After a smoke' the men put a buoy on a line and towed the carcass back to the shore. With assistance from whalers 'Messrs Moore, in the *Tairua*', the small crew got the carcass onto the beach. By this time the blubber was 'getting ripe' but with the help of two tides the men floated and dragged it higher onto the beach. Only then was the expedition deemed a success.

Bullen, writing as 'Lonehander', summed up his descriptions of this small catch with some interesting comments on the experience and the effort required by whalers:

It was hard work shore-whaling in those days, especially in the winter season. Men stood waist deep in the water and stripped the whales of their blubber and then carried it up the beach clear of the sand. This was the worst job of all and it accounts for so many men having been whaling without ever becoming whalers. One experience generally was enough for the average man, principally because there was no adequate offset in the way of cash. It was the spirit of adventure only that held men to the whaling business in the old days—that is the rank and file, four-fifths of whom would never make a second voyage.[7]

Technical changes to whaling in New Zealand were being applied as early as the 1890s when H. F. Cook set up a factory for processing whales at Whangamumu. Here the migrating humpback whales sometimes passed between the tip of Cape Brett which juts out into the sea and a cluster of rocks slightly farther out. It was an ideal place to lay nets and catch the humpbacks as they swam through the narrow channel.

Cook and his men used open longboats to chase or herd the humpbacks into nets strung across the channel. Once caught in or impeded by the nets the whales were harpooned. The nets were 150 to 180 m long and dropped to a depth of 60 m. They hung on cables buoyed by large floats and drogues. About ten humpbacks a year were caught using this method, with the largest annual catch being nineteen whales. Later steel was substituted for the rope and the nets were stronger and more durable.

It was an interesting whaling technique and although not unique—Japanese whalers used nets for catching humpbacks off their own islands—it attracted much interest from newspaper and magazine writers. An early twentieth-century eyewitness account of a capture was written by journalist D. Fagan, of the *Wide World Magazine*:

When the nets are in position the launches and attendant whale-boats, with their crews, take up their stations at some distance to watch for the upheaval and dancing float line that marks the 'striking' of a whale . . . Suddenly a sort of shudder runs through the sea. There are tossing billows and wild commotions away by the bobbing float-lines. 'Hurrah! She's struck!' is the cry.

Away go the boats, each racing to be first 'fast' to the struggling 'fish' and so earn the bonus that rewards the winning crew.

A mighty gray-black head, entangled in a clinging web of wire, rears from out of the water. Up, up, it goes till a huge bulk of body towers a good fifty feet in the air, its side fins thrashing wildly in a smother of foam. It curves in an arch and then, like an arrow, down go whale and net together for the 'sound'.

Not for long, though. The upward drag of the bunched net-floats, and its necessity for breath, bring the 'fish' quickly to the surface— a spouting, snorting, wallowing mass; mad with rage, wild with terror of the unknown, clinging horror that envelopes it.

Bang! bang! go the guns from each boat, in quick succession. Both irons are home and well placed. A wild quiver of flukes and fins, and the whale either 'sounds' again or 'races' along the surface, towing the boats after it at express speed. But the net holds fast, and at each new effort for freedom the victim becomes more hopelessly 'wound up' than before.

Soon, exhausted with futile struggling, the whale comes to rest, and there is a momentary cessation of the mad fight as the leviathan pauses for breath. Huge, panting air-gasps are plainly audible aboard our launch at a distance of half a mile.

The crews are quick to seize the opportunity. With the lance-men ready in the bow, the boats sweep in, one on either side. 'Steady with the lance.' 'Now!' Eight foot steel blades drive deep for the heart behind the pectoral fins.

A shiver, a hissing spout of water and blood, a wallow and roll of the huge, wire tangled carcass, flashes of red and white foam in the sunlight, and the black heave of a twenty foot fin that for one dread instant, scimitar-shaped, a falling wall of bone and sinew, hangs over the boat and its occupants. The boat's crew back out like lightning, just in time. Down crashes the mighty flail, missing its blow by a bare foot. There is a roar and clap of many thunders, and jetting spurts of spray leap high into the blue.

The boats, backed clear, still hang to the lines, the crews watching events and waiting the end. It may be that the dying whale will 'sound' again or 'race' in a final effort.

But, no. The lances have gone home. A few more wallows of despair, the great tail-flukes thrash the water with lessening force, and presently the huge body, inert, lifeless, lies quietly on the surface. Hawsers are made fast to the dead whale, and while the boats return to their stations to watch the remaining nets it is towed by the launch to the flensing jetty ashore.[8]

In 1910, Cook purchased a Norwegian type steam chaser, to chase the whales and tow the carcasses back to the factory. The introduction of these techniques marked the first 'modern whaling' in

New Zealand. The new launch was being used by the whalers when journalist George Walker visited Whangamumu in November 1910. Walker's description of the hunt, similar in tone to Fagan's, was published a little later, in *Life*.

Walker noted that once the whale was dead the whalers worked quickly to free the carcass from the net. Unshackling the parts of the net did not take long. It was moved out and the net shackled together again and relaid. Walker continued, 'a hole is cut through the whale's nose, the steamer's heavy tow rope is attached, and before long the whale is placed alongside the slip at the trying-down works. When a capture has been effected, a message "Get steam up", is sent through to the try-works, and by the time that the steamer arrives with the catch the powerful winch is ready to haul the immense body up the slip.'

The men were assisted in removing the blubber by a winch, which was used to pull large pieces away once cuts had been made with long-handled spades. These were cut into pieces, 'junks' about 3 cm square and thrown into try tubs. The whole carcass was put to good use. The meat of the whale appeared like a coarse beef to Walker, who noted that a whaler looked approvingly at some fresh whale meat and commented on his desire for a slice of this with onions. The bones were crushed into bonedust, the best whale meat was tinned and exported. What remained became manures.[9]

Netting was abandoned in the 1920s. A steam launch enabled Cook to pursue and catch the humpbacks using more commonly used methods. He increased his catch to 70 whales a season, a rate he maintained until 1931, when he died and the station closed.

Scientists at Whangamumu

During the winters of 1911 and 1912, D. Lillie, biologist to Robert Scott's 1910–13 National Antarctic Expedition, visited New Zealand. While there, he was able to make what he described as 'a fairly close study of thirty seven' humpback whales. Lillie talked to whalers and was able to obtain information 'concerning the distribution and migration of whales in the Southern Seas'. His systematic work contributed to the rapidly growing body of information about Area V humpback whales. His report, *Cetacea*, edited by Sir S. F. Harmer, was published in 1915 by the British Museum as part of the scientific papers of Scott's expedition.[10]

During October 1911 he visited Cook's whaling station at Whangamumu, and examined seven individuals of the New Zealand humpback whale, then scientifically described as *Megaptera nodosa*. During the winter of 1912, Lillie spent four months on the two Norwegian floating factories SS *Rakiura* and SV *Prince George*, belonging to the New Zealand Whaling Company. The vessels, the first modern whaling vessels to operate in seas close to New Zealand, were then working near the Bay of Islands. On these ships he was able to examine 30 more specimens.

Lillie's work was thorough. He measured seven humpbacks as the carcasses were on the flensing decks of the whale station. (At that time the carcasses of humpbacks were cut up while they floated beside the factory ship and accurate measuring was not possible.) Lillie listed the average length of the males as 35 ft (11 m), and females 40 ft (12 m). Although his sample was small, he felt confident to note that these measurements were 'almost identical' to those of 94 humpback whales taken off the northern coasts of Norway and Russia in 1885 and 1886 ($35\frac{1}{2}$ ft for males, 40 ft for females). Using four adults and one large foetus, Lillie extended his comparison with other humpbacks, this time for 'Body Form'. He tabulated 21 proportional measurements, such as length from tip of snout to eye, greatest breadth of tail flukes, length of pectoral fin, height of dorsal fin and distance from eye to ear, expressed as percentages and compared them with measurements of specimens taken from Finmark (1880 and 1885), Newfoundland (1899) and Iceland (1867) and again found remarkable similarities. Despite individual differences in the shape of the dorsal fins, Lillie found that 'in each case a basal portion could be distinguished which was surmounted by the fin proper.

An Area V humpback as depicted in zoologist D. Lillie's report on the humpback whales that migrated past New Zealand in 1912. Note the barnacles on the skin and pectoral flippers. (D. Lillie, Cetacea)

The variations in the outline of the dorsal fin were quite independent of the variations in the amount of pigmentation.'

One of the most distinctive distinguishing features of the world's humpback population is the difference in pigmentation. Yet, in the first decades of the twentieth century while scientists were working on a comprehensive picture of the world's humpback whales, they continually commented on the variety of this pigmention, which initially led them to believe that the different populations may have intermingled. Lillie's work supported the view of a wide variety of pigmentation within a population.

After his examination Lillie was another drawn to the conclusion that the New Zealand humpbacks were no different to those Northern Hemisphere specimens previously described in the scientific literature.

Discussing the migrations of the humpback whales, Lillie noted, 'The first whales began to pass the Bay of Islands on their way northward about the middle of April. They continued to go north until the end of August. The greatest number passed northward of this locality in May and the early part of June.' During October and

The grace of a humpback swimming is charming. Nineteenth-century whaling captain Charles Scammon described it as being like a 'swallow in flight'. (photolibrary.com)

Mother and calf have a close relationship during the first year of the calf's life. (Australian Picture Library/Midden Pictures)

The killer whale, sometimes known as grampus. (*Natural History of the Ordinary Cetacea*, 1837)

Whalers mixed adventure and peril in their stories. This upset in the northern whaling grounds was pictured in 1837, in a book of general information about whales. (Natural History of the Ordinary Cetacea, 1837)

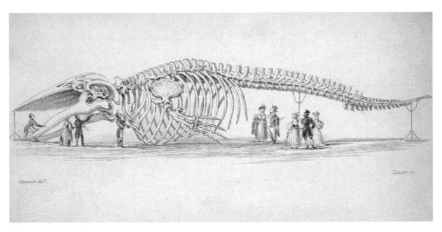

The overwhelming size and grandeur of the whale has drawn people to museums for centuries. In 1837, this skeleton was depicted—possibly a little larger than it should be—in Natural History of the Ordinary Cetacea.

Many whalers' tales were published during the nineteenth century. This drawing is from A Whaleman's Adventures in the Southern Ocean *(1849), a richly illustrated story which told of the romance and adventure of a whaling voyage on the* Commodore Preble.

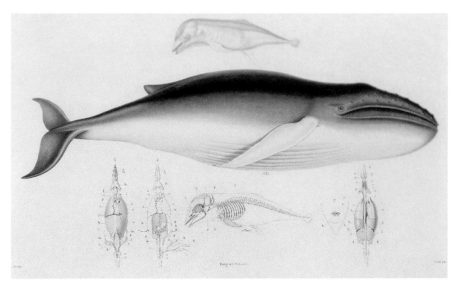

*Scientists of mid-nineteenth century voyages of exploration and discovery
collected and described the nature they encountered on their travels. This image
of humpback whale and embryo from Saint-Vincent was published in the record
of the voyage of the French expedition of 1837–40, led by C. Dumont d'Urville.*
(*Voyage au Pole Sud, Zoologie, Mammals,* plate 24)

The first catch of the 1922 season, Norfolk Island. Once landed, the carcass was cut up on the beach, the scene attracting a small crowd of onlookers.
(Mitchell Library)

Whalers with flensing sticks watch from the beach as a whale chaser steams to the wharf at Tangalooma whaling station, 1957.
(Sven Hudin photograph)

The Perano's whaling station in the 1950s, Fisherman's Bay, Tory Channel.
(William Dawbin photograph)

Processing a humpback whale carcass on a beach in Tonga, 1950s.
(William Dawbin photograph)

The harpoon strikes. Tongan whaling in the 1950s.
(William Dawbin photograph)

November the whales are travelling southwards. Lillie continued, 'After the middle of September, at the Bay of Islands, the first members of the long procession were seen going southwards. The majority passed south of the Bay during October and by the middle of December they were all south of this place.'

At the start of the season most of the females were carrying foetuses and this provided Lillie with the opportunity to examine the young and development of the humpback whales. He saw a foetus 3.9 m long (the length of a newborn being about 4.5 m). He added that as during the southward migration the majority of the cows were lactating and that the calves were only slightly longer than 15 ft (4.5 m), they had probably been born to the north. He also recorded a foetus of 51 mm in length in a southbound cow, indicating that conception had occurred farther north.

Another New Zealand shore station opened not far from Whangamumu in 1957. After two years of disappointing results, the station closed. Whaling was revived at the same station in 1960 but this venture closed too after poor catches.

New Zealand whaling effectively ended in the 1960s, and it was the collapse of the humpback populations and IWC bans, followed by poor results for sperm whaling, that compounded the poor whaling situation. The humpback whales that now pass along the coasts each year are fully protected. They are the targets now of tourists and interested scientists.

Twofold Bay

Travelling up the coasts of east and west Australia, the pods of humpback whales continue the northerly migration. Those Area V whales that go to the Great Barrier Reef pass Tasmania, or strike the east Australian coast near southern Victoria, and migrate north-east, following the coastline and rarely more than 10 nautical miles from land. They swim steadily, within small pods, bound by social activity and the sounds of whale song.

The sea around Twofold Bay, on the southern coast of New South Wales, is a very rich source of nutrition for plankton, and many sea animals frequent the area seeking fish and shrimp. Many species of whale, including the blue whale, the southern right whale and humpback whales snack-feed in these seas. Southern right and humpback whales migrate past Twofold Bay and often swim into its sheltered waters. The southernmost point of the bay is Honeysuckle Point. Lookout Point, close to the present town of Eden, divides the two bays. North Head is the northern point of the bays. In winter it can be cold, as bitter south and south-easterly winds drive up the coast and into the bay.

Killer whales (*Orcinus orca*) are occasionally seen in these waters and along the eastern Australian coast. They live throughout the Southern Ocean and along the coasts of Australia and New Zealand. These predators, sometimes known as 'wolves of the sea', are large dolphins. Adult males and females may reach 9.8 m and 8.5 m respectively. The pigmentation varies with individuals, but generally they are black above with white extending underneath the body from the chin to about two-thirds of the body length. The white extends upwards and backwards along the flanks. On the broad body is a distinctive dorsal fin which in adult males may be 1.8 m tall. The female's dorsal fin is smaller and more rounded. Killer whales attack their prey fiercely and tear chunks from their victims, whether it be seabirds, marine turtles, whales, seals or, in the Southern Ocean, penguins. They live and hunt in pods, usually up to ten strong but some packs may be much larger.

The killer whales that came regularly to Twofold Bay attacked young, old or sick whales, particularly humpback whales as they migrated along the coasts. In the past, they also herded whales into the shallows before attacking them.

European whalers were probably the first to anchor in Twofold Bay, attracted more by its shelter than the prospect of whales. In 1797, George Bass came into the bay and formally 'discovered' it for the European settlement. Later, whalers set up their tryworks on the shores and extracted oil from whale carcasses. An article in the *Sydney Gazette* of 15 August 1828 notes that Australian shipbuilder John Irvine had experimented with Twofold Bay whaling. It reported that the schooner *Darling* had returned to Sydney after three months with sixteen tons of oil. The *Gazette* also reported the news that 'whales flock into the bay in shoals owing to which there are now eighty and ninety tons on the beach ready to be brought to Sydney'.[11]

In 1828, Thomas Raine successfully established a small whaling industry. In 1832, others established whaling businesses. Merchant and farmer Peter Imlay secured land in the district and with his two brothers Dr Alexander and Dr George set up a bay whaling station and planned to also raise sheep and cattle in the hinterland. Businessman Benjamin Boyd saw Twofold Bay, 240 miles (380 km) south of Sydney, as a viable port and established two towns on the Bay, Boydtown and East Boyd. Competition for the many whales was strong. The Imlays and Boyds had shore-based operations and sailing vessels visited the area in search of whales.

The New South Wales Government chose a site for a settlement near the middle point of the bay. Later called Eden, the settlement was formally approved in 1843, but it did not grow rapidly and by 1848 the population was only 63. By 1849 nine whalers were working from East Boyd, then the main settlement with its economy based on whaling, the supply of whaling ships and the export of agricultural produce from the hinterland. By the mid-nineteenth century, Twofold Bay was widely known as a port of refuge from the fierce storms that blew up from the south.

In 1844, Boyd's vessel the *Wanderer* was in Twofold Bay with artist and traveller Oswald Brierly aboard. He noted his descriptions of the region and its activities in notebooks, making several references to the whaling. Brierly remained in Twofold Bay for two years as manager. In 1844, he noted that 30 boats operated from Twofold Bay prompting the remark that he 'pitied any whale who would show his nose here'.[12]

The whalers were both Aborigines and European settlers who

would supplement their seasonal income with work in the nearby bush, cutting timber and working on the farms developing in the region. It was in many ways a frontier existence, with the whalers establishing themselves and their occupations in a new land.

On 11 August 1844, Brierly described a whale hunt, recording one of the first European references to the presence of killer whales near the action. The men had:

> . . . started early and went round the whole bay and found this whale . . . close to the beach—here he threw an Iron which missed and the whale took off out of the bay—followed closely by Jos who fastened to it in the north bay . . . Toby behaved very well on this occasion lancing the whale repeatedly. The whale died at some distance outside the heads and the Boats had a very long tow of seven or eight hours against the wind . . . seven boats ahead and one astern to keep lancing the killers which would otherwise have taken it down—as it was they breached right on to it and it was entirely underwater—not a bit of it to be seen above the surface—and I expected every moment to see it go down entirely. However they got it safely about 2 o'clock. They say it is one of the largest there has been seen in the Bay for this season and is what they call a Magpie whale [southern right whale]— all the belly being beautifully mottled with irregular patches of the purest white—these generally turn out the best blubber—I expect this will be nearly twelve inches [30.5 cm] thick.[13]

During the 1840s, the colony of New South Wales was in depression. By 1844, the Imlays were in financial difficulties and Boyd had over-extended his businesses. In 1848, the Boyd lighthouse was being built of sandstone blocks brought from Sydney by ship, and nine sperm whalers now operated out of East Boyd, from where they went into the rich sperm whaling grounds of the Pacific. By 1849 Boyd's whaling business in Twofold Bay had ceased. His business and buildings passed into other hands. The lighthouse, which stands today, was never used as a lighthouse but was often used as a lookout by whalers.

Like the whaling established and conducted by the Perano family in New Zealand, the industry that developed in Twofold Bay in the late nineteenth century and which continued till 1930 was profoundly influenced by one family, the Davidsons. In 1842, Alexander Walker Davidson, his wife, three sons and three daughters arrived in Sydney as bounty immigrants. After working through his bond as a carpenter in Sydney, Davidson took the family to Boydtown, and in 1847 to Kiah inlet, where, near the sheltered mouth of the Towamba River, they built a small house and garden. In 1861, with equipment purchased from Boyd's now defunct operation and whaleboats bought from George Barclay and S. Solomons, Davidson and his son began shore-based whaling.

The Davidson family built a long-term successful whaling business based mainly on the southern right and humpback whales that passed by or sheltered in Twofold Bay. Alexander passed the operation on to his son John and to John's sons. George Davidson continued the business until operations ceased just before 1930.

As whaling developed in Twofold Bay and as the stories of killer whales were disseminated, journalists periodically visited the regions and published their accounts of the industry in newspapers and journals. But the whale carcass was occasionally put to other, less conventional use. A journalist of the *Pambula Voice* published an account of the medicinal uses of the carcass in the issue of 25 October 1892. People were placed into holes cut into the carcass, the males nude and the females 'covered with a loose gown' for about an hour. It could get hot with temperatures reaching 40°C. If the patient could bear the heat and smell, he or she could stay for many hours. Some returned for more than one treatment.

Although no-one knew exactly what caused the relief, the general opinion was that it was the oil and some of the gases which accumulated in the decomposing carcass. Dr Eddie of Bombala was quoted as comparing the effect and technique with that of a large poultice opening the pores of the skin. Almost miraculous cures were attributed to the treatment. 'A man from Bega' who walked with sticks, was known to have to walk unaided after a session in the whale. He later returned, walking, for second treatment.

This use of the whale carcass continued well into the twentieth century. But whaling was the main attraction for visitors and journalists, a steady stream of whom came and witnessed the experience before writing their stories.

The killer whales of Eden

The often reported relationship between whalers and the killer whales of Eden is one of the strangest stories in whaling history. As whaling in and near Twofold Bay developed, the stories became widespread, and different versions appeared in newspapers and books for many years. Given the fame of the killer whales and the power of the central theme of the stories, it has been almost impossible to separate fact from fable.

The relationship, and its consequent accounts stemmed in part from the relationship between the local Aborigines and killer whales, one that existed before Europeans came to Twofold Bay. The Aborigines around Twofold Bay held the killer whales in high esteem. They saw these fast swimming and aggressive killers as spirits of dead warriors. Journalist James Morgan reported: 'An old Aboriginal, many years dead, used to say that he heard his Grandfather speak of the Beowa (the Aboriginal name for the killer) . . . He used to relate how, when the Beowa came inshore his countrymen stroked their backs with long spears, the animals enjoying the operation in cat-like fashion. This statement is borne out by early whaling men.' There are stories of Aborigines offering food to the killer whales and calling them by slapping the surface of the water with spears.[14]

With the presence of Aborigines among the whaling crews, it was not long before the killer whales entered European whaling techniques and myths.

At this stage, whalers would sometimes attempt to catch killer whales, despite Aboriginal beliefs, and their reluctance to participate in such hunts. Brierly noted that, on Saturday 14 September 1844, a pack of killer whales was seen in the bay. One male of 'very great size' possessed a fin two and a half to three metres high on its back. The men went after the whale in their boats but could not kill it.[15]

A graphic and colourful description of a killer whale attack was published in the *Bega Standard* on 20 August 1895. The author noted that the killer whales would arrive in the area in June and remain until October. In packs of 15 to 30 they would lie in 'ambush' among the rocks on the southern side of Twofold Bay. When a passing whale making for shallower waters was seen, the killers swam out:

Like Furies, usually two or three in front, one on each side of the head, and a few following in the wake; the remainder spread across the bay . . . they twist and turn the whale . . . Should a killer be near when the whale rises to spout or breathe, the fiend throws himself plumb on the vent hole on the top of its head to prevent the whale taking air. When thus treated, the whale begins to roar (the noise is similar to a loud foghorn) from actual nervous dread of this most rapacious enemy. The killer has enormous teeth . . . and should a chance offer he will make a bid for a lump of blubber from off the whale's cheek or shoulder and probably make its mark by tearing out two or three hundred pounds weight. The tit bit to them is the ponderous tongue and lips. These they frequently attack when the whale is just killed and . . . sinking . . . They seldom if ever catch them in the open sea, for the whale swims with rapidity equal to that of the killer and can remain longer under water, so when the whale gets to sea he sinks and the killer departs again to his lair among the rocks at the entrance of the bay . . . The killers if they come to a calf, torment the poor thing to death after the cat and mouse style.

The author completed his story with the note that 'the whalers never destroy their friends and coadjutors, the killers, and these in turn will not touch a whaler should he fall overboard'.[16]

In 1903, the whaling techniques were described in the *Sydney Mail*. By then George Davidson was operating from Kiah and caught about 'half a dozen whales a season'. In this account, the killers sometimes harassed the dying whale back up to the surface for the final killing either by lance or by explosive bullet fired from a gun.[17]

Journalist Albert Dorrington visited Twofold Bay in June 1908.

Repelled by the stench of the whaling station, but perhaps also influenced by a desire for sensation, Dorrington wrote a lurid description of the station, commenting that 'Whale offal clings and rots where it holds. On Judgement Day, when the Angel of the Apocalypse has poisoned the land and sea, the Devil will smother mankind with the vitals of the whale.' As he walked around the station, covered, as he saw it, with oil and grease, he was moved: 'Wherever I grasped a boulder in my ascent there was a handmark—in oil. If I held a straggling limb to steady my footing, the oil was there where a whaler's hand had clutched. The oil-rotted grass afforded no footing, the very reefs glistened with white hump-grease. And a great smell of whale seized the eyes and filled the heart with pain.'[18]

The stream of visitors continued; their stories not always as dramatic as that of Dorrington. In 1919 the *Eden Magnet* published a description of the hunt. In this account the killer whales herded a right whale, 'maddened with pain' and attempting to escape from whalers, back towards the shore where whalers could complete the task. The following Tuesday, a humpback whale and calf, 'likewise coerced by the killers, came into the harbour, where they were effectually held up under a fierce attack by their pursuers pending the arrival of the Kiah whalers. In due course George Davidson got home with the harpoon and, after a lengthy chase which was followed by a large number of highly interested and excited spectators, succeeded in securing his prize, which it is believed will prove to be of considerable value.'[19]

The killer whale 'cooperation' which had continued for decades, was witnessed by many. The killer whale's distinctive fins enabled observers and whalers to identify and become familiar with individuals. They gave nicknames to the killers; Old Tom was a well-known male pack leader and Hookey had a bent fin. They became favourites in the area and the wider community read of their exploits in the many published accounts.

True to whaling tradition, the stories were embellished and became ever more fanciful as they were related. Some made attempts to find the basic truth behind the narrative. David Stead, expert in the New South Wales Fisheries Department, recorded his assessment of the killer whales in two articles in the *Sydney Morning Herald*. He, like many others who learnt about the killer whales' activities, was both amazed and sceptical, explaining to his readers that many of the stories would 'only be . . . accepted in the inner circles of the disciples of Isaac Walton'.

He continued 'there is one anecdote, for instance, of an occasion when the killers having failed to draw the whalers' attention (at night time) to the fact that there was a whale in the bay, by their usual process of striking the water loudly with their tail, placed oyster shells in their blowholes so as to make a siren-like sound!' No proof of this activity has been found.[20]

Thankfully, interested observers, such as Stead and zoologist William Dakin retained their scepticism and endeavoured to accurately record accounts of this extraordinary relationship. Members of the prominent Twofold Bay whaling family, the Davidsons, knew much about killer whale activity. J. Davidson, interviewed in 1984, provided further balance when he said that often the killer whales were a nuisance, attacking carcasses being towed by the whalers and pulling on ropes trailing in the water during and after a hunt.[21]

In the late 1920s Roy Bell was visiting Eden and on 5 November 1930 described the death of a large 'Black or Bile' whale, which after a long struggle was harpooned in the bay to the south of Middle Head. The whale, probably a southern right whale, 'kicked up a great commotion and made north, towing the boat behind it'. Before long:

it was attacked by two of the killer whales which are always about Eden. One with a long strait [sic] back fin known as Tom & one with its back fin bent to the right known as Hookey. These two farsoned [sic] onto the whale like bulldogs one on either side. The whale started to roll over & over & so got the whale line completely tangled about its body in the end the line parted but the two killers held it when another harpoon was driven into it & a bomb fired which did not seem to have much effect.

The real struggle now commenced the whale was now turning & lashing out with its tail in all directions & several times the boat missed destruction from these mighty lunges by a few feet only. Had it not been for the killers which never let go the boat would not have had a chance. The struggle started at about 3.30 & continued until long after dark. All the launches in the place were following up the chase to pick up the men in case the boat was smashed. The whale went north though only in a general way for it kept continually turning back & going round in circles. When half way across North Bay the boat got a chance with the lance which soon killed the monster . . . As soon as it was struck with the lance it began to spout blood in streams & soon died. But before it was quite dead the killers forced their heads into its enormous mouth & devoured its tongue. The whale when quite dead sank to the bottom when strong anchor were let go on the whale line to keep it from moving away when it should float which they usually do 12 hours after death. It was found to be afloat next day & was towed to the try works at East Boyd where I saw it on the rocks & where I took several photos. The length of this whale I was told was close on 60 feet [20 m] while it measured 19 feet [6 m] across the tail . . . This whale yielded about 6 tons of oil & about £400 worth of bone. It was a cow whale with a large calf. Other wise it would have yielded much more oil.

Bell knew that the whaling operations and equipment had not been changed to take advantage of newer or more efficient modes. 'But the whole whaling plant at Twofold Bay' he wrote, ' is more than out of date, in fact on its last legs or stages of decay'.[22]

In 1929, the last whale killed commercially by the Davidson family was brought in and processed. With the closure of the Davidsons' station, 'old style' whaling—from whale boats rowed out to intercept the prey—finally ceased on the Australian mainland. The closure may have marked the end of a unique whaling method, but the stories of killer whale hunts endure.

When the last of the killer whales which accompanied or assisted whaling (probably Old Tom) died, in September 1930, the event and pictures of the carcass were published in newspapers. Accounts, like those of James Morgan in *The Australasian* (1930), read like obituaries: 'There is not a person in Australia who has seen the killers at work, or knows of their wonderful doings, but will deeply regret that the last of those intelligent animals passed away at Twofold Bay on September 17. The loss to the whaling crews is irreparable.'[23]

Modern whaling begins in Western Australia

Soon after the small groups of Area V migrating humpback whales reach the South Island of New Zealand, and the southern coasts of Australia, Area IV whales are moving north towards the south-western coast of Western Australia, from Albany west to Cape Leeuwin. Some humpbacks from Area V are known to move west and swim along the southern Australian coast to Western Australia and to group with these animals.

The coastline along Western Australia, running north-west and north from Albany past Point Cloates to North West Cape and north-east towards Broome acts as a guide for migrating humpback whales. In late April and early May, the first small pods of humpback whales arrive from the south and south-west and move north to the warmer breeding and birthing waters off the coast that stretches from North West Cape.

During the nineteenth century, European whalers took seals and whales—southern right, sperm and some humpback whales—from the seas off western and southern Australia. The products from this work were mainly whalebone and whale oil. Often their vessels would land seeking water and food and the crew set up temporary camps on the strange shores. As the whalers became familiar with the whaling grounds and as they listened to previous experience, their knowledge of the whales' movements grew. By 1833 for example, American whalers knew that humpback whales appeared seasonally off the West Australian coast. They knew that by following the migrating humpback whales to the Monte Bello Islands and the Dampier Archipelago off the north-west coast of Western Australia, they would find great concentrations of whales. They also knew one of these concentrations occurred at Shark Bay, on the mid-west coast.

In 1840, thirteen whalers were reported at anchor in Swan River, Western Australia. A large whaling industry, based mainly on southern right whales and sperm whales, developed off the coasts of South Australia.

Modern whaling techniques were brought to Australia in 1909 by Norwegian companies which had established shore stations on the west coast of Africa and then moved across the Indian Ocean to try whaling in Australia. Although committed by licence to construct shore stations, they came with factory vessels and chasers—vessels that gave a freedom to whaling operations first experienced by deep sea whalers of the nineteenth century.

Following the example of whaling licences issued by the Falkland Islands Dependencies, the Western Australian Government introduced licences of its own. These were designed to both regulate whaling within its coasts and seas and to stimulate the growth of the West Australian economy. Licence conditions included an annual levy of £50, the stipulation that shore stations be built, and that the entire carcass be utilised, and a ban on the killing of females with calves of a 'non commercial size'.[24]

In certain cases the administrative structure of Norwegian marine companies saw a managing company overseeing the work of discrete whaling companies, each of which might operate in a different region, yet each being associated with the central management in Norway. At times these companies would share equipment. Each company would apply for and receive exclusive licences to whale in different regions, thereby appearing on paper if not in fact to be applying a form of cartel over a whaling ground. One such company was Christian Nielsen Company of Larvik, which conducted the affairs of the Spermacet Company and of the Western Australian Company, which had secured an exclusive licence to hunt whales in north-western Australia. This licence was not taken up and managers sent the Spermacet company vessels to the north-west. Norwegian consul August Strang acted as Australian representative and the experienced Captain Bull as whaling organiser. Already successful on the west coast of Africa, the management of the Spermacet Company sent the factory ship *Vasco da Gama* and chasers *Fynd* and *Klem* to Western Australia.

The arrival of the Spermacet whaling ships on 23 June 1912 marks the beginning of successful modern whaling in Australia. Soon after the ships entered Fremantle Harbour, expedition leader Captain Siegwarth entertained politicians and businessmen on board the *Vasco da Gama*. The expedition was celebrated as a new and useful enterprise for the west of Australia.

A few days later, the expedition went north, and attempted to find a harbour on the barren, inhospitable coast near Point Cloates. Shark Bay was tried without success. Adequate and protected anchorages and fresh water were both difficult to find. Wells sunk in the dry coastline held some fresh water, but if dug too deep the water became salty.

However, some whales were killed and more was learnt about their migrations. On 10 July 1912, men of the *Fynd* killed the first humpback; on the 11th the *Klem* killed another. By the end of July 34 whales were taken. In August, the catch improved and 113 whales were killed. The humpback whales were still travelling north during July and early August. In the third week of August they were seen swimming south, a return migration which continued until the end of September. The last whales were caught on 2 October. The 'season's' total was 224 humpbacks, which provided 5696 barrels of oil. On 5 October the vessels returned south, to hunt for sperm whales along the southern coast of Western Australia.

Frenchman's Bay

The Spermacet whaling vessels reached Frenchman's Bay on 29 October 1912. Soon after work was commenced on building a shore station. Frenchman's Bay, on the western side of King George's Sound on the southern coast of Western Australia had many of the natural features needed for a successful shore station. The bay gave protection from storms to the whale chasers and access to the seas through which sperm, right and humpback whales travelled. A small stream runs down to the sandy bay providing the much-needed water for drinking and for the steam processing of blubber. It is an attractive place, surrounded by eucalyptus trees and scrub.

In 1915, Sydney-based zoologist and whaling historian William Dakin visited the Frenchman's Bay station. He found it well established, but isolated, with only a few bush tracks out. A two-storied wooden building containing the boilers in which whale meat and bones were digested under steam pressure stood at the end of the wooden flensing platform. Opposite this, in a shed, were the open boilers for rendering blubber. An engineering shop had been built at the end of the jetty. Here all repairs were carried out, including the manufacture of new heads for explosive harpoons, and parts for the motor launch engines. Wooden houses, home for the men during their stay at the station, were dotted throughout the surrounding bush.

The 167-ton whale chaser *Fynd* was 31.6 m long and 6 m wide. As with other chasers, her bows were high and she was low in the stern. When hunting, a short gun mounted over the forecastle was loaded with a heavy 2 m metal harpoon. This had four large barbs and a pointed screw-on cap containing the bomb. In the hands of a good harpooner, brought to within 18 m of a whale, it was an accurate and deadly weapon.

On one trip at sea, with Dakin aboard the *Fynd*, the men saw two humpbacks and followed them. The harpooner, in this case the skipper, took his place at the gun. His job was to forecast the place at which the whale would next rise and then to fire the harpoon into its side, just below the flipper. The humpbacks heard the chaser's engines and swam quickly away. The whales surfaced only briefly to breathe before continuing the escape, following a zig zag pattern. The chaser, however, closed in and as the whale surfaced close to the bows the harpooner shot his weapon. The harpoon went cleanly in and the bomb exploded, killing the whale. Dakin's response was one of curiosity and awe:

The muscles and tissues were still alive, practically as full of life as they had been a minute before when the creature was, if not a thing of beauty in appearance, a marvellous living mechanism. She was now like a wound-up clock with nothing to put the pendulum in motion, a vast mass of living cells still ready to do their duty, but with the central nervous system shot away and the amazing telegraphic system of nerves completely out of gear. Some tissues were still doing their job. Here and there a muscle quivered and twitched. She was a hulk of dead and living tissues, each cell craving for the oxygen and food supplies which were being denied it. A little longer and the great beast would be a dead mass, a thing of value only in terms of industrial processes; workmen in the chemical factories of far-off lands would earn wages by treating the fatty compounds, the products of its former living activities.

Dakin recorded his reflections on the kill. While there remains an element of literary convention in his sentiments, his thoughts display a genuine concern.

It is always after the excitement is over that regret and depression come, and I think it would be impossible for even a seasick landlubber to miss the thrill whilst a whale hunt is on. But one later has other feelings. No one who has seen a whale die can ever think of it unconcernedly as a fish.[25]

Once the whale was dead it was hoisted tail-first to the bows and a heavy chain cable passed around the carcass. The flukes were cut off and the carcass pumped full of air to prevent it sinking. The compressed air grotesquely inflated the whale carcass and the large tongue extended from the mouth in a large and almost ridiculous fashion. It was marked with a small flag and set free to be collected and taken back to the station once the day's hunt was over.

While these Norwegian companies were establishing their businesses, others came to Australasian seas. Two vessels of the New Zealand Company (another subsidiary of the Larvik-based C. Nielsen), the *Prince George* and the *Rakiura* had spent some time whaling in the Bay of Islands in New Zealand, before returning home in 1912. The hunting in New Zealand was not successful and the ships were transferred to Western Australia, where Mr Stang had obtained a licence for the coastal stretch from Cape Leeuwin to Steep Point. Again the returns did not match expectations and the largest factory ship and two chasers were sent back to the Congo, while the factory ship *Prince George* and two chasers were retained to work for the Spermacet company.

Meanwhile, modern whaling vessels attempted whaling off the east coast of Australia. The Australia Company, established by the Monsen firm of Tonsberg, sent the factory ship *Loch Tay* (8000 tons) and three chasers *Sorrel*, *Campbell* and *Lionel* to Australia. In 1912, the *Campbell* and *Sorrell* left Norway and the *Loch Tay* left Cardiff for Fremantle. However, the chasers saw no whales and the *Loch Tay* was diverted to Sydney, arriving on 10 August 1912. As the chasers sailed to join the ship they found whales at Jervis Bay, at latitude 35°S.

A licence was obtained from the New South Wales Government and the *Loch Tay* arrived in Jervis Bay in September. Only a few whales were caught, producing 3000 barrels of oil. Management decided to try again next season and achieved moderate success in New Zealand with a catch of 30 sperm whales. On their return to Jervis Bay, in May 1913, they found that residents, and the personnel at the newly established naval base had complained about the pollution and the smell arising from whaling in the region. The company caught humpback whales in May and June, before the local peak of the humpback migration which occurred in July. Five hundred barrels of oil were produced before the *Loch Tay* returned to Norway. The Norwegian consul for Sydney expressed doubts about the feasibility of Australian whaling but in his letter home, written in October 1913, he noted that 'if a company could carry on whaling south of Australia, on the edge of the ice, it would certainly find lucrative fields'.[26]

In the west, the Spermacet Company again went north in 1913. Captain Bull and Mr Stang had made further investigations and decided that Point Cloates would be a more profitable place to hunt the humpback whales. A small harbour formed by a natural breakwater of a coral reef was chosen as a temporary shelter. The bay was unnamed and Captain Siegwarth called it 'Norwegian Bay'. The factory ships *Vasco da Gama* and the smaller *Prince George* anchored in the bay. Freshwater wells were dug in the barren and low-lying coast.

By 24 June only a handful of whales had been caught. However many humpback whales arrived in the area in late June and the catch soon increased. It subsequently exceeded all expectations and the factory ships were overloaded with carcasses. The *Vasco da Gama*, with a capacity of 1600 barrels of oil a week was pushed to an output of over 2000 barrels a week. The *Prince George* was similarly occupied. On 28 July, twenty humpbacks were processed and by the end of that month 320 humpbacks were brought in. The southern migration commenced in early August and by the 17th it had reached a peak. By the end of August, the expedition capacity was almost reached and chaser captains were told to restrict their catch to two whales a day. By season's end, 654 whales had been taken, producing over 16 500 barrels of oil. The factory ships returned to Frenchman's Bay via Fremantle.

The 1914 season was equally as successful. This time the Spermacet Company, the Fremantle Whaling Company and the Western Australian Company planned to work in concert, using the three ships *Vasco da Gama*, the *Perth* and the *Rakiura*. From late June to the end of September, 1900 humpback whales were killed. The change from the days of bay whaling, with its seasonal catch expectations of no more than twenty whales, was dramatic. The eventual outcome of such success was not lost on the Norwegian Whaling Company which noted in its annual report for the year that the humpbacks 'regularity in migration lends ease to their extinction'.[27]

By 1914, the West Australian Government had granted to the three whaling companies exclusive licences that extended south from Cape Lambert on the north-west coast. At that time there was a belief within the government and Fisheries Department that the humpback whale breeding grounds lay to the north-east of these areas and that they should be protected. This protection was one of the earliest forms of whale sanctuary in Australian waters.

Having met with limited success on the east coast, the Australia Company attempted to move across to the west coast but it had no licence. Captain Andersen of the Australia Company saw that there were prospects for good whaling off the Albrohos Islands. The islands, however, fell within the licensed area of the Fremantle Company although that company had not acted upon its permit. Andersen made a claim for the region on the grounds that the Fremantle Company had not fulfilled its lease conditions in that it had not constructed a shore station. Subsequently, a licence was granted to the Australia Company to take whales in the north-west despite opinion that it was a breeding ground. Naturally the Fremantle Company was concerned.

The subsequent discussions became political and finally the Legislative Assembly of Western Australia established a Select Committee that attempted to resolve this dispute, and examine the issues surrounding the West Australian whaling industry.

Select Committee on whaling in Western Australia

Less than two years after Major Barrett-Hamilton was sent to South Georgia to gather information on whales for the British Government, and two years before the initial meetings which led to the Discovery Committee, the West Australian Government established the Select Committee on whaling. It was set up to inquire into the 'whaling industry generally, the granting of licences, the obligations imposed on such licences, and the standing and operations of the companies to whom such licences have been granted'.

Inquiry members asked the whalers, pearlers and seamen who gave evidence before the Inquiry a range of questions, the responses to which provided valuable information about the humpback whales that migrate along the West Australian coastline. Often witnesses were employees of particular companies involved in the disputes.

Some of their evidence was contradictory and some of it uncorroborated. Some witnesses made it clear where they stood in relation to whaling. For example, after some discussion about the killing of calves, Captain Carl Hendrik Bjerke Andersen of the Australia Company was asked by an Inquiry member, 'It seems to me that you fellows go in for wholesale slaughter?' Andersen's reply was as succinct as it was revealing: 'I never knew a whaler who made any scientific study of a whale.'

The evidence from the Inquiry was published in 1915 and it collated information about feeding, migration, breeding and calving. It stands as one of the first bodies of information published about Area IV humpback whales. The following excerpts indicate how much—and how little—the whalers knew their prey.

Witnesses stated that whales migrated from the Antarctic in a regular pattern, swimming north during the summer to breed in the seas off north-west Australia—although witnesses were unsure about the exact boundaries of the breeding grounds. Opinions varied as to which part of Antarctica the whales left, and some nominated the Ross Sea, noting that the whales came with the current which flows from east to west across the bottom of Australia, and turned north. Others thought that humpback whales also came from the west, from Antarctica or from South Africa, where it was known humpback whales also migrated along the coast.

Captain Bull described his view of the migration routes:

> Some tracks come in on the east part and the others on western part and the whales join up further north and go up in one stream along the North West coast. They are maintaining the same speed all the way. They go round the Monte Bello Islands and eastward of the Dampier Archipelago. When they reach Dampier Archipelago, they have got to their breeding ground. Some of them go further up as far as Bedout Island. Very few go further north . . . I would say that the breeding grounds are between the 117th and 119th parallel.

The breeding and birthing season continued from late June to late September/early October. While on the breeding grounds, the young whales which appeared to have been born the previous year, called yearlings by the whalers, were observed to be close to their mothers, but 'quite able to look after themselves'. On or near the breeding grounds 'five or six males' had been seen fighting for one female.

The last of the humpback whales would have left these areas for the south by early November. One of the most interesting observations was from Captain Andersen, who stated that the migration was staged: 'whales one year old generally go south early. The bigger whales go later on and as regards the cows, we do not see them making south while we are up north.' As cow and calf migrate, the calf travels 'just above' the cow, following her movements closely. An interesting indication about pregnancy rates is revealed in the Inquiry evidence. Whalers noted that about one-third of the females caught on the southerly migration had 'fosters' (foetuses) in them. The issue of opportunistic feeding patterns during the southern migration was indicated; witnesses noted that food, in the form of small shrimp, was available along the coast and one noted that he had seen similar food at Jervis Bay, New South Wales, 'at about the same latitude'.

Once in Antarctica, according to Captain Bull the whales 'eat a certain variety of small shrimp. If a current happens to change and the shrimps are not carried into the islands [he had experience of whaling in the Kerguelen Islands] the whales are unable to get any and go away.' It was believed that the shrimp 'originated in the spring time'.

The witnesses answered many questions about the practice and impact of whaling on this population. The whaling usually finished in October. About 70 per cent of the catch was male; whether this was the result of policy, which restricted the catching of females with calves or due to an absence of females was not discussed. Despite these statements, calves appear to have been accepted as a fair catch by some whalers.

Most of the witnesses agreed that killing whales in the breeding grounds would be very harmful to whaling stocks. One witness noted further that it would be possible that the whaling stocks of the West Australian coast could be subject to 'slaughter' on more than one point on their migratory path, a fact which would be even more harmful to the stocks. Witnesses agreed that the economic potential of the whaling grounds was about ten years.[28]

During 1915, the Western Australian Company and the Fremantle Company worked together in the north, with the *Perth* and the *Prince George*. In accordance with licence requirements, construction of a shore station had commenced. The season was not as successful as previous efforts. Again, almost all of the whales caught were humpback whales. A total of 21 300 barrels of oil was produced, less than half that of 1914. The Fremantle Company sold out at the end of the 1915 season, leaving the Western Australian Company on the northwest and the Spermacet at Frenchman's Bay. In 1916 the Western Australian Company gained only 3700 barrels of oil. In 1916, it too closed down. The 1916 season for the Spermacet Company produced a total of 10 000 barrels from a catch of humpback and sperm whales. They also sold out.

Humpback whaling concentrates in the north-west

Throughout the twentieth century, Australians relied on Norwegian skill and knowledge to establish whaling operations and in some cases to operate these establishments. The main difficulties were the lack of Australian expertise and inadequate capital to set up the enterprise. However, in 1921, the North-West Australian Company was established in Perth using Australian personnel and finance.

The new whaling company was a popular project and company shares were subscribed within two days. Although underfunded due to inexperience in planning such ventures, operations began from Point Cloates. Unfortunately, the business was not a success and Mr Strang, the experienced Norwegian Consul-General, went to Norway to secure further financial support. Strang was successful. The Norwegian Bay Whaling Company agreed to assist and took over the licence for a share in any profits. The very experienced Norwegian Captain Bull took up the management of the operation. After some initial difficulty, the new company began to show a profit, a proportion of which was used to pay off the £28 000 debt of the original operation.

On 15 August 1928, the Western Australian Government debated a bill 'to regulate whaling and the business of the treatment of the carcasses of whales for the purposes of obtaining commercial products therefrom and to impose a royalty on whales taken in or brought into Western Australian waters, and for other relative purposes'.[29] The Bill was another attempt to regulate an industry which was almost beyond regulation and another demonstration of concern at whaling excesses. One of the counter-arguments to the Bill, expressed in parliament that day, was that factory ships would simply operate outside territorial waters. The migration of humpback whales, the argument ran, was the property of all, and was in parts outside territorial waters. The debate and associated prospect of regulation and of a £1 per whale royalty worried the Norwegian management.

The Bill was defeated, but the discussions it aroused were prophetic. Factory ships were being produced with slipways in the sterns, up which the whale carcasses were drawn to a flensing deck. This adaptation to the vessels made shore stations in inhospitable and remote regions almost obsolete. Whaling expeditions with chasers and factory vessels could operate anywhere in open seas, a fact then being demonstrated in the Southern Ocean. Here were seemingly plentiful whales, factory ships and chasers, and expeditions near Antarctica were more profitable than the smaller operations in Western Australia. In 1928 the Norwegian Bay Whaling Company closed its operations in Western Australia.

Whaling in West Australian waters did not recommence until 1936. From 1936 to 1938 three foreign fleets operated off the north-west coast, outside territorial waters. In 1936 the factory ships *Anglo-Norse* and *Frango*, each with six chasers, took whales from the area near or within Shark Bay. They killed 3076 humpback whales. In 1937 the West Australian Government permitted operations within coastal waters by the factory ships *Frango* and *Ulysses* and their chasers, with inspectors on board, and 3251 humpback whales were killed. In 1938 the *Frango* returned and killed 913 humpback whales.

Despite a subsequent lapse in the Australian whaling industry many continued to lobby for its resumption. These efforts were carried out amid genuine concerns for whale conservation and the growing success of Antarctic whaling, some of which was operating in the Ross Sea and along the coasts of what was soon to become Australian Antarctic Territory. Japanese whaling fleets, to much concern, had begun to operate in these waters in 1937.

Although reluctant to provide financial support for whaling, the Australian Government was aware of the economic potential of the industry and of the need for regulation. In August 1936, the year Australia assumed responsibility for the Australian Antarctic Territory, the government brought down legislation to control whaling in southern waters. The regulations, laid out in the *Commonwealth Whaling Act*, required that a licensed vessel despatched from Australia call at an approved Australian port and produce a copy of the licence. It further regulated that vessels be capable of processing all the catch into commercial produce within 48 hours of delivery to the factory ship. The provisions of the Act were incorporated into international covenants that had been first drawn up by the League of Nations in 1931.

The *Commonwealth Whaling Act* was a legislative instrument which again demonstrated the willingness of some national governments to take some responsibility towards conservation, but which could only be applied or enforced in territorial waters. It was therefore very limited in its impact and it was widely ignored.

Sir Douglas Mawson, who had for many years advocated both the exploitation and conservation of whale stocks, in 1938 summed up the feelings of many in Australia when he said: 'I still think that one of Australia's most glaring oversights is that it has not come into the whaling business. It seemed that because few people in Australia know much about whaling they had left others to explore the industry.' Mawson later noted that 'a heavy toll was being taken of whales today, and the only hope of maintaining them was not to kill the mothers with suckling young'.[30]

Post-war whaling in Western Australia

Despite these efforts and concerns an Australian whaling industry was not recommenced until after the Second World War. In 1947 the Albany Whaling Company, an Australian company, using a 10-ton chaser, *Wadjemup*, began operations. They killed their first whale—a large humpback—off the entrance to King George Sound. The catch was not easily won and the whale, though wounded, dragged the chaser for many hours, and close to reefs, before two more explosive harpoons killed it.

In 1952 the Cheynes Bay Whaling Company set up operations in Frenchman's Bay close to the site of the old whaling station. At first it was granted a quota of 50 humpback whales, but this was later increased to 175. The chasers from this company took the humpbacks from the seas off King George Sound, as they came to the West Australian coast. Although this company continued to take humpbacks, in 1955 it began to take sperm whales, eventually moving to hunt exclusively for those whales. From 1952 to 1961, the company took 1079 humpback whales.

Shark Bay, Carnarvon and Point Cloates

The western arm of Shark Bay is a peninsula. It leads to the nearby narrow Dirk Hartog Island which lies in a north-westerly direction. These landforms are the westernmost point of the Australian continent. Migrating humpbacks must move around these before swimming north to Point Cloates, at the bottom of North West Cape. Once around the tip of the cape, the whales swim north-east towards the Monte Bello Islands and along the coast towards Dampier and to the islands off the Kimberley coast. The seas off these coasts are the birthing and breeding grounds.

The Shark Bay World Heritage Area, 600 km from Perth, is a place of remarkable beauty. The area is bounded to the north by Carnarvon on the Gascoyne River and extends 200 km to the south and includes Bernier, Dorre and Dirk Hartog islands. A wide diversity of marine mammals live in its sheltered bays, including dugongs which feed on the extensive beds of marine grasses. Dolphins frequent the bay and killer whales come in to feed, sometimes attacking the dugongs. There are many sharks in the bay and off the adjacent coasts. Green and loggerhead turtles and graceful manta rays live in the region. Enormous whale sharks, up to 15 metres long, feed on the abundant plankton as they cruise along the coasts off Shark Bay.

This part of the coast is the point at which the first known European contact with Australia was made. Dirk Hartog landed on Dirk Hartog Island in 1616 and left a pewter plate to mark his landing. William Dampier visited the area in 1699, and in 1801 and 1803 the French ship *La Géographe* visited the area. Dampier named the bay Shark Bay after the abundance of sharks he found there. While searching for fresh water, Dampier sailed along the coast and landed on a shoal of coral rocks where the men scrubbed the bottom of the ship free of barnacles. Continuing north-east on 18 August, he anchored at a shoal, 22°22'S, at 36 m deep, later recording:

> . . . we had in the Night Abundance of Whales about the ship, some ahead, others astern, and some each side blowing and making a very dismal Noise; but when we came out again into the deeper Water they left us. Indeed the Noise that they made by blowing and dashing the Sea with their Tails, making it all of a Breach and Foam, was very dreadful to us like the Breach of the Waves in the very shoal-water, or among the Rocks.[31]

In November 1945, the Australian Commonwealth Government approved plans for Australian participation in whaling in the Southern Hemisphere. The government invited Norwegian Captain A. Melsom to advise and assist in the establishment of an Australian whaling industry. It had already heard the advice of Perano from Cook Strait, New Zealand on whaling on the east coast of Australia. Captain Melsom was very experienced. He made his first whaling trip aged eighteen to Spitsbergen and six years later was a gunner captain. He had visited Point Cloates in 1914 and between 1919–29 was with the Japanese whaling company Toyo Hogei Kaisha. Experienced in many seas of the world, including the Southern Ocean, Melsom was reported to have killed about 3850 whales. He recommended the purchase of a factory ship for work in the Southern Ocean and if this was not possible, to establish a shore station near the normal track of the whales. It was decided to establish a shore-based enterprise in Western Australia as a government-owned enterprise.

In an attempt to regulate the proposed whaling, the Australian Government amended its *Whaling Act* of 1936 and prescribed minimum lengths for some whales (the humpback minimum being 35 feet [10.6 m]) and a closed season of six months with a prohibition on the taking of females with calves. It was a condition of the licence grant that factories could process all the carcass of a whale. This brought the government's regulations into line with those of the International Whaling Commission.

In 1948, requests for information were published in the *Fisheries Newsletter*, a publication of the Fisheries Branch, Department of Primary Industry. The department required the 'date when whales sighted, locality, number of whale species, apparent size, whether with or without calves, direction in which whales were travelling', and the fisherman's name and address. This would provide some idea of the place and size of whale populations in post-war Australia. Reports back to the department were useful. They indicated that whales passed Rottnest Island off Perth on their northward leg from May to August. They were also found off the Queensland coast at Lady Elliot Island, Double Island and Stradbroke Island, from July to the end of September when they began the southward leg of the migration.

Modern whaling returned to Point Cloates in July 1949, with the work of the Nor'-West Whaling Company. The men established themselves in the old whaling station buildings left behind by the Norwegian Bay Whaling Company. These buildings and some equipment were renovated and a meal mill was built to produce protein meal which, with guano made from the whale offal, was sold in Western Australia. In the first year of operation, 190 humpbacks were taken. Although it was an Australian venture, employing Australians and backed with money raised in Australia, two Norwegians, Captain Larsen and Captain Jenns Andersen were crucial to the operation. The main chaser, the *Norwegian Bay*, was a converted Fairmile naval vessel.

South of the Point Cloates operation, another whaling station was established. In May 1949 the Whaling Industry Bill was passed through Parliament and the first publicly owned whaling station, to be governed by the newly established Australian Whaling Commission, was initiated. As both a supportive and symbolic gesture for the new Australian industry, whale steak was on the menu of the Canberra Parliament House dining room in October 1950.

Babbage Island, at the mouth of the Gascoyne River near Carnarvon, and near the open mouth of Shark Bay, was chosen as the site for the new station. Unlike many other sites on the West Australian coast, this one had an adequate supply of fresh water. Fifty-nine experienced Norwegians were contracted to establish the business and train Australians. This was reduced to ten by the second year of operation. The company used three modern whale chasers, the *Carnarvon*, *Gascoyne* and the *Minilya*. It was expected that the catch could be taken within a 50 mile (80 km) radius from Carnarvon. The processing plant, capable of handling 1000 whales a season, was to run from June to October, catching humpbacks on both the northerly and southerly legs of their migration.

During the first season, 1950, 190 humpback whales were taken by the Australian Whaling Commission. In 1951, quotas, derived from an estimate of that sustainable for the population were allocated to whaling stations. The 1951 humpback quota for Carnarvon was set at 650 whales, 600 for each of the next three seasons, and for 1955, 500.

The future for a regulated and well managed industry appeared sound. The writer of an article, 'They've got a £2 mil. harvest', published in the *Argus*, noted in a review of the 1951 season: 'At Babbage, the Commission treated 650 whales, for a yield of 5200 tons of oil valued at £821 600. Additional by-products yielded about £200 000. Farther north at Point Cloates, Nor'-West Whaling, with a catch limit of 600, showed a return of about £750 000 . . . So there's real money in humpbacks', concluded the journalist.[32]

Australian writer Peter Lancaster Brown worked on the flensing deck of the Babbage Island station, beginning in the first year of operation. His account of his experiences of Australia's coast of coral and pearl was published in 1972. He and the others worked the seasonal hours of operation, twelve-hour shifts, seven days a week. During each shift, Brown and the other flensers waited for the carcass to be towed in by the chasers. When it arrived, bloated with compressed air, tongue grotesquely inflated and extended, it would be drawn by winch up onto the flensing deck. Brown particularly remembered the tongue, the thin barnacle-encrusted pectoral fins and the eyes, 'tiny' and 'opalised in death'.[33]

Whalers and scientists

Biologist Graham Chittleborough, then with the Australian Commonwealth Scientific & Industrial Research Organisation (CSIRO), visited and worked at the shore station beginning in the 1951 season. Working on many aspects of humpback whale migration and anatomy, he was based in Perth and received information and specimens from the West Australian whaling stations. He made several field trips, one of which was to the Carnarvon station where he appeared on the first day 'a fresh faced lad in a brand new boiler suit, shiny rubber boots and a neat beret'.[34] His initiation to a whaling station was similar in tone to that of

William Dawbin in New Zealand. Chittleborough once fell, and as he slid on the fresh blood across the flensing deck, a 4 m long flipper cut from the carcass of a humpback fell near him.

Brown wrote in his account that Chittleborough, with whom he later became acquainted, angered the workers with his desire for precise measurements. The men were also concerned that Chittleborough's work, if it revealed too much about the destruction of whaling stocks, represented a threat to the viability of the industry. In 1972 Brown reflected that 'Chittleborough's pursuit of scientific exactness was misinterpreted by the ignorant flensing crews as a personal crusade to find undersized whales'. Brown explained his reaction to the situation:

> Conservation of whale stock is a subject which immediately separates the professional whaler from the biologist or ecologist. It was a subject guaranteed to raise the hackles of most whalers, who felt their economic livelihood was endangered by the meddling scientific community. Whalers have never listened to the advice of wiser scientific counsellors since the immediate profit was their only prime requisite.

The flensers established an informal committee to sabotage Chittleborough's work. Two 'accidentally' slashed his measuring tape when they could. Organs vital for Chittleborough's research were mutilated and therefore rendered useless before he could work on them. However, Brown notes, Chittleborough's failure to react to these tactics—his 'apparent cool indifference and lack of animal anger . . . won him the day'. The flensers' jokes and sabotage dropped away and only a few whales were totally sabotaged.

Chittleborough, like Dawbin in New Zealand, survived the 'initiation' to be accepted as a part of the work of the flensing deck. Despite difficulties with some deck crew, he formed working relationships with some and friendships with others. 'Young Dusty' Doust, leading flenser, learnt to make long cuts in the carcass and expose the various organs Chittleborough required for his work. Chittleborough sought

out testes and ovaries of the whales, from which he could make assessments for his research into reproduction and age determination. The
testes of the male sometimes weighed 13.5 kg each. He became known
as 'ball-boy' or 'balls'. Chittleborough also counted the number of
scars on the females' ovaries to ascertain the number of ovulations and
therefore the age of the whale. He was used to handling the large
organs of the whales, but when a bulge on the ovary indicated recent
ovulation, he was obliged to search the large Y-shaped uterus for an
embryo probably no more than 10 mm long.[35]

Chittleborough's work added greatly to the store of knowledge
about humpback anatomy and about the shape and size of group IV
humpbacks throughout the 1950s. But—however successful—and
Chittleborough's publications and reputation attest to that success—
his work clashed with the priorities of the whaling station. Although
whaling inspectors were at all stations, their work was less exact
than Chittleborough's scientific requirements. In 1952, his careful
measurements of carcasses was not appreciated by a management that
preferred to have less stringent assessments, particularly for those
records that indicated carcasses slightly smaller than the legal limits.
Conflict over this issue saw Chittleborough initially removed from
the station—his measurements indicating shorter whales than the
figures officially supplied to authorities in Canberra. For the remainder
of that season, he worked at the Point Cloates station just to the
north. A workable compromise was reached and Chittleborough
continued at Carnarvon in 1953. He had received, however, his first
lesson in the power of an industry threatened by the knowledge
produced by competent and principled scientists.

Chittleborough also worked from a light plane, an Auster, used
by the Nor'-West Whaling Company to spot whales, and to make
direct observations of the migrating humpbacks. With pilot Jim Pekin
and sometimes accompanied by others such as Peter Brown, Chittleborough plotted tracks and speeds of whales, recording data concerning
the time of calving, the proportion of whales giving birth and the
changeover from the northward to the southward migration.

In May 1963, Western Australian whalers prepare for the work of modern whaling: left, a whaleman sharpens his long-handled flensing knife; below, members of a whale-chasing crew adjust the head of an explosive harpoon. (*Walkabout* photographs)

There was other cooperation from station management. When the season's quota had been filled, Chittleborough and others on board the chasers followed the humpbacks and shot 25-cm markers into the whales. Fired from close range into the back muscles of the whale, this stainless steel dart was engraved with a unique number. If the whale was later taken by whalers, and the dart found during processing, it was returned to be registered, with details of location and time of catch. In this manner researchers could build up a picture of the extent and range of humpback migration. One dart Chittleborough recovered at Carnarvon had been shot by others into the whale, 23 years before.

Chittleborough's work led him to believe, as early as 1953, that the quotas were too high, and that the humpback whale population was being seriously depleted. Each year he published a report about the impact of whaling. The whaling industry response to his concern argued that the questions required more scientific evidence, and that if Australia cut quotas, other countries would kill the whales marked for Australian stations.

In 1956 Chittleborough became a member of the Scientific Committee of the International Whaling Commission. Each year the statistics of the whaling indicated declining whale populations. Each year vested interests, including some scientists, avoided the obvious conclusions that something more would have to be done to avoid a total collapse of the humpback whale population. In 1957 Chittleborough was transferred from Perth to Cronulla in Sydney. From here he continued to work with whales, using information from whaling stations at Tangalooma, Byron Bay and Norfolk Island.

When the humpback whale population finally collapsed Chittleborough moved on to other work, but his current position today, as an ardent advocate for the environment owes much to his work on the humpback whale. It was strengthened by his contact with those elements of the whaling industry, in Australia and internationally, which did their best to hamper efforts to conserve whale stocks and protect the industry for as long as possible.

In 1956, despite much opposition from those who wished to see a stronger government role in the industry, the Australian Government sold the Australian Whaling Commission to the Nor'-West Whaling Company for £800 000. Surplus funds from the sale were allocated to the Fisheries Development Trust Account to assist the development of the professional fishing industry. The Nor'-West Whaling Company site was not as good as that at Babbage Island, and its equipment there was worn out. Management moved the station to the Babbage Island site and took up its quota of whales. In 1957, the plant processed 1120 whales.

While sperm whaling continued at Albany, from the 1960s humpback whaling continued to decline. After 1962, and the closure of the stations on the east coast of Australia and Norfolk Island, Cheynes Bay retained a humpback quota of 100 whales and Carnarvon 450 for 1963. After this the IWC ban came into effect. Despite the use of spotter planes, both companies experienced difficulty obtaining a reasonable number of humpback whales, the total catch being 87, nineteen at Albany and 68 at Carnarvon. In 1964, the *Fisheries Newsletter* reported in its summary of the year's activities that the value of whale oil and its by-products had dropped from £1 006 000 in 1962 to £512 000 in 1963. The author noted bluntly: 'Sperm whaling, which the Cheynes Bay Whaling Company pioneered in 1955, is now the only commercial whale fishing in Australian waters.'[36]

CHAPTER 5

North to warmer seas

T he whales continue their migration north, swimming night and day, many within sight from the land. As they move north the seas warm to subtropical temperatures. The whales' undersea world is more evenly divided between light and dark than the days of their southern stay. Despite the long swim north the healthy whales are still fit and in fine condition with heavy coats of blubber. Singing is often heard along the migratory thread as males make a claim for mating rights. The singing is forceful and carries through the sea. It is a unifying and encompassing sound, recognised by all humpbacks as they move north. Pairs are sometimes seen and early courting or mating may begin. The pregnant females, at the rear of the procession, are close to giving birth. In fact some cannot make it to the breeding grounds and they may give birth in these seas. If kept safe from sharks and killer whales, the newborn calves have a good chance of survival.

The whales move steadily until they reach Cape Byron, the most easterly point of the Australian continent. The first humpback whales are seen off the cape in May; the bulk of the migration passes during June and July. To reach the breeding grounds the whales must swim around Cape Byron, before swimming a little more directly north to the seaward of the coastal sand islands, Stradbroke and Moreton, at about 27°S.

In the 1950s and 1960s, this section of the coast became the last place where modern whaling was undertaken in eastern Australia. The prey was humpback whales and the kill decisive.

Byron Bay

Cape Byron headland juts out into the Tasman Sea at latitude 29°S. It is a beautiful spot with sweeping views over the sea. When examinations into the feasibility of post-war whaling in Australia began, Byron Bay headland was seen as an ideal site for whaling, as it was so close to the humpback whale migration routes. This period of Australian whaling was to be supervised by the Federal Department of Primary Industries, Fisheries Branch, a representative of which attended the regular meetings of the International Whaling Committee.

Whaling had begun slightly further north at Tangalooma in 1952 and the decision was made to begin whaling operations at Byron Bay two years later. A. W. Anderson & Co., owners of the meatworks at Byron Bay, formed the Byron Bay Whaling Co. A few years later the company was sold to the North Coast Whaling Company Pty Ltd.

The company was given an annual whale quota of 120 humpback whales. Later, in 1959, it was increased to 150. The IWC imposed certain requirements on the gunners of the new whaling enterprises on the east coast of Australia, as they had done in the west. The gunner was to observe the minimum legal size which was 35 feet (10.6 m); a cow with calf was not to be killed; when he made a kill, he was to note the exact time and location of the kill and his name. The whalers knew that whales moved from the Antarctic north to the warmer seas off the coast of Queensland, and that the whales fed mainly on the plankton in the southern seas. They knew that humpback whales moving north were fatter and therefore better catches than the thinner beasts swimming south. Although the whalers concentrated on the whales in the northerly migration, the 'season' was from 1 May to 31 October each year, thus covering both legs of the whales' journey.

In February 1954 a cyclone destroyed 600 m of a long jetty and destroyed the fishing fleet at Byron Bay. The jetty was repaired and a ramp from the water to a railway built. The track led to freshly constructed buildings near the meatworks alongside the railway.

These were to operate as the whale processing factory. A powerful winch was used to haul the whale carcass from the water and onto a flat-top railway truck, which pulled by a diesel locomotive nicknamed the 'green frog' delivered the carcass to the factory. Two Fairmile Naval Coastal Patrol Boats with a harpoon gun on each bow were used as whale chasers. The *Byrond 1* was used as a working boat with the *Byrond 2* as a reserve. Both vessels were based at the nearby port of Ballina.

In 1954, Stan Nolan, Primary Industry Meat Inspector at the meatworks, accepted the additional responsibilities of Whaling Inspector at the new whale factory. He continued working with the whaling company until it closed in 1962. His long account of the operations is held in the Byron Bay Public Library.

The first whale was killed on 29 July 1954. It was taken 5 miles offshore. The chaser *Byrond 1* took two hours to bring in a 40-ton, 40-ft whale to the jetty. The annual quota for that year was reached in 61 days. The original gunners, the 'elite' of the whaling community, included Norwegians Captain Andresen and Laurie Mills.

Stan Nolan explained some of the operations:

> The *Byrond 1* would sight and chase the whales which would have to come up to breathe and reveal their location. When close enough and the gunner judged the whale to be big enough not only in terms of legal size, but suitable for the factory's requirements, he would shoot it. The whale was then roped to the side of the boat, tail flukes were cut off and jettisoned so as not to interfere with the steering, air would be pumped into the whale to make it buoyant and the whale would be delivered to the jetty. On rare occasions two whales were brought in. The whales travelling north in pairs, male and female were vulnerable for a double capture if the female was shot first. The male would remain around the area and become an easy second kill. If the male was shot first, the female kept going.

If a whale was illegally caught, Nolan was to notify the station manager and get a written report from the gunner responsible. One of Nolan's many duties was to examine the mammary glands of the female and to remove the ovaries to verify if the whale had been legally taken. Nolan learnt to discern between any residual milk in the glands and the fresh milk indicating a recent birth. He thought that there had been only a few times when a gunner 'had a whale which had recently calved'. He added that as the calf mortality rate was high, 'it was quite probable' the cow had no calf when the gunner shot it. There was no way that whalers could determine whether a whale was pregnant and some were killed by the gunners. Some of these had completely formed foetuses measuring about 4.2 m long.

Although there were penalties, including fines or loss of bonus, in the *Whaling Act* for any gunner who killed milk-filled or undersized whales, Nolan could not recall an occasion when these were enforced. 'It was a moral pressure' on the gunner. He added that the company didn't want undersized whales. It meant one off the quota. In a particularly Australian twist to regulations, the quota was increased by one when, in 1957, the proceeds of that whale were used to build a retirement home at Ballina for members of the Returned Servicemen's League.

The whales had to be processed within 33 hours of capture, or the deterioration of the carcass would affect the quality of the oil. They were brought quickly into harbour. Sharks were a minor problem, both when the whales were first killed and when carcasses were brought into the jetty. Nolan recalls:

> In the 9 years the whaling station operated, some of the whales were shark damaged on their arrival at the jetty. The majority were not. It was difficult for the shark to eat the whale unless the blubber was broken. It was like a dog trying to bite a piece out of a motor tyre. However, the tongue was vulnerable as it was the softest tissue in the body and the air which was pumped into the whale to make it buoyant, entered the tongue and caused it to protrude from the mouth. The sharks which followed the whales to the jetty . . . would then patrol around the jetty until the whale was taken away.
>
> However, there was one memorable afternoon at dusk when a pack of whaler sharks followed the whale under the jetty and as it was

hauled up the ramp, they jumped like Australian Rules players taking pieces out of the whale. The whale had to remain on the ramp as the flat top had a whale on it and the flensing floor was full. The sharks were ravenous and appeared crazy. They were not cautious or hesitant in coming up the jetty to tear chunks out of the whale.

Aub Harris (one of the jetty gang) tied an old rag, which had been used to wipe his arms, to a meat hook which was attached to a bollard by a thick rope. He threw it over but it was a couple of feet out of the water, [when] one shark leapt out of the water and grabbed the rag and hooked itself.

When the carcass was brought to the jetty, it was dragged to the ramp, pulled up onto the railway truck and taken by the 'green frog' to the factory. Here, the carcass was winched onto the flensing floor. Nolan then measured it, and noted the sex for his inspection. If it was a female he checked the mammary glands.

Little of the carcass was wasted. Whale bone was crushed to meal and used as fertiliser. Less frequently bone was carved into ornaments such as chess sets or shoe horns. Gelatine extracted from the process was used in photographic film and jellies. The endocrine glands were used in medicines and pharmaceuticals. The livers went into pet food, the tendons used as tennis racquet strings or surgical stitches. The whale oil was used for glycerine, and in soaps and margarines. The meat was sold as pet food, stock feed and put into soups and gravies for human consumption.

When processed, the whale oil was like cod liver oil, it was viscous, and tan in colour. It was stored near the factory in 300 000-gallon tanks before being shipped by rail to Brisbane and then to the United Kingdom.

Scientists also saw opportunity in the resumption of whaling and Nolan sent to staff at the Fisheries Division of the CSIRO at Cronulla in Sydney, regular information about the size of the whales and samples of the organs and ear plugs, then used as an indicator of age. Nolan found that his earlier methods of obtaining the ear plugs involved pushing at the surrounding flesh, a method which resulted in the crushing of the soft plug. The workers at the factory devised a new method and intact plugs were then sent to the CSIRO. Scientists from the Soviet Union, the United Kingdom and Japan had been marking whales with darts and these would occasionally be found in the carcasses brought in for slaughter and sent on to relevant authorities.

For the first few years the personnel at the factory were a mixture of locals and itinerants, some with valuable experience in other whaling factories. Gradually, an experienced and stable workforce was developed. In 1956 modern whaling commenced at Norfolk Island, in association with the Byron Bay Company. Using the *Byrond 1*, the company operated out of Norfolk Island on a quota. Workers from Byron Bay worked at Norfolk Island and some from Norfolk worked in the factory at Byron Bay. Nolan remembers the surnames of Christian, Quintall and McCoy, descendants of the *Bounty* mutineers, on the timesheets. The work was hard, dirty and noisome but there were some memorable moments. Nolan recalled one 'late wet night as I was waiting for a pregnant whale to be eviscerated. The Norfolk Islanders were on shift and as they worked they conversed among themselves in their soft Old English, French-cum Polynesian patois. We were the only people present and the steam from the winches, coupled with light rain, blotted out the surround- ings, creating a scene that was impressed upon my memory.'[1]

In the first few years the quota was quickly filled and the average weight of whales was over 10 tons. The price for oil was around £100 stg (then £125 Australian). In the 1959 season, the quota was filled in just 44 days. One hundred and fifty whales were processed with an average length of 13 m. In 1960, it became much harder to fill the quota. Captains had to sail farther to make the kill. Gunners could not afford to be as selective as the average length of whales caught dropped. In addition, the price received for whale oil fell, making it less commercially advantageous to hunt for the whales.

By 1962 the situation had changed again for the worse. The quota was not filled despite 144 days searching for the whales. One hundred and seven whales were processed, but now the average length was 11.7 m. The oil total was less than half that of 1959.

In 1962 whaling finally ceased. There were obvious concerns about the collapse of a local industry and the consequent loss of employment, but business was also concerned about the reduction in tourism that accompanied the withdrawal of the popular drama of whale butchering.

Moreton Island whaling—Tangalooma

Two islands, Moreton Island and North Stradbroke Island, form the eastern edge of Moreton Bay, on the western shores of which lies the city of Brisbane. Moreton Island is a sand island, covered with vegetation. The eastern seaward beaches are windswept and the dunes are threaded with tough herbs and grasses. To the west between Moreton Island and the mainland, the waters are shallow and protected. The islands lie near the routes of the humpback whale and humpback whale carcasses have been found stranded on their shores.

In one remarkable case, in 1919, naturalist Thomas Welsbey undertook to obtain the skeleton of one stranded 11 m whale for the Queensland Museum in Brisbane. The task occupied Welsbey in fifteen months of hard labour. During that period, he endured the taunts of passers-by and 'odours of a mephitic nature' until he had the bones dried and stored to be sent to Brisbane. This he did successfully, and whenever he viewed the skull of the whale in the museum, he thought: 'I see it wink and smile at other anatomical surroundings, aye even at me.'[2]

During the Second World War, a naval station was built at Tangalooma on the protected western side of the island. A large shoal just off Tangalooma forced vessels to approach the station from the south. Cold winter westerlies would sweep across Moreton Bay and push up a dangerous swell, making sea journeys from the station cold and dangerous.

On 15 December 1950, Whale Products Pty Ltd was established in Sydney to hunt whales off the east coast of Australia. After much research, the company decided to base its operations on land leased from the Queensland Government at Tangalooma, close to the migratory routes of humpback whales. A whale processing plant was soon erected. A log ramp ran up from the sea to the flensing deck, which surmounted a large factory. Staff were accommodated in nearby buildings. The station was built in an idyllic setting, amid large eucalypts and surrounded by dense scrub. On a calm day the waters of Moreton Bay were a clear, green blue.

Experienced Norwegian whaler Captain Melsom was appointed whaling manager and in 1951 he arranged the purchase of factory equipment and whale chasers. As in the case of many new whaling operations, Norwegian experience proved vital and Melsom engaged experienced crews and workmen. Whale Industries Ltd remained as a subsidiary company responsible for the catching and processing of whales. A five-year licence was obtained from the State and Commonwealth governments. The whalers were permitted to kill 500 humpback whales a year during the season, from 1 May to 31 October. Although the hunting area extended a radius of 240 km north, east and south of Tangalooma, it was initially never necessary to venture far, as the quota could be obtained from the migration routes close by.

Three whale chasers were purchased in Norway and these were manned by experienced Norwegians. *Kos VII*, *Kos I* and *Kos II* arrived at Tangalooma in May 1952 and on 6 June the first humpback was killed by Captain Melsom aboard *Kos VII*, 3.5 km north of the Cape Moreton lighthouse. Two days later all three whale chasers were at sea when they encountered a pod of 30 humpback whales. They killed eight 12.2 m whales and returned. On 7 July 1952 the hundredth humpback whale was killed. The whalers soon learnt the exigencies of whaling at Moreton Bay. Low tides delayed the landing of whales and sharks mauled carcasses left in the water while others were processed.

It was a successful season. The Tangalooma whalers easily filled their quota, plus an extra hundred granted to them when the Byron

*Onlookers watch as a humpback whale carcass is winched up the ramp to
the Tangalooma whaling station flensing deck in 1957.*
(Sven Hudin photograph)

Bay whaling station could not open in time for the season. The
whales, caught on the northern migration, were fat from the months
of feeding in the Antarctic. In this season the largest humpback then
killed in Australian waters was brought back to the factory. It was
15.8 m long. The last 100 whales were caught in little more than a
fortnight. The 124-day season closed on 7 October 1952. Products
sold overseas from this season's harvest realised nearly £400 000.

Most of the meal and dried solubles produced from the carcasses
of humpback whales killed in Australian waters was consumed
locally. The meal and solubles were used as a dietary additive for cattle,
poultry and pigs. The meat meal was used in Australia for stock and
poultry feed, the oil was exported and used in the manufacture of
margarine and edible oils, in the tanning trade, for tempering steel
and in the manufacture of nitroglycerine.

Seven hundred whales were caught in Tangalooma's second season. The quota for 1954, when the Byron Bay whaling station came into operation, was reduced to 500—Byron Bay received a quota of 120. Earlier that year, new factory equipment had been installed. Also in ˋ1954, after a chase of nearly 3 hours, men on *Kos II* caught a 20.4-m long blue whale. The capture caused great excitement among the men. It was then only the fifteenth blue whale killed in Australian waters. It also caused some embarrassment as it was found to be an illegal catch under the International Whaling Commission regulations for length.

In June 1954, the Sydney journalist Gavin Souter, then in his mid-twenties, was sent by the *Sydney Morning Herald* to report on the whaling station and its operation. The journalist came to the assignment full of excitement and anticipation. When he arrived at the picturesque location he was hit by the stench of a working whaling station. The atmosphere was like that of wet, long-enclosed fur—thick, muggy and cloying.

Undeterred, Souter went whale chasing next day on the powerful 243-ton vessel *Kos II*. At 8.50 a.m. the Norwegian seaman in the lookout spotted the spouts of two humpbacks, a male and a female, both about 13 m long. Captain Bredo Rimstad immediately gave chase. *Kos II* was a small vessel, not much larger than an oceangoing tug with a high bow on which was mounted a harpoon gun, usually angled down. Captain Rimstad, like many others who worked at Tangalooma, was a Norwegian who came from home to Queensland for the season. Their skills were well rewarded; Rimstad's fares were paid and he received £3500 for the three months. To sharpen the skills and productivity, bonuses were paid. In an echo of the shared payment of the sailing whaling days the men were paid partly by the number of whales harpooned and partly on production from the factory at Tangalooma.

The *Kos II* closed in to 20 m and Rimstad moved quickly to the gun platform and scanned the water for the whales which had sounded. The whales surfaced again, off to the left, 250 metres away. They dived again, this time moving towards the clear blue shallows where they could be seen by the crew. The chase continued for an hour and a half before Rimstad felt he was close enough to fire a harpoon into the side of the whale. A spurt of blood from the wound was followed by a muffled explosion that forced smoke from the wound, blowhole and mouth. The whale surged out of the water and began to swim in circles, tethered to the boat by the rope.

According to Souter, 'The harpooned whale broke water again, roared as it sucked in its last gulps of air, and died'. It was less than a minute after the explosion of the grenade. A winch began winding the carcass in closer to the *Kos II*. The accompanying male was nearby. He was killed instantly by another harpoon and grenade. Blood from the wounds quickly spread out into the sea, colouring it so red as to shock new whalers and passengers.

Spears were plunged into both carcasses and compressed air pumped into the bodies. The tail flukes were trimmed with a long flensing knife. At this stage, bronze whaler and white pointer sharks arrived, attracted by the blood flowing from the wounds. At first they circled the carcasses cautiously, then quickly rushed in and tore out a piece concentrating on the belly, lips and flippers. While shark attacks did not mean a total loss of the carcass, they were a loss of potential oil and meat and the whalers used a .303 rifle to deter the sharks. Rimstad ordered the *Kos II* to move on; sharks rarely attacked the carcass once the chaser was moving.

That day *Kos II* returned to Tangalooma with three carcasses; its sister ship *Kos VII* had taken two. Although the men could easily have killed more humpbacks, the factory could not process more. After leaving the whale carcasses near the ramp at Tangalooma, at 3.30 p.m., the men of *Kos II* sailed out into the channel to fish for schnapper.

The two whale carcasses were left in the shallows until it was time for them to be dragged up the concrete ramp. At 5 p.m. a steel cable was placed around the tail of one whale and the carcass dragged up the slipway. Water sprayers kept the slipway wet and reduced the friction as the great animal was dragged up to the concrete flensing deck below, on which were the large Kvaener and Huse cookers imported from Norway. The flensing deck was the size of several tennis courts.

As the whale carcass was slowly dragged up, Souter noted that the only sign of life were the feathery feelers of the barnacles on the whale skin, waving in vain as they sought sustenance from the passing air.

Two flensers set to work on the carcass, with long-handled and very sharp cutters. Chains were attached to the cut blubber which was winched off aided by the flensers who followed the stripped piece as it was torn from the carcass, cutting at the join of blubber and flesh occasionally to ease the strain on the winch. Blood spilled out onto the slipway. They started cutting the white belly, slicing quickly and easily through skin and blubber. When the belly was cut, the flensers moved to the back blubber, then the lower blubber and finally they removed the jaw and the top baleen plate. The carcass was turned over to cut away the remaining blubber, the lower baleen plate and the head. Then the ribs were separated and the backbone taken out.

A skilled pair of flensers with men working on chains and winches could finish their task in about half an hour to an hour depending on the size of the whale. Once finished, the lemmers moved in. These men had a good knowledge of whale anatomy and they carved the meat and cut out the organs of the whale. Bones, blubber and flippers were dropped through holes in the deck into cookers in which they were cooked for about four hours to produce the oil. Leftovers from the process were ground and cooked into meat meal.

As Souter watched the carcasses being flensed and butchered, others watched for their own reasons. A government inspector checked to see if the animal was over the size limit, or if it was a lactating female. Also watching were scientists or their representatives. These men were examining whales and slowly building a database of the anatomy, sizes and diseases of the humpback whale. In 1954 the CSIRO scientist Jack Robbins was at Tangalooma working on age, life span and maturity age of the humpback. He had looked at 800 whales since 1952.[3]

The quotas for Tangalooma and for Byron Bay remained unchanged until 1959, despite concerns from members of the scientific community that whaling was having a harmful impact on the populations of humpbacks. In 1959 world prices for whale oil began to fall. The Tangalooma quota was increased to 660 to try to offset this setback. This was achieved in only 65 days.

The 1960 season quota was again quickly filled, the whales caught and processed within two months. But the signs of an exhausted supply of whales began to show more clearly. The chaser captains had to search over a wider area for the whales and spend more time to fill a day's quota. Each chaser was now longer at sea, putting in two hours per day more than before.

Inevitably, the shock came. In Tangalooma in 1961 the whales were nearly gone due mainly to the effects of Soviet whaling. Despite spending twice the normal time at sea, the quota had not been filled. At season's end, 31 October, 591 whales had been taken. Now the whalers were searching from 35 km north-east of Maroochydore to Southport. They were as far as 152 km from Tangalooma and the towing chaser was now a necessity to pull carcasses into Tangalooma while the catchers sought more whales. A light aircraft was used to spot whales. As the stocks declined, captains were now obliged, in order to meet the defining commercial pressures of quotas, to kill every whale they could and the earlier caution, the earlier husbanding, was abandoned.

The significance of this season was realised. The board chose to purchase two more modern and fully equipped whale chasers. These arrived late in the 1962 season, and whaling again commenced on 18 June. However, the stocks of whales had been reduced more seriously than believed. Only 68 whales were caught by 5 August, 185 less than the same period in 1961. The economic reality forced Tangalooma to stop whaling and close down on 5 August 1962. (Byron Bay and Norfolk Island closed down soon afterwards.) Whale

Products Pty Ltd closed their Brisbane Office in Mary Street. The three newest whale vessels were quickly sold to other companies. The two remaining Kos vessels were eventually scuttled in Moreton Bay, where they remain as an interest site for scuba divers. Some of the factory equipment was sold off. On 21 June 1963 the remaining buildings were sold to a syndicate of Brisbane businessmen who converted them into a tourist resort which opened in December 1963.

For many years afterwards, whale skeletons lay in the gardens of the new resort and photographs of the whaling days adorned the walls of the bar. Until recently the rectangular concrete flensing deck was used as the resort tennis courts, the large holes through which blubber dropped into cookers were filled with concrete and the cookers area was a games room which included table tennis facilities.

Norfolk Island

Those Area V humpback whales that swim past New Zealand leave the islands and head north-east towards Norfolk Island and New Caledonia. Others may swim more directly north to the islands of Tonga and Vanuatu. The other main stream, which migrates along the east Australian coast, rounds Cape Byron and swims north-west towards the Great Barrier Reef and the breeding grounds.

Norfolk Island lies about 1450 km off the coast of eastern Australia. New Caledonia lies 450 km to the north, and 1100 km to the south-east is the northernmost tip of New Zealand. Most of the island's coastline is high rocky cliffs washed by surf. Many of the bays are difficult to reach by road, and anchorages are suitable only in fair winds. The main port is Sydney. The small but important humpback whaling industry was based at Cascade Bay, on the north of the island.

Norfolk Islanders were involved in whaling from the mid-nineteenth century. The methods of hand harpooning from small open boats and towing the carcass back to shore continued into the twentieth century. The whaling was perilous, arduous and scarcely profitable, and the industry periodically lapsed until it was finally abandoned in 1964. The prey was mainly humpback whales.

Captain James Cook landed on Norfolk Island on 10 October 1774. Arthur Phillip, governor of the newly established colony in Port Jackson was instructed to establish a settlement and on 29 February 1788 the first European settlers reached the island. After some initial problems with supplies and establishing a viable agriculture, a settlement was properly established. Many convicts were sent to Norfolk Island and after some trouble, including attempted rebellions, the island became known as a place of convict hardship and punishment. In 1803, orders were given by Lord Hobart (Secretary of State for Colonies) to abandon the settlement. Despite the reluctance of some settlers, by 1809 most had transferred to the new colony in Van Diemen's Land and by 1813 the island was totally abandoned. In 1825 a second wave of Europeans came to Norfolk Island. This time the convicts were second-offenders and Norfolk's reputation as a penal establishment was confirmed.

American whaling ships were operating in nearby seas in 1804 and possibly earlier. The numbers of whaling ships from many nations swelled as whalers came to the Pacific, and by the late 1840s over 600 American whaleships and others from ports in Britain, France and Australia were working in the Pacific Ocean. During the final convict period of Norfolk Island, the administration permitted contact only with supply vessels and vessels in distress. Whaling resupply was not permitted, as whaling captains often sought new crew and convicts no doubt saw a position on a whaling ship as a means of escape.

When the convict era finally came to an end in 1856, the remaining prisoners from Norfolk Island were transferred to Port Arthur in Tasmania. By then, Norfolk was widely known as a beautiful island sometimes described as a paradise, or as Scottish-born journalist David Burn noted in 1844, a 'terrestrial Eden'[4] but still tainted with the record of a brutal past. In 1856 Norfolk Island's entertaining history took another turn when Queen Victoria offered the island as a home to the descendants of the *Bounty* mutiny, who had outgrown the limited resources of Pitcairn Island.

The Pitcairn Islanders settled and with the visiting restrictions no longer in force, the new residents began resupplying whalers operating in the nearby seas, a business which grew over the following years. Some of the islanders joined the crews of whaling vessels and whaling became established on Norfolk Island. The Reverend George Nobbs, an Englishman who had settled on Pitcairn Island in 1828, moved to Norfolk Island with the other Pitcairn Islanders. By 1858, two years after the transfer from Pitcairn Island, Nobbs wrote: 'Our people are now busily engaged in killing humpback whales, and have succeeded in securing one hundred and twenty barrels of oil; but', he added, 'it is somewhat dangerous work'.[5]

Sir William Denison, Governor-General of New South Wales, visited Norfolk Island, then in his jurisdiction in 1857 and in 1859. Denison was anxious to promote the small settlement's economic development, and he was interested to see what he called a 'form of communism' among the Islanders, who collected and shared the many birds' eggs that could then be found on Norfolk. In his accounts of the visits, he also noted that in 1858, 33 men had joined together, formed a company and purchased two boats and whaling equipment from an American whaler. These men, Denison wrote, had 'gone energetically into the business of bay whaling, and had killed whales enough to furnish fourteen tons of oil, which at present prices may be worth nearly five hundred pounds'. These and other products were traded with whaling ships that brought supplies for the Islanders. There were other trades, as Denison noted: 'I found a keg of whisky had been purchased from an American whaler, of which many had par-taken so freely as to be very unwell, the captain having, for the interest of sobriety I suppose, abstracted half the whisky, and filled up the keg with sea water.' Perhaps more in hope than expectation Denison made a law prohibiting the introduction of wine or spirits into Norfolk Island.[6]

Whaling and resupply continued to provide some income for the

Islanders. Reverend Nobbs noted in 1859 that 120 barrels of oil had been secured in 1858. One hundred barrels were sent to Sydney and £240 realised. While this was a good price it barely covered the costs of new boats, lines and casks to be used in an expanded operation. Despite the financial difficulty, four boats were prepared and 24 men to work them readied for the next season. Thirty-five whaling ships arrived between 1857 and 1859. In 1859 Rev Nobbs made £50. He could, he wrote 'suffice' with this amount. But whaling captains were canny and wished to barter rather than part with cash.

Denison continued an active interest in the development of the small settlement and in 1859 wrote to Nobbs recommending that to achieve better results with oranges, the 'ground must be carefully prepared, must be trenched two feet deep, should be well manured with animal refuse every fourth or fifth year. The stuff from the boiling down of your whale blubber will answer admirably. By the by', he added, 'I hope that you will be wise enough to reserve, not only the refuse from the trypots, but the whole carcass of the whales for manure. Your land will pay you twice as well if you add this rich dressing to that which you can get from other sources.'[7]

Agriculture, whaling and resupply were the main economic activities throughout the 1860s. Manufactured goods, including tools and clothes, were traded from whalers in exchange for whaling oil, wool and vegetables. However the income dropped sharply when the American Civil War, fought between 1861 and 1865, drew American-based whaling ships away from the Pacific. In 1865, only £30 worth of produce was exported. A mission to train Melanesians in agricultural techniques was established in 1867. This provoked some unease among Pitcairn Islanders who were concerned at the new encroachment on their small island economy, but the change does not appear to have affected whaling. Returns show that for 1868, 300 barrels of oil were processed. Despite the potential, whaling was always a dangerous and financially risky occupation and in 1868 two boats were lost as Reverend Nobbs described in a letter to Admiral Moresby:

We have had an adventurous whaling season. About three hundred barrels [of oil] have been taken, or at least preserved; two boats destroyed entirely . . . and one crew of six persons were for three hours in the water, without the aid or knowledge of the other boats. The boat in question, Frederick Young's, was some three miles from the shore, and having imprudently fastened to a cow whale, no other boat being in sight, she very quietly turned the boat bottom up without staving a plank, and then went off some distance. The crew set about righting the boat, but of course could not free her of water; however, they got the oars lashed athwart, and though the gunwale was level with the sea, commenced paddling (each boat always carrying a set of paddles besides the oars) very comfortably towards the shore . . . about a league distant. The current was against them, and they did not make much progress, still they were gaining ground, when to their surprise they saw the wounded whale coming towards the boat. As soon as they were convinced the boat was the object which engaged her attention— she either supposing it to be her calf, which lay dead some miles distant, or actuated by a desire for vengeance—the crew lept overboard, and the irritated monster placed her head on the boat and then remained motionless for some time. Then she retired to a short distance, and the headman swam back and got a lance ready, determined to use it if the whale came again within reach. She did return and Young actually thrust the lance several times into her 'spout hole'. Feeling the smart, the whale settled down some fathoms, then came up swiftly and smashed the boat and oars to fragments.

There was now no alternative but to strike out for the land. One of the crew, an English sailor, could not swim, but two of our people bid him put an arm on each of their necks, and they would not leave him while life remained. The last time they saw the whale she was in a very weak state from loss of blood, but still remaining by the debris of the boat. And for now three long weary hours, did they exert their energies to the utmost; but, the current setting off, they had not gained more than a mile. The poor sailor was almost exhausted, and most began to think their ultimate safety doubtful. There was also a lad of sixteen, one of our own people, who was beginning to weary, so that the other two of the crew were obliged to keep by his side to encourage him. That which seemed to alarm the lad more was the presence of immense sharks, whose fins were continually coming in contact with his legs. At this time their perilous situation was unknown to the other boats, or to us on shore.

At length my son Fletcher, seeing nothing of Young's boat for several hours, left off chasing whales and went in quest of him. After a search of some time he concluded that the boat must have landed, and began to think of doing so himself, as what was technically called 'the chances' of the day were over. While rowing leisurely along the shore, about a mile from the land, Fletcher, who was standing up steering, fancied he heard something like a distant shouting or calling. Having mentioned this to the boat's crew, they ceased pulling, and surveyed the adjacent ridge, which came down nearly to the water's edge, thinking it might be someone desirous of telling them what direction the other boats were. But they could see no one. Presently they heard the same sounds again, and then after a short interval a third time.

Fletcher and his crew were now of the opinion that it was from seaward the voices proceeded. Having come to this conclusion, the boats head was turned in that direction, and 'Spring, boys there's help needed somewhere' was the prompt conclusion and they bent to the oars with a good will. After pulling nearly a mile, the steersman, who had perched himself on the gunwale of the boat, fancied he saw three black spots on the water, about the size and appearance of cocoa-nuts, and quickly assumed they were human heads.

Thinking these were all that were left of Young's crew, he became so affected that he sank down in the stern-sheets, and could not utter a word. This, of course, alarmed the boat's crew, but he speedily recovered himself, and simply said 'Pull boys; there they are, just ahead.' Soon they had the three on board, but they were actually afraid to ask what had become of the other three, fearing they were either drowned or eaten by sharks; but one of the escaped men said, 'Pull on; the others can't be far off,' and about half a mile farther on the others were happily met with, but in a most sad state: humanly speaking, another half an hour would have sealed their fate.

And now for ourselves, who were on shore. Many of us, both male and female, were assembled on the pier, looking at a young whale which had been killed the day before, when a boat appeared rounding the 'Windmill point'.

All eyes were directed towards her, and someone remarked, 'There are more than six people in that boat; some accident has happened'. Our faces blanched, and our hearts beat quick on hearing these remarks. A few moments' silence, and as the boat drew nearer, we attempted to count the number on board. Having no glass at hand, we could only perceive nine. Three are gone was the mournful conclusion; but whose husband, son or brother? I now ventured to ask, but with bated breath, 'Who's steering the boat?' 'Fletcher' was the prompt reply—the only son I had out that day. Did I feel relief? Wasn't it selfish? I can answer the first query, let causists decide the second.

After a little further scrutiny of the quickly approaching boat, a tenth person was discovered, and then the eleventh; they were seated among the rowers. At last the twelfth was discerned seated low in the stern, with his head resting on the gunwale. Yes, they were all there. But this last undoubtedly injured. Well, the pier was soon rounded, and as soon as they came within hail, 'Allright?' was our half hearted interrogatory. 'All right, thank God!' was the subdued but cheerful response. No one was hurt, and the man leaning on the side of the boat was the English sailor, still weakened and pallid; our people stuck by him, to the endangering of their own lives. What a picturesque appearance they exhibited; some with trowsers and no shirts, others with shirts and no trowsers, for the swimming party had divested themselves of all incumbrances, even to nudity, and those in the boat had shared their garments with them, which were not many, as the weather was intensely warm. However, here they were, all mercifully preserved. And I am sure all hands were unfeignedly thankful, for tears of joy plentifully bedewed the faces of all present.[8]

While it was uncommon, men died while whaling. During October 1877 two died; Jacob Christian as a result of a bad cut received while flensing and Isaac Christian from exposure after being in the sea all night.

Thomas Rossiter left an account of Isaac's death in his diary. On the evening of 30 October, a few whales were seen in Cascade Bay. Christian's boat pursued a whale and harpooned it, making fast soon after. However the crew did not return and a search boat went out, followed by another at about midnight. On the 31st Rossiter wrote:

Nothing heard or seen of Isaac's boat or crew this morning and three more boats are sent down. 12.15 pm News came that the boats were returning with signals set showing 'all right' and everybody felt immensely relieved but a little later the signal in the boats said 'something wrong' and great anxiety was felt. A boat soon came in bringing the sad news that Isaac was dead. Soon after fastening to the whale the calf stove the boat and she filled at once. They held up the waif [a small pennant] to signal for help but folks on shore said they were towing the whale. The poor fellows were in the water all night standing in the stoven boat. The night was very windy and [the] sea rugged. Six times the boat rolled completely over. They suffered much

Whale bones and boats lie on the stony beach at Cascades whaling station, Norfolk Island, 1920s. (Mitchell Library)

from cold and about 6 in the morning Isaac died from cramp. Gregory and Earnest were also very near death when Johnson and his crew found them from 8 to 10 miles off shore. Isaac was buried this afternoon deeply regretted by everybody.[9]

During the late 1860s and 1870s Islanders' whaling companies developed further. At the end of the season the proceeds from whaling were divided among families whose members worked in the industry. Joseph Campbell visited Norfolk in 1879. He commented on what he saw, noting that the population of just over 400, 250 of whom lived 'in town', depended upon whaling, stock and garden produce as their only sources of income. He described the organisation of the whaling industry, divided into two whaling companies, the N.I. with about 50 members and the I.J. with 30. Rules of chase had developed between the companies, the boats of the first company to see a blow had rights to that whale. Sometimes the others were invited to join in which case the shares of the oil were divided. Each company had a boiling down establishment at Kingston, and at the Cascades, on the other side of the island, was one large building used by both companies.[10]

Whaling continued in the two decades before the twentieth century, the small catch making significant contributions to the island economy. In 1882, the Islanders caught eighteen 'black whales' which yielded 70 tons of oil worth about £25 a ton. By 1894, whaling was the most lucrative industry on Norfolk Island, with whalers now organised into four companies. Each company earned about £2000 a year, an amount which returned £15 to each company member. By 1896, the population had risen to over 800, one-third of which was attached to the Melanesian Mission. The economy was still mainly agricultural, with the main exports being whale oil and whale bone, onions, potatoes, bananas and oranges. In 1900 the four whaling companies made satisfactory catches but whaling continued to take its toll. In 1902 Byron Adams was killed by a whale and Frank Bates Evans died in a whaling accident in 1908.

In 1913 Atlee Hunt, the Secretary for the Ministry for External Affairs in the young Commonwealth of Australia, visited Norfolk Island to report on local conditions. His report was comprehensive and he strongly recommended the stimulation of the whaling industry through the introduction of up-to-date methods, and the use of small government loans; however, the First World War (1914–18) interrupted whaling on the island and Hunt's recommendations to modernise the industry on Norfolk do not appear to have been comprehensively regarded. Whaling using traditional methods continued throughout the following years.

Norfolk Island's beauties attracted a small number of tourists and in 1923, school teacher J. Barnes visited the island. Then, the whaling season was four months, and began in early August, when the first humpbacks were seen. At the time of Barnes' visit, the whalers were still divided into companies. In a good season up to twenty whales

Norfolk Island whalers pose in their boats before a hunt in the 1920s.
(Mitchell Library)

were caught, in a bad season none. One whale yielded 5 or 6 tuns of oil at £30 a tun. A season of 10 whales was considered a good year.

The techniques used by the young men were those of the bay whalers. The boats, made on the island, were strong and well made, about 6 m long and wide in the middle. Each end was swept up to a sharp point making the line of the boat's rail a gentle curve. In the middle of the boat was a tub with about 230 m of coiled rope. When the harpoon was fast the line ran out of the tub, round the loggerhead at the stern, back past the whole length of the boat between the rowers and out through an eyelet at the stern. It was vital that the line ran clear when fast, as the least hitch would throw the whole boat's crew into the water.

Barnes persuaded the whalers to take him out, provided he did as he was told, an essential attribute for a visitor in a small whaling boat. 'Whaling' Barnes wrote in his account of the visit, 'is not child's play'. He was told to keep quiet, for the whales could hear the whalers, and to keep out of the way. Two boats, one to hunt, the other as a safety backup, left Cascades early one morning and soon after reaching the 'whaling grounds' the lookout saw a whale, about 2 km away. Using sail and oars the men got closer until about 50 m away. Then the steersman took up the harpoon and when the moment was right threw it into the whale. Another was thrown. Barnes was thrilled:

> The result was wonderful, the whale made off at a tremendous rate, and the boat flew through the water like an express train. The line ran out of the tub like wind but was checked by a half hitch round the loggerhead which only allowed it to surge out gradually and so we followed where the whale led at a pace that is inconceivable to those who have never experienced it.

After a ride of 3 km the whale tired and rose to the surface blowing 'with a roar like thunder'. As this happened the men would draw in the rope and coil it in the tub, bringing the boat closer to their prey. Again alerted to the men's presence, the whale dived again and when it rose the whalers repeated their efforts until close enough for the captain to throw his lance in an attempt to reach the whale's 'life' or the heart of the whale. It was a skilful procedure requiring knowledge and timing and on this occasion, was successful, as Barnes described:

> Ah! there it goes and like a flash the lance flew straight for the whale entering the mighty body about $1\frac{1}{2}$ yds [$1\frac{1}{2}$ m] behind the great flapper which was momentarily raised, only to fall on the water next instant with a crash like a rifle shot, the boat seemed to spring away from the great beast only to be sucked back by the backward swirl of the water. And now for the first time blood was drawn and we had proof that the keen weapon had been well placed, but not vitally, and the whale, who appeared to recognise the fact that the matter was assuming a serious aspect, redoubled his exertions to get away, diving deeply and making short darts in different directions and everywhere

In the 1920s, a Hotchkiss gun was examined for possible use for killing whales. (Mitchell Library)

leaving a trail of red in the swirling waters which were lashed to foam round the boat . . . The lance was again buried in the whale's body and again we sprang back out of reach of possible happenings. And this time the keen weapon had reached the 'life'. And the next time the whale rose to the surface to blow, clouds of blood were blown yards into the air further staining the already blood red water . . . which extended for an acre around the boat.

Imagine, if you can, a creature over 70 ft long wriggling like a sprat on a line and there you have an idea of the death throes of our whale. Rising almost perpendicularly out of the water & crashing down on his side he struck the blood red water alternately with head and tail and vast sheets of pinky red foam came flying from beneath the mighty blows which roared like cracks of thunder and created such a vortex as threatened to swamp our boat already half filled by the blinding, bloody spray.

A few moments later the whale died and the captain stepped out onto the body and roped the mouth shut as the dropping of the enormous lower jaw made the whale very hard to tow back to the factory. The men returned to shore, singing to make the work easier. At the beach the carcass was tied with ropes and the men in their boats, 'the scene of so much toil, hardship & danger with bared and bowed heads sang the Doxology as I have never heard it sung before'.

The next day the men would return to the rocky beach and process the carcass. Barnes concluded his account with some appropriate comments on the effect of modern whaling.

> Modern methods of whaling have been advocated by visitors and others but the islanders do not approve for various reasons, but their most important contention is that modern methods would, in a few years, so far decimate the numbers of the whales that the industry would automatically cease in these waters as it has done elsewhere, and this view is no doubt a correct and sound one to take, and the islanders are to be congratulated on their foresight and so the introduction of modern methods would have to be accompanied by laws to restrict the number of whales taken each season and so guard against the inevitable consequences.

Barnes commented that 1923 had been a poor season. In 1924, the four whales caught returned £400 and the oil took a year to sell. By 1927, the industry ceased. It was revived in 1936, and again halted during the Second World War.[11]

A resumption of whaling was planned in 1949 as the South Seas Whaling and Sharking Company was established to hunt for humpback, blue and sperm whales, using a 11-m chaser capable of speeds up to 30 knots. Assets and some equipment from previous whaling enterprises were acquired. The organisers, Mr and Mrs Pickard of Hamilton, New Zealand, were assisted by Captain Hassan, who supervised the erection of most of the buildings and the plant, including winches, petrol engines, choppers and cutters. A factory was set up at Ball's Bay. Prospects for the next season were good. The value of the whale to Norfolk Islanders was now about £500 a carcass, up £400 from the values of the late 1920s. Islanders and visitors were optimistic. Visiting journalist Vernon Wheatley concluded his article 'Norfolk island whaling is not for weaklings' with the comment, 'If the Company meets with the success it deserves, it will automatically have a bearing on the future economy of the island'.[12]

However, the venture collapsed. In October 1950 a disastrous fire—lit, one rumour noted, by Islanders unhappy about the influx of New Zealand capital to exploit whale stocks—destroyed the new boat, boat shed and buildings. In two seasons, only a few tons of oil were produced.[13]

Six years later, another group attempted to set up whaling based on Norfolk Island. In 1956, the Norfolk Island Whaling Company at Byron Bay, New South Wales, was established. While oil was seen as the most profitable product, meal for poultry or stock feed would be derived from the unused carcass which was dried and ground down. Other by-products foreseen by the administrators were vitamins from liver extracts, bone meal for fertiliser and glandular preparations. Whale steak was considered a possible source of food for humans and animals.

In the late 1950s the whaling season was May to October inclusive. The quota for Norfolk island was 150. There were other restrictions on the catch. As a calf left to fend for itself would usually die, no lactating females were to be killed. A season's quota in these productive years took perhaps half a season to fill. A season produced about 1000 tons of oil and as much meal as could be sold.

The Norfolk Island Whaling Company purchased a small oil tanker, the *Forso*, which was used to transport whale oil to Sydney and to return with fuel oil and petrol. Frozen whale steak was a separate venture. In 1958, the whaling seemed prosperous and the potential for other fishing seemed good. New jobs were provided for Norfolk Islanders. Captain Brett Hilder concluded positively 'A prosperous era seems at last to have arrived for their idyllic Norfolk Island'. However, there was a strong body of opinion against whaling. Hilder expressed his own feelings:

To the sensitive observer who is not a Shareholder in a whaling company, the killing of the world's largest and most harmless animals is very sad, but we need have no fear that the species will be killed right off, for when the total number of whales is reduced to half, the chase becomes uneconomical.[14]

Only a few years later it became obvious to all that something was drastically wrong with the population of humpback whales. The sudden decline in numbers appearing off the east coast of Australia and New Zealand was also observed off Norfolk Island. Whaling from Norfolk ceased in 1962 and it has not resumed. Although it is hard to get a full total of the humpback whale catch from Norfolk Island, scientist William Dawbin estimates that for the period 1956–62, 880 humpback whales were caught.[15]

It is not known exactly where the Norfolk Island whales move on to, but their probable destination is further north to the islands of Tonga and Fiji. Some may swim west and strike the Australian coastline before moving north along the coast to the sheltered waters of the Great Barrier Reef. In the warm and sheltered waters of these locations, the pregnant females give birth, males continue the fight for the right to mate with a receptive female. Others may remain in the area or wander, some swimming farther north to the northern parts of Fiji or to the northern limits of the Great Barrier Reef. On the western coast of Australia, the whales swim as far as the waters off the rugged and beautiful coast of the Kimberley to give birth to the light-skinned and dependent calves.

CHAPTER 6

The birthing and breeding grounds

Between June and October each year, the humpback whales gather in loose concentrations in the tropical seas off northern Australia. The boundaries of these regions are indistinct, but the seas and bays are relatively shallow and are often protected from the open sea. The water temperature is about 25°C and sometimes higher, a marked contrast to the temperatures in the feeding grounds. They are ideal locations in which to give birth and suckle defenceless calves. Calving generally occurs between July and August. Slightly later, between August and September, courtship and mating takes place. Off the north-west coast of Australia, the whales gather north of about 21°S, past the Monte Bello Islands and north along the stretch of coast which runs from Exmouth Gulf north-east to Broome and on to the islands off the coast of the Kimberley. Off north-east Australia, the breeding grounds are the protected waters of the central Great Barrier Reef which runs from near 22°S to about 15°S, with a probable concentration around the Whitsunday Islands. In smaller groups, the whales occur east across the Coral Sea, near New Caledonia, Tonga and slightly farther north to Fiji and Samoa. Courtship has been observed in these birthing grounds and farther south, near Point Cloates at 22°S and Hervey Bay at 25°S. Mating behaviour has been seen in both these localities and it seems that while birthing takes place further north, courting and mating extends south to at least 25°S.

The whales arrive at the breeding grounds progressively. The first to arrive are the immature whales closely followed by the cows with yearlings, the calves that have just completed their first full circuit of the migration. These calves are now about 8 m long, and they continue to feed from their mother's milk for a short while longer. While in the breeding grounds, as they approach $10\frac{1}{2}$ months, they will stop drinking the milk. The next main food they eat will be the krill, in the Antarctic. Weaning is probably a gradual process, the calf suckling less and less until it stops altogether. Later, they will join the pods of immature young. They remain in these groups for another three and a half years, when they will be sexually mature. As they have completed a full circuit of the migration, they will have experienced the range of oceanographic and coastal influences in their migratory routes, and their first lessons in behaviour and navigation will be complete. They have heard the songs of their group and have a rudimentary sense of belonging to a social, migrating population. Their pod relationships, first established in the firm bonds with their mothers, and broadened in the loose communal feeding in the Southern Ocean, will change further in this season as they move into another stage of their growth.

Next to arrive are the adult males and the non-pregnant females. The males, which may have begun their singing as they leave the Southern Ocean—certainly during the continental sections of the migration—are moving towards the peak of their season. In the months after their arrival at the breeding grounds they will compete with other males for the right to mate. The sexually mature males are at least 11 m and will be over four years old, the females 12 m and also over four years old. There is however more growth to complete, the males reach physical maturity at about 13.7 m, the females at 14 m.

Labour, birth and the newborn calf

The heavily pregnant cows are the last to arrive: their need to give birth in these waters is paramount. Sometimes the safety of these waters will not be reached and calves are born just south of the birthing grounds at places like Coffs Harbour and Byron Bay.

Although susceptible to attack by sharks and killer whales, calves may survive birth this far south. Occasionally calves are born farther south. In 1955, a newborn calf was seen off Albany in Western Australia. It may have survived the remaining leg of migration as it was seen swimming north a few days later.

Females carry their calves for 11 to 12 months. Sometimes they give birth in the presence of an escort, either a female, or a male waiting to mate. The birth begins when the amniotic fluid floods into the sea and, after a labour of 30 to 60 minutes, the calf emerges, tail first, and with the long pectoral fins folded forward. Very soon afterwards the umbilical cord is broken and a few hours later the placenta is expelled. Although the calf is born with its eyes open and with good hearing, it has to be assisted to the surface to take its first breath. At birth the calf weighs approximately 680 kg, and is from 4 to 6 m long. It has fine, hair-like down which shines silver or gold in the sun. Both calf and cow are exhausted and they remain at shallow depths resting and feeding.

Births are very rarely observed. However, in October 1994, scientist R. Paterson watched a probable birth from his observation post on Moreton Island, south-east Queensland. The cow was seen remaining stationary for a while before 'rising horizontally as if being inflated. Approximately ⅓ of its body was above the water and its head and flukes were visible.' It then 'subsided' and soon after a small grey coloured calf 3–4 m long appeared at its side close to the pectoral region. The pair then moved away.[1]

Soon after birth, the calf takes its first drink of rich, high-fat milk. The cow's nipples are two-thirds of the way along the body, on either side of the genital slit, near the stem of the tail. The mammary glands are within the body. In a lactating female of 14 metres they are 2 m long and half a metre wide at their broadest. The milk produced in these glands passes from ducts into a spacious central reservoir, and along to the nipple. The whale's milk is 40 to 50 per cent water, 35 to 50 per cent fat, 10 to 12 per cent protein, with lactose, salt and vitamins. Usually the calf holds the nipple between tongue and lower jaw, at the corner of the mouth near its eye. Unlike other mammals, the calf is unable to draw off milk by sucking, and it is expressed forcefully into the calf's mouth by the contraction of the cow's compressor muscles.

The calf consumes milk voraciously and it rapidly gains weight. At first it must breathe frequently and it feeds in short bursts between surfacing. Calves may nurse as many as 40 times a day, drinking litres of milk each session. Over the next few days, it consumes up to 40 kg of milk a day and may gain weight at the extraordinary rate of a kilogram an hour. Within a week the first indications of the black and white markings have emerged on its body.

During the first season, the bonds between cow and calf become strong. They remain within eyesight and touching distance of each other. Socialising the calf is a fundamental aspect of this relationship, which is maintained in part by the calf's dependence upon its mother for food, and by physical contact. Calves often swim just behind their mother's dorsal fin, or beneath her pectoral fins. The cow will use her pectoral fins to touch, and to 'caress' the calf. When necessary, she will protect the calf by extending her fin over its body. The mother will often stroke the underbelly of the calf and will sometimes tumble it off her upper jaw.

Humpbacks will forcefully defend and protect their calves. In 1953 helicopter pilot Jim Pekin was flying near Exmouth Gulf, north-west Australia, and watched as four or five killer whales attacked a small pod of two adult humpbacks and a calf. One adult kept the calf close while the other went for the killers, driving them off with powerful swipes of its tail flukes. A similar incident was observed in 1952, near Point Cloates. In neither case were the killer whales successful in their attacks.[2]

Mating

Mating is rarely observed but it is accompanied by a range of intense and physically demanding activities. Ovulation is stimulated by a number of factors, including hormonal activity as the animal reaches sexual maturity and external cues such as daylength. Humpback females ovulate once a year, although they may only reproduce every two to three years. A female in oestrus quickly attracts males that compete with others for the right to escort and mate. These active, competitive groups may remain together for a few hours but the groups break up as the stronger whales dominate. Females may mate after giving birth, those with yearlings just weaned will mate again.

In the mating regions, several males may chase a female and fight among themselves for the right to mate. Fights are aggressive and the noise of these conflicts is transmitted through the water to others and signifies the intensity of the ritual. During a fight, a male will attempt to hide himself or his mate by blowing air into the sea, creating a confusing screen of bubbles and noise. The immense tail is slapped onto the water as a warning. Males charge rivals, swimming just below the surface to create a bow wave with their broad heads. The physical contact is hard and they use their heads as a ram, often dragging their chins, encrusted with resident barnacles, across the skin of the opponent, drawing blood. The whales may dive and twist away from attacks, breaking the water in large and noisy splashes.

One observed behaviour is a synchronous and exuberant dance. Once thought to be a courtship ritual it is now believed to be another contest between rival males.

As this begins, the rivals position themselves, heads slightly tilted towards the surface. Together they swim upwards and powered by three or four mighty sweeps of their tails, break into the air in a tremendous surge, seawater streaming down the long pleats of the throat and from the flippers. At the peak of the breach their bodies may be almost clear of the water. They hang momentarily suspended— ready to fly—before toppling back or sideways and crashing into the water. The dance may include eight or more simultaneous breaches between two rivals, each a little less vigorous than before. It continues with the whales swimming side by side, on their backs with raised flippers, or side by side with one flipper each extended and slightly curved, in concert. The pair may swim in high-speed chases and indulge in tail slapping. As they lie together on their backs they will slap their fins on the surface of the water. The ritual may last for 30 minutes or more, an enchanting and complex pattern of communication.

Mating may occur after the fight to escort is won, or sometimes during a break in the conflict. Intercourse is brief and observations of mating are rare, but it seems that positions vary. The whales sometimes face each other, hanging vertically in the water using flippers to clasp each other, heads emerging to breathe. They hold this position for about 30 seconds and then submerge. Mating in a horizontal position may also occur. According to some reports, humpback whales may copulate belly to belly just as they emerge from the water at high speed. Some scientists reported that the animals mated a number of times within three hours.[3]

The song of the humpback

The competition for a mate may begin earlier, along the coastal migration routes and on the approach to the mating grounds as males begin singing during the journey north. Singing humpback males hang balanced in the sea, or move slowly, flippers held out away from the body. They may sing alone for long periods. The song, which is forcefully produced, is heard by many humpbacks within range, and it could be attractive to females. They may judge a 'better' suitor, based on breath capacity as demonstrated by the length and strength of the song. If so, it could be one explanation for the fact that each season, as one male changes his song, all males within the population change theirs to match.

Although humpback whales have a larynx, they have no vocal cords and most of the song sounds are produced from bursts of air shifting through sinuses and passages in the body. The frequency range of the song is wide, from 20 to 9000 Herz. It is forcefully produced, and has been measured at 100 to 110 decibels and even at 185 decibels.

The song sounds eerie, sometimes slow and tuneful to the human ear. Sailors have heard it through the wooden hulls of boats, and in the sea, when diving. Scientist Lyall Watson, studying humpbacks near Tonga, heard the song while under water. 'On one occasion', she wrote, 'we found ourselves surrounded by underwater leviathans that made the breeding lagoon thrum almost painfully despite the fact that there was not a whale in sight'.[4]

Analysts use musical terms to describe the song. Each unit of sound, or note, is arranged into a phrase. Each phrase is repeated several times before another is produced. This is then repeated and so on. Each sequence of repeated phrases is a theme. On average a song contains between five to eight themes, and each time the song is sung, the order of themes is the same.

Doug Cato, an Australian scientist working in the field of humpback song, published a set of tentative rules which govern the song pattern and sound character of the songs heard off eastern Australia. He classified song sounds, using terms such as moans, whistles, sighs, violins, squeals, gulps, chugs, chainsaw, yaps and chirps. Cato's and others' analysis has shown that the rules of composition are fundamentally the same with all humpbacks, but that each population works out particular variations. Researchers can determine where a song was produced by listening to it.[5]

Humpbacks sing along coastal migration routes and in the mating grounds. Some researchers, such as Jacques Cousteau, see the changing complexity of humpback whale song, and the fact that the songs are recognised and changed by other males of the stock, as evidence of a form of language. Others are not as sure and are not willing to see it as anything more than a stylised display. Whatever the motivation for the singing it remains as a regular, identifiable and unifying thread through the humpback's migration.

Whaling in Tonga

The islands of the small South-West Pacific nation of Tonga are divided by two narrow channels into three groups, Tonga, Ha'apai and Vava'u, the most southerly being Tonga. Most of the islands are coral or volcanic in origin.

Humpback whales are in Tongan seas from June and population numbers peak, including new calves, in September. They appear to congregate mostly but not exclusively near the Ha'apai group. Here in waters restricted and protected by reefs and narrow channels and which also accommodate dolphins, sperm whales, sharks and highly coloured fish, humpback whales rest, suckle calves and mate. Others move through the islands, swimming a little farther north or south on the first stages of the migration to the Southern Ocean. Most of the humpbacks caught by Tongan whalers were on their way south to the feeding grounds.

The Tongan reception of European sailors was mixed. Europeans first noted Tonga in May 1616, when the two high-pooped Dutch ships of Schouten and Jakob Lemaire landed at Niua-tobutabu. Navigator Abel Tasman arrived in the region in January 1643. He reportedly found a paradise of peaceful inhabitants and rich fields. Captain James Cook claimed the islands for Britain in 1773, naming them the Friendly Islands because of the welcoming reception he received when he landed. But in 1806, when the English privateer *Port-au-Prince* stopped at Ha'apai for repairs, the ship was captured and most of her crew killed. William Mariner, the son of one of the ship's owners was on board, and was spared. He stayed on Tonga for four years and an account of his experiences was published in 1817. The description of his experiences and of Tongan customs and beliefs was widely read. Mariner saw no Tongan whaling but noted that stranded sperm whales were sought after for their teeth and that when putrefaction was not spread throughout the stranded carcass, the meat of the whale was taken for food.[6]

Whaling near the Tongan breeding grounds began in the nineteenth century, as news of the availability of sperm and humpback whales spread. Humpback whales were hunted, although the oil from these whales was not as prized as that of sperm whales. United States based whaling crews took substantial numbers of humpbacks from the reefs to the north-west of New Caledonia from July to October and around Tonga from July to November.

The whalers brought their techniques to other Pacific islands and sometimes attempted to build and administer small shore stations at these bases. During the 1870s small stations operated on Aneityum in the New Hebrides, now Vanuatu. There was another station on Erromanga.

Whaling Captain Charles Scammon reported that the whaling season in Tonga was between August and September, adding that off 'Tongataboo . . . the females were usually large, yielding an average of forty barrels of oil, including the entrail fat, which amounted to about six barrels. The largest whale ever taken at this point, during the season of 1871, produced seventy-three barrels, and she was adjudged to be seventy-five feet in length. It is worthy of remark that a large majority of the whales resorting thither were white on the under side of the body and fins.'[7]

During the 1880s there was a humpback fishery off the Tongan islands. In 1886 a New Zealand whaler was based on the island of Nukupuli in the Ha'apai group and over the next two years took many barrels of humpback oil. About the same time, Albert Edward Cook, born in New Zealand in 1863, built a whaleboat, made harpoons and lances and took up a form of bay whaling, based at Ha'apai. At first Cook and his sons sold oil to passing ships. Later they began to trade in fresh meat with the Tongans. The Cook family continued whaling in Tonga until 1981.

In 1890 journalist Frank T. Bullen was fourth mate of the whaler *Splendid*. The men, who had been hunting sperm whale without success, decided to sail to Vava'u searching for humpback whales. The methods used by the men of the *Splendid* were similar to those used by the other nineteenth-century open sea whalers around the world. Bullen's account graphically—at times sensationally, in the tradition of whalers' tales—describes the chase, killing and butchering of humpback whales in Tongan waters.[8]

Bullen and his crewmates were experienced whalers and this

knowledge shaped their hunting techniques. They knew that the best time to chase cows was when they were near to giving birth, when they were less able to defend themselves: that gravid humpback cows sought out the shallow waters and sheltered bays in which to give birth. Experience had also taught them that the cows, which could destroy small whaling boats and endanger lives, would be aggressive if with a calf. To avoid this aggression, the whalers killed the mother first, which often died, according to Bullen, 'clutching the young one to her bosom with her huge pectoral fins'. The males were quicker to escape and the whalers rarely pursued them.[9]

Reaching Vava'u, the men of the *Splendid* found a sheltered bay and anchored. Each morning the boats, with a crew of six, made their way into the seas, looking for whales. A boat contained 300 fathoms (549 m) of line in two tubs, four harpoons and three lances, five oars and a large steering oar, a mast and sails, drinking water and biscuits, baler and a lantern.

The boats spread out in their search, the men rowing when the winds did not allow sailing. One day, while near the coast, they found a cow and calf in a narrow cove in cliffs.

Down came the mast and sails as if by magic, and in less than one minute we were paddling straight in for the cove. The water was smooth as a mirror, and the silence profound. A very few strokes, and the order was whispered 'stand up' to the harpooner. Louis rose, poising his iron, and almost immediately darted. The keen weapon was buried up to the socket in the broad, glistening side. 'Stern all' was shouted, and backwards we swiftly glided; but there was no need for retreat. Never a move did she make, save to convulsively clutch the calf to her side with one of her great wing-like flippers.

We carefully approached again, the harpooner and officer having changed places, and, incredible as it may seem, almost wedged the boat in between the whale and the rocks. No sheep could have more quietly submitted to slaughter than did this mighty monster, whose roll to one side would have crushed our boat to flinders [sic], and whose death-struggle, had it taken place as usual, must in so confined a corner, have drowned us all. Evidently fearful of injuring her calf she quietly died and gave no sign. Case-hardened blubber hunters as we were we felt deeply ashamed, our deed looked so like a cold-blooded murder. One merciful thrust of a lance ended the calf's misery, and rapidly cutting a hole through the two lips of our prize we buckled to our heavy task of towing it to the ship. We were soon joined by the other boats, but all combined made no great progress, and we had seven hours of heavy labour before we got the carcass home. Securing it alongside we went to a hard and well earned meal, and a good night's rest.[10]

The next day the crew cut in the blubber, surrounded by a growing crowd of Tongans anxious to get some of the meat. The carcass was cut adrift and the local people took it to the shore, where it was cut up and either cooked and eaten or taken away for future consumption.

During the following days the crew sought more whales. Not all humpbacks died quietly and the battle between whalers and prey was dangerous. On one occasion a harpooned whale:

. . . rolled swiftly over, raising his tremendous tail in the air, and delivered a diagonal blow that would have crushed in the side of the ship herself. It just reached the boat's bow, and chopped off about three feet of her as cleanly as with a huge scythe. The mate saw the blow descending, and immediately hove the line off the loggerhead in the stern round which it runs. In doing so he accidentally cast the bight over the after oarsman's neck with a half turn. Poor Peter snatched at it with both hands to free himself, but at that moment the whale plunged furiously downwards and our shipmate was snatched from our midst before we could realise what had happened . . . we never saw our shipmate or whale again.

The men repaired the boat and returned to the ship. Despite the 'great horror' that overwhelmed them, they resumed work the next day, 'for nothing is allowed to hinder whaling when fish are about'.[11]

Hard work was required to chase, kill and tow a whale back to the ship. However there were times on the calm sea when the searching became tedious. There were distractions, as Bullen recorded:

Sometimes as the boat glided gently through the lagoon-like passages, the whole crew, with the exception of the coxswain, would strip . . .

and take to the water like so many tritons and nereids attending the progress of some ancient sea-god. Or they would slip nooses of line over their shoulders, and be gently drawn through the limpid, tepid wavelets without effort and attended by every sensation of languorous bliss.[12]

On another occasion the crew of the whale boat, seeing no whales, explored a gorge between two cliffs through a small entrance. The cliff edges almost touched overhead and the sun that shone through the gaps illuminated the deep bottom. It was quiet and cool. The whispers of the men were amplified and thrown back at them from the gorge sides. A sudden blow from a humpback (described by Bullen as an 'awful, inexplicable roar') shattered the silence and scared the men. As the whale rose again beside the boat, the harpooner threw his harpoon into its back. 'A hideous uproar' followed as 'the big mammal seemed to have gone frantic with the pain of his wound, the surprise of the attack, and the hampering confinement in which he found himself. His tremendous struggles caused such a commotion that our position could only be compared to that of men shooting Niagra in a cylinder at night.'

Fortunately, someone cut the line, but the whale continued to thrash about in the small space until it was still. In the excitement no one had noticed that the tide had risen and that the small entrance was now covered. The men sat out the night half expecting the whale to arise again but increasingly convinced that it had died and sunk, or that it had swum out into the sea.

Bullen continues:

That being settled, we anchored the boat, and lit pipes, preparatory to passing as comfortable a night as might be under the circumstances, the only thing troubling me being the anxiety of the skipper on our behalf. Presently the blackness beneath was lit up by a wide band of phosphoric light, shed in the wake of no ordinary sized fish, probably an immense shark. Another and another followed in rapid succession, until the depths beneath were all ablaze with brilliant foot-wide ribands of green glare, dazzling to the eye and bewildering to the brain. Occasionally, a gentle splash or ripple alongside, or a smart tap on the bottom of the boat, warned us how thick the concourse was that had gathered below. Until that weariness which no terror is proof against set in, sleep was impossible, nor could we keep our anxious gaze from that glowing inferno beneath.[13]

The men were neither killed by sharks nor drowned, and when the tide dropped they rowed out of the narrow gorge and back to their vessel.

Despite the lack of early success, blamed by some on the 'unquiet spirit' of crewman Peter Lindhstrom, seven large whales were caught, producing 500 barrels of oil. The *Splendid* returned to port.

Tongan shore-based whaling continued sporadically throughout the twentieth century. In the 1930s Albert Cook handed over much of his whaling business to his sons Albert and Ned and the base moved to Tongatapu. Whale meat was popular and whale oil was used in lamps and for cooking. Cook's whalers experimented with a harpoon gun at this time and in 1937 caught 27 whales. However, that year the gun accidentally exploded, killing a whaler, and it was not used again.

Patricia Ledyard who stayed in Tonga for several years during the 1950s noted that while there was no whaling on the island of Vava'u, there was in Nuku'alofa a family which continued whaling. She wrote: 'The Nuku'alofa whales are butchered on the beach and the meat has a ready sale among the Tongans, but not among the Europeans who are driven away by the overwhelming smell which fills the whole town whenever the whalers come home with a catch.'[14]

In the 1950s and 1960s a crude form of bomb lance was used by some whalers in Tonga. Dynamite, introduced as an aid to excavation for building works, was quickly adapted to other purposes. A stick of the explosive with a slow fuse was attached to the spear and it was supposed to explode and kill the whale after it had been thrust into the animal's body. Some whales were killed in this way, but many were also injured and escaped with gaping wounds. The practice was dangerous to whalers. Scientist William Dawbin, in

Tonga to study whales, remarked, 'It is a great wonder that human mortality did not also increase'.[15]

In 1954 a preliminary report on a fisheries survey in Tonga reported briefly on the whaling then undertaken in the nearby waters. The whaling season was then August to September, as the humpbacks passed through the Tongan islands on their southward migration. The authors, Hon. Vaea, Inspector of Agriculture and W. Straatmans, Head of the Department of Agriculture, noted that the cows travelled with their calves, more slowly, and therefore separately to the males which also moved south in groups. The Tongan whalers avoided the male humpbacks and attacked the females with calves.[16]

William Dawbin works in Tonga

In the 1950s New Zealand based biologist William Dawbin travelled into the South-West Pacific in his research. Here he studied many forms of cetacea, and in particular worked on the movements of humpback whales. His trips to Tonga were remarkable for the long-term association he built with Kuki Cook, of the Cook whaling family. In order to obtain a better picture of the humpback migration patterns in the region, Dawbin placed small advertisements in magazines such as the *Pacific Islands Monthly*, requesting any details of sightings, and asked local sailors and fishermen to report sightings to him. He also worked with some tagging of the humpbacks.

Dawbin studied and photographed Cook's methods. Cook used two whale boats built in Tonga, but of New England design. One was for hunting and the other was a standby boat in case of accident, and to assist once the whale was caught. Cook used sails, centre-board and tiller rather than rowing to get close to the whale. He and his crew sailed right up to the whale, a practice requiring tremendous skill, before the sails were quickly dropped and centre-board raised while the harpooner struck.

Dawbin estimated that the Tongan catch was between 10 to 20 animals a year. While this does not appear to be a large number, it has to be recognised that calves and cows were taken, and that this was the third and possibly fourth time the humpback population had been attacked in the one migratory cycle. Later estimates of the whale catch include the possibility that as more whales were harpooned than finally killed the mortality rate might have been up to three times the 'hit rate'. All the meat and blubber was consumed locally. It was much relished for its flavour and reduced the need to import frozen or tinned red meat. When the crew caught a calf it would often be cut up and ready for sale and distribution by the time the boats reached the land.[17]

On 29 August 1957 Dawbin aboard the launch *Aliamoana* accompanied the Cooks on a regular whaling trip. He recorded the experience in his diary. At 7 a.m. they saw the first spouts of a humpback cow and calf. Dawbin transferred to a whale boat which began to track the whales.

> As we neared, the mother & calf started breaching & made a staggering sight with both in the air on occasion. They were cruising—not stationary & it took a lot of tacking to & fro to get up ahead & even then had to wait until they turned downwind. On turning they still didn't stop but Kuki set sail for top speed & we swept down on to them. All four lances were hurled but it was too late to get the harpoon fast & only two lances struck—enough to cause a great tail lash alongside as the whale sounded and vanished. Kuki just kept saying too late too late & all lances were wrapped again in tapa [cloth made from beaten tree bark] & stowed while we stood off back towards Aliamoana. The whaleboat was again taken in tow . . . [while we] resumed searching.

The whales were again sighted and the boats pursued them, men ready with the lances:

> Ben must have hurled the harpoon instantly after his lance as we were suddenly fast with line hissing down the centre of the boat with Kuki taking turns on the loggerhead & watching the big coils between his & my feet. It wasn't in a tub this time as the last big whale had taken it all out & wet it before getting away & the damp rope would no longer

coil in the tub. The sail was let down & furled at high speed while we shot along towed by the whale with water flying all over us & Kuki straining to let out the minimum of rope. The moment the whale started to surface again, all boys hauled frantically while Ben at the bow with a lance egged them on more & more excitedly as we gained & brought the boat into range for him to hurl the lance once more. Time and again this was repeated without much visible effect on the whale & Kuki in exasperation took another turn around the loggerhead to put the brakes on.

The rope was almost immovable & it creaked & the boat strained as the whale surged on & then dived with such taut line that the harpoon pulled out & it was again free & treavelling at high speed. Kuki signalled the Aliamoana to go & tow the standby boat over to help.

The whale was resighted and pursued:

We were soon near it, but its turns and antics made it impossible to get a chance of a further harpoon. The calf was still with it & finally the calf came head on towards us & as it passed Tom fastened with the harpoon. Kuki quickly played out a lot of slack, but even so we were spun around as it tightened with the whale going past in the opposite direction & we heeled over & took water until once more lined up in position behind. There was more hauling up & soon Tom had lanced the calf & it was dead at our bows with the wounded mother arching & circling around us continually. The boys cut the hole through fin and jaws by long handled spades wielded from the boat as it was hardly necessary to dive over for such a small catch. Lines were passed to the Aliamoana & they swung the calf tail first to tow behind. Meanwhile the mother had re-appeared so it was almost impossible to tell which was her.

Kuki thought she must have died & sank & we were already heading towards Malinoa on return watching the various spouts around when Kuki decided to cast off and have a closer look at a group of 3 not far off us. When near I could see two lance marks on one & knew we had again found the big mother but was baffled to see how Kuki could tack & pick her out of the group. However after more manoeuvres we again ran up with all 4 boys set with lances & Ben following immediately with harpoon to make fast. As they hurled I could see that it was indeed the same whale as we started with at 7 am . . . again we were fast & took off but with only 2 turns on the loggerhead this time & it was played more carefully . . . Ben & Bert resumed to finish off.

It started to roll so we backed off frantically & were just out of reach as it gave a last tired flurry on the surface & the flippers turned out. By this time it was after 3 pm . . . we were in the swell of the open sea with a gradually rising wind so the boys worked frantically, diving over to get the holes cut in the 2 jaws for passing through the lines with the surge they had to dive repeatedly & we all got on the rope to try to turn the whale somewhat as it was partly on its side & to bring the mouth closer to the surface. Finally lines could be passed to the launch & the whale was tied alongside about 4 pm. The calf was cut free & we saw a 12 ft shark approach & others joining as we started moving back towards Malinoa now in the distance—both whale boats also in tow with head wind & rising sea. Progress was slow & the launch & ropes were straining & the whale buffeting. As darkness fell we were still well off Malinoa & set Tom's boat to return home by sail. Next the head rope to the whale tore out & Kuki's boat swung over to it while he frantically called the launch to stop. It was an even harder job to get new holes cut & lines through in the half dark. Once completed I went on board the launch & we restarted.

Eventually, by 11.30 p.m. the whale had been dragged onto the beach and the cutting up began, a process which continued till past 4 a.m. when Dawbin 'called it a day'. He measured the whale at 46 ft (15.3 m), 'a really big one anywhere'.[18]

At the time Dawbin worked in Tonga with the whalers, there were some, like whaler Tom Cook, who began to notice a decline in numbers of humpbacks in the region. Although they were not widely circulated at the time, such personal observations were another warning of the impending crash in numbers of Area V humpbacks.[19]

Tongan whalers

The Tongan whalers were skilful hunters and stories of their exploits became widespread. One such tale is told of Totau. A popular whaler, Totau was about 40 years old in the early 1960s. During the 1958 season, he and others were based in the small island group of Ha'apai. One day the crew saw a large cow with calf. The men approached quietly and Fa'aui, the harpoonist, struck the cow with his first throw. While other crew members worked to get the boat closer to the animal, Totau took up the lance and attempted to kill it. He was not immediately successful, stabbing a lance many times into the cow's body before sensing that it had weakened.

Throughout the kill, the 10 m calf stayed near its mother, moving away and circling back. Totau took up another harpoon and threw it into the calf. He harpooned it again, and watched as the calf dived beneath the surface. Now attached to the calf by 22 metres of rope, Totau was dragged through the sea. When the calf dived, Totau held on, hoping that the whale did not sound deeper than the length of the rope. When the whale surfaced, Totau shortened the distance between the two, at times managing to push the harpoon farther into the whale. At one point in the chase, during a particularly deep dive, Totau let go of the rope, and swam in the direction he thought the calf would next surface. He caught the rope and remained with the calf until it died.[20]

The whale meat was used as a source of protein and every digestible part of the body, including skin, blubber, entrails and meat was consumed. Blubber was sometimes fried and eaten as a form of crackling. Humpback calf meat tasted like veal, better than that of older whales, and the first baby whale of the season was offered to the royal family. Even the bones were baked and eaten.

Teacher J. W. Taylor's account of whaling in the 1960s was published in the *Christchurch Star* of 1978. Taylor was one of many now concerned about the impact of whaling. The whale death he witnessed was long and hard, filled with a pain and fear that made him feel ill. He described the butchering: 'a long incision was made the full length of the spine. At right angles to this was a series of cuts about a metre apart, down through the black skin and white blubber to the flesh beneath.' The skin and blubber were then peeled back—'like rolls of turf on a lawn'—so that the underlying meat was accessible. The butchers now 'clambered about on the carcass and in the water, cutting off huge chunks and passing them to a waiting rowing boat'. The price for a chunk of meat was then four shillings. When the heart, liver and flesh were sold the remainder was left for those who could not afford to buy the best pieces. By nightfall all that remained was the skeleton, which by law had to be removed. It was floated out to sea and sunk. For days afterwards fish fed from small pieces of rotting flesh which sometimes floated back to the beach; fishermen caught sharks near the sunken skeleton.[21]

Taylor arrived in Tonga in 1962. In that year twelve whales were caught; the year before, sixteen. In 1963 five whales were taken, two in 1964. Tonga was not a member of the IWC and each year since the ban on killing humpbacks came into force, a small number of humpbacks had been taken. Local whalers continued an annual subsistence harvest of between five and fifteen whales. This catch returned valuable protein to the islanders and a good financial return to the whalers. The procedures and rituals of the catch and distribution strengthened cultural bonds within Tongan society. Whaling continued until 1977. Many whales were wounded but escaped, possibly to die. It was another factor in the sudden decline of whale numbers. However small, Tongan whaling was an influential attack on the breeding stocks of the humpback, then still considered as a vulnerable species. Tongan whalers chose the slower or weaker animals to kill. This method meant attacks on lactating females, or calves, those individuals most needed by a population struggling to survive.

A moratorium on whaling in Tonga

As numbers of humpbacks declined, population studies became increasingly important, both for whalers and for those interested in the survival of a species. Verifiable statistics concerning numbers of whales were presented to international bodies accompanied by emotional and scientific arguments concerning the desirability of protecting a species of whale. In 1979, the Government of Tonga imposed a two-year moratorium on all subsistence whaling. During this period of 'calm water'[22] the humpbacks would get a chance to stabilise their numbers and scientists an opportunity to count the remainder and begin observations on the rate of population growth of these whales.

Between July and October 1979, scientists M. Cawthorn, Ronald Keller and William Dawbin completed a preliminary survey of humpback whales in Tongan seas. The funds for the project came from a number of sources, including the New Zealand Government, and the World Wildlife Fund, now known as the Worldwide Fund for Nature. Keller determined that humpback numbers then were 'not significantly in excess of 300', 312 adults and fifteen calves, and that 'the ratio of calves to adults was disturbingly small . . . It took no great acuity to conclude that any resumption of whaling was out of the question.' Keller added that a 'minimum of five catches a year would be a major blow to the population, but one good year of fifteen kills, the bulk of them females and calves, could be disastrous'. Keller concluded that it would take 'considerably more than two years to assess whether the population was declining, stable, or growing'.[23]

The Tongan king was sympathetic to the preservation of whales despite opposition from whalers, and in December 1979, the Whaling Act that established the original moratorium was amended to require direct permission from the king for killing a single whale. Whaling was finally banned in Tonga in 1981. When Tongan whaling ceased, these Polynesians were among the last of the whalers using nineteenth-century whaling techniques. At this time there were eleven small whaling operations in Tongan waters involving about 176 people.

In his report to the World Wildlife Fund, published in March 1982, Keller outlined his reasons for supporting a continuation of a moratorium:

It is vital to distinguish between what we presently know about the humpback population in terms of absolute numbers and what we do not know in terms of what this number means for their future. The latter question—whether the population is declining, stable, or increasing—is by far the most important one; . . . In my view, a minimum of ten years would be required to discern a measurable change in the present population. Assuming that no harvesting takes place in the next decade, a count of whales in 1990 ought to be revealing as compared to the results of surveys taken in 1979 and 1980. If at that time the population is about the same, or even less, than the current estimate, that would be ominous. But if it is significantly higher, say by as many as 150 individuals, then we could be more assured of the group's recovery.[24]

A growing tourist industry which developed around the spectacular diving locations in the seas around Tonga has now added the equally spectacular and rarer opportunity for divers to swim with the humpback whales which return to the islands. Tourist numbers to these islands are growing and a new generation of Tongans is trained to assist the tourists see the humpback whales.

Humpbacks protected—1963

The slaughter of humpback whales officially ended in 1963. As the humpback whaling operations collapsed and as the IWC decision to ban whaling became known it was time to take stock and reflect. Despite the small numbers of whales that continued to be taken by Tongan whalers, it was believed by many that at last there would be a respite for the Area IV and V humpbacks. However, pirate whalers in the Southern Ocean continued operations throughout the 1960s and 1970s and more humpback whales were taken from these stocks, increasing the pressure on these two populations. Pirate whalers simply altered statistics and reports to the IWC. Although recently produced figures reveal the extent of the false reporting, the final figures of humpback whales killed in the two areas may never be known. Those statistics of the kill that have been calculated lie sober on the page. They do not reveal the pain and disruption caused to whale populations by this level of killing.

In 1965, Chittleborough published statistics for the humpback whale killings. From 1949–62, at least 18 180 humpbacks had been taken from Area IV stocks, those that migrate along the West

Australian coast. In addition to these, estimates indicate that many more were taken from this stock in the period of modern whaling. From 1936–38, at least 12 673 whales were taken in both the Southern Ocean and Western Australia. Others were taken by pirate whalers. And many thousands more could be added from the early seasons of 1912–16 and 1925–28. Such figures are staggering but they are made more so when compared to Chittleborough's 1965 estimate of Area IV stock size. He estimated that in 1934, the population was 12 000 to 16 000, in 1950, just before the final onslaught, 9400 and by the end of 1962 just 800 individuals, many of whom were immature.

The statistics for Area V reveal a similar story. The total from 1949–62 is at least 15 577 killed. Chittleborough estimated the population size in 1934 to be about 10 000. It was about the same in 1950, but by the end of 1962 it had dropped to an estimated 200. Not only did the catch numbers decline, but during the same period, 1949–62 the average length of whales caught also declined, a sure sign of a seriously depleted population.[25]

Severe as these statistics are, the devastating figures of Soviet pirate whaling add thousands to these tallies, from an overall total of 44 795 humpback whales. At present the tallies are not divided into areas, but many were taken from Area V humpbacks, particularly those which migrate past New Zealand.

Australian fisheries expert D. J. Gates, Project Officer in the Fisheries Branch of the Department of Agriculture, wrote in the *Fisheries Newsletter* for February 1963 that:

There is no doubt that the Antarctic catch in 1958–59 of 1796 humpbacks from the Group [Area] IV population accelerated the decline of this population. The illegal whaling in the Antarctic carried out by the Olympic Challenger is a further example of the problems facing the management of an international resource . . . the International Convention for the Regulation of Whaling 1946, aimed at establishing on an international level a management program which would conserve the world's whale populations. However, in this field of responsibility one can only conclude that the Convention failed.

[*199*]

Gates outlined a number of reasons for this failure. Two of the most important were the fact that nations that objected to IWC rulings could simply lodge such objection and not be bound by the determination, and the fundamental powerlessness of the commission to enforce its decisions. He concluded:

> The cessation of humpback whaling off the east coast of Australia and Norfolk Island in 1962 . . . is an example of the need for more effective control of the world's whale resources, of which, because of their habits, no country can claim sole ownership. Because of this lack of proprietary right, it is difficult to enforce proper management measures when the nationals of many countries seek to exploit these resources in different parts of the world.[26]

Management of the failed Tangalooma whaling company on Queensland's Moreton Island was equally critical. Directors had warned shareholders about the ineffectiveness of international control of whaling and the consequent over-exploitation of whale stocks in 1960. Secretary of Whale Industries Limited, R. Shannon, reported in the annual report of Whale Industries Limited for 1962:

> These excessive pressures on the stocks of humpback whales in the Antarctic first became apparent on the East coast of Australia in 1960 when the catch took 73 days compared with 63 days in the previous year . . . The matter [of declining stocks] was discussed with the Commonwealth Government and with the Commonwealth Scientific and Industrial Research Organisation. The scientific advice is to the effect that stocks have been reduced to a level that could sustain a total catch of between only 50 and 150 humpbacks in the Antarctic and all Australian, New Zealand and Island stations. A continuance of whaling at such a level would further postpone any regeneration of stocks. The advice was that even if whaling ceased completely in the areas mentioned, which is considered highly unlikely, the stock would not regenerate to a level to permit sustained catches of the order of 400 to 1000 per year in less than ten years; and possibly longer.

When the company was incorporated whale oil prices stood at £120 stg per ton. Early in 1962 prices had dropped to £60 stg per ton. In addition margarine manufacturers, long purchasers of whale oil for their product, had switched to other cheaper oils. Whaling was no longer profitable.[27]

Stan Nolan, inspector at Byron Bay, had his own views on the sudden decline in humpback whale numbers:

> Experts had determined that there were five definite areas in the Antarctic that the humpbacks occupied. Each area was separate and distinct. One of these fed the west coast of Australia, another fed the east coast. The other three areas fed the Pacific away from the Australian coast. It was in Australia's interests to know how the two relevant areas were whaled in the Antarctic during the annual international season. The overkill was done in the Antarctic. The whaling fleets that harvested them comprised many nations. They were equipped with the most sophisticated gear, spotter planes, sonic systems and the humpbacks suffered more slaughter than was presented to the International Convention. It was generally agreed that the humpbacks were being logged under other species to conceal they were being taken. The International Whaling Commission was a failure. Any international organisation is only as effective as its members allow it to be. The profit motive and international rivalry and suspicion would have to be eliminated before a successful conservation program could be effective. Modern techniques have made the capture of a whale a mere formality and any relaxation of the present ban in humpbacks would see their exit from the scene.[28]

Nolan hoped that humpbacks would never be harvested again.

Later, in the late 1970s, when Chittleborough wrote an account of Australian humpback whaling for an Inquiry by Sir Sydney Frost into Australian whaling, he again commented on the role of the Scientific Committee of the IWC. Although there were scientists concerned about whale conservation on the committee, he noted, the conservation movement did not have the momentum that it later achieved and other influences took effect. The issues of maximised profits, energetically argued by representatives from major whaling nations, dominated meetings of the IWC. Chittleborough pointed to other inadequacies in the management that led to the collapse of the humpback whale resource. There was insufficient knowledge about humpback whales to make accurate assessments of stock size and predictions about stock recovery. And even when the fact of stock depletion was known, there was 'an unwillingness of decision makers' including those within the IWC, to accept the seriousness of this decline.[29]

The returns to science from the modern period of humpback whaling were great, although many scientists were aware of the costs. Many whalers had cooperated with scientists and research had been carried out by officers of the CSIRO Division of Fisheries and Oceanography and scientists in New Zealand. Whaling inspectors located at each station contributed by collecting ear plugs and ovaries, by making observations such as the weight of testes and ovaries and by measuring whales as they came into the factory, although the measurements may have been erratic and in some cases deliberately falsified.

Many papers by prominent scientists such as Chittleborough and Dawbin in Australia, and Omura in Japan, together with the mass of details issued through the work of the Discovery Committee, had created a large and coherent body of information, which if at times contradictory or uncertain, was usually well researched and documented. Two major papers that were published, one each by Dawbin and Chittleborough, were almost a summing up of the modern whaling era knowledge of the Australasian humpbacks. Later, in 1996, Dawbin published another paper, the result of years of work on humpback migration.[30]

This work covered aspects of the anatomy, physiology, growth rates, feeding patterns and breeding cycles of the humpback whales. Significantly, it made public, in a coherent and verified manner, the patterns of humpback migration from Areas IV and V north to tropical seas. As these papers were published it became quite clear that two of the world's significant populations of humpback whales lived in distinct regions of the Southern Ocean, and that they migrated periodically and in a regular manner between feeding grounds and breeding grounds. The suppositions and 'fieldcraft' of whalers had been replaced by thorough, independent and careful work.

The image of the humpback whale presented by this body of information was of an intelligent, social mammal, with complex behaviours and a sophisticated, elegant and extensive migration. It was a picture of an animal that migrates through different oceanographic systems, and that possesses physiological and behavioural mechanisms to adapt to these environmental changes. The humpback whale had been pictured as a truly remarkable mammal.

These works, however significant, were not the end of scientific humpback research, but it was not until the 1970s and the gradual reappearance of the humpback whale populations that research, in different forms, and in an almost completely changed social context, was to regather momentum.

CHAPTER 7

The southerly migration

In late July or early August the southerly migration begins in the seas to the north of Tonga and the breeding grounds off the northern coasts of Western Australia and Queensland. In August, the first of the Australian Area V humpbacks move down the coast, leaving the protection of the Great Barrier Reef soon after latitude 22°S, and swimming towards the easternmost stretch of the Australian continent, the 400 km from Hervey Bay to Cape Byron. At 25°S the whales come to Hervey Bay. On the west coast of Australia they move south-west from the breeding grounds to the North West Cape, and Exmouth Gulf, where cows and calves may rest. Then they swim south. They follow the coast until they come to Shark Bay slightly south of 25°S. At Shark Bay and Hervey Bay, both sheltered and shallow bays at the ends of the continent, many of the humpbacks stay for a few days, some to rest, others to mate. From Tonga and Fiji, the route is not as well known. The whales swim south towards New Zealand, possibly following the relatively shallow waters along undersea landforms that extend to New Zealand. Those whales from the Coral Sea between the east coast of Australia and New Caledonia may follow the Lord Howe Rise and the Norfolk Island Ridge which extend south-east to New Zealand.

There are intriguing reports of humpback whales in tropical seas, near the Murray Islands, being seen between October and January. If accurate, it may be that not all humpback whales migrate south each year.[1]

The southerly migration may be difficult for the whales with depleted blubber reserves and which have not eaten for many months. Some will be weak and vulnerable, with a long journey to complete. Nursing mothers must produce large quantities of milk for their quickly growing calves. Active males have used precious energy reserves in fighting and mating, pregnant females in producing and nourishing a small foetus. The newborn calves are stronger and growing quickly on mother's milk.

While the whales are hungry, the diffuse pattern of the southerly migration suggests that factors other than hunger, such as daylight length, may stimulate the onset of migration. Humpbacks probably snack-feed in certain places along the migratory path. While this feeding is not the enormous and concentrated feeding of the whales in the Southern Ocean, it supplements the reserves for the southerly migration. There have been reports of humpbacks snack-feeding on small fish off Fraser Island and there is a considerable amount of plankton off Shark Bay. Farther south, the whales opportunistically feed in the waters off Eden and possibly Jervis Bay on the eastern coast of Australia, off Rottnest Island, Western Australia and in the Foveaux Straits, New Zealand. During October and November, humpbacks feed on coastal krill off south-eastern Tasmania. They may find food in other, as yet unidentified locations.

As with the northerly migration, the humpbacks return south in pulses according to sex and stage of reproductive cycle. There is a change in the migration timing for some, as the newly pregnant females, carrying young conceived in the tropical waters, are now the first to leave. These whales are followed about three days later by young males and females and the mature adults and resting females. Sometimes older females have been observed with groups of sub-adults. Approximately thirteen days later, the mature males begin swimming south. The mothers with calves have stayed the longest in the warmer waters, but they too must return and they begin their journey about nineteen days after the others. Of the returning whales, they are the ones which travel most slowly, often stopping to rest and play in sheltered bays, river mouths and harbours.

[*205*]

On their first migration the calves stay close to their mothers. Although they learn to swim soon after birth, they are not familiar with the sustained effort required to migrate south. Calves have been observed 'hitching' a ride near their mother's back. Here the small calves benefit from reduced drag on their bodies, induced by the effects of water flow across the mother's back.

The humpback whale is usually free from predators, but when sick, old or young it may be attacked by sharks or killer whales, sometimes also known as grampus. Attacks occur along the migratory path from the breeding grounds to the Southern Ocean. They have been observed and reported by whalers. Whaling Captain C. A. Larsen recalled, 'I saw grampus, the worst beast of prey among whales. It goes for the young humpbacks swimming with their mothers. I have often seen them attacked and killed in ten minutes. By the Sandwich group [islands near the Antarctic Peninsula], I have even seen the grampus kill a fin whale swimming in the whale-blood. The sea was full of pieces of blubber: the whole thing lasted half-an-hour.' Twofold Bay whaler Jim Davidson remembered how killer whales had trouble taking humpback whale calves from their mothers. 'They get underneath', he told William Dawbin in 1984, 'she'd carry it under her side fin and as soon as they came round her she'd roll over and they couldn't take it'.[2]

The killers may not kill the whale, and they have been observed swimming away from the victim before it dies, perhaps sated or sensing that the animal is crippled and that its carcass will sink and be available as food for the next few days. The humpback may survive or die. If mortally wounded, it will proceed slowly, exhausted and probably bleeding, its fins, tail and flippers scratched and torn. It becomes increasingly defenceless. When it dies the carcass will sink to the bottom of the sea and be eaten by sharks, fish and smaller bottom scavengers. As gases produced by the rotting body build up in the carcass, it will rise to the surface, and be eaten by seabirds, or sometimes wash ashore.

Not all attacks result in death or wounds. In July 1987, observers, including New South Wales National Parks and Wildlife marine mammal expert Dave Paton, in a boat 6 km east of Cape Byron watched as a small pod of killer whales attacked a pod of humpbacks. A large male killer and two other smaller killers swam past the boat and then swam quickly at an estimated speed of 20 knots at a group of humpback whales. The humpback whales unleashed an 'awesome display of power and violent upheavals', Paton recalled. 'The humpbacks, twice the size of the killer whales, closed ranks and thrashed the sea into huge water spouts.' The killer whales continued south and the humpbacks north. There was no blood shed.[3]

Hervey Bay and Shark Bay

Hervey Bay is a large (4000 km sq) horseshoe-shaped bay open to the north. Its boundary is the south-east Queensland coast which curves east, is broken by the Great Sandy Strait and then curves north again as the western side of the large sand island Fraser Island. The bay is shallow with a sand or mud floor less than 18 m from the surface. Close to the easternmost point of the continent, the bay is a catchment for many of the southbound humpbacks that come in to play, rest or court and mate. Dolphins frequent the calm, protected waters of the bay and are often seen 'playing' with the humpback whales. Thousands of dugong feed from the undersea grass meadows that grow on the bay floor.

The humpback whales are familiar with swimming in shallow waters and they have even been seen among sandbars, moving back into deeper waters as the tide turns. One story is told of a humpback crossing a very shallow sandbar with the incoming tide. It was on its belly, with both pectoral fins working forcefully until it had cleared itself into deeper water.

On the southern migration, the humpback whales enter and leave Hervey Bay from its northern mouth. Most whales spend a short time, usually only two to three days in the bay but individuals may stay longer. One whale was observed to be in the area for fourteen days. While in the bay the whales tend to keep to their pods, the size of which varies from mother and calf to three or more individuals. The small pods keep separate, about 6 km apart.

Many young males and females visit the bay, which appears to be a significant location for courting and mating. Here, males are often heard singing, and seen fighting and chasing females. Seeking to mate with cows accompanied by calves, the males may swim close to the mother–calf pods.

During August the population in the bay is mainly adults, then the juveniles arrive. The cows bring the four- to six-week-old calves into Hervey Bay from early to mid-September and numbers reach a peak in late September or early October. As the adults and juveniles leave, the bay is occupied during October by mothers and calves with a possible escort.

During the period from mid-September to October, when the nursing mothers visit the bay, the calves, now familiar with feeding routines and patterns, are quickly fattening. They drink up to 120 gallons of milk a day. Feeding usually takes place with the mother submerged in a horizontal position for approximately 8 minutes during which the calves surface for air four or five times. Older or heavier calves have more difficulty submerging and so are sometimes fed as the mother adopts a vertical position; the head down and tail flukes above the surface of the water allowing the calf easy access to her teats, which are just above the tail stem.

After a feed a calf may become playful and breach. While this is often interpreted as play, it also a form of training. The cow may complete a few breaches followed by its calf. The cow will also demonstrate pectoral slaps and tail slaps. These lessons are not confined to Hervey Bay and they continue along the migration path to the Southern Ocean.

Shark Bay, Western Australia is another area where the whales have been observed courting and mating in a sheltered region. Like Hervey Bay, it has an open mouth facing north. Although observations of whale behaviour in Shark Bay have not been as extensive as those in Hervey Bay, it is known that the humpbacks near Shark Bay rest here with their calves, before continuing the southerly migration.

Population recovery and new perspectives

After the cessation of whaling, the humpback whale migration continued in a small and fragmented manner. The populations were devastated. In some spots—such as Tory Channel and off Byron Bay, they were not noticed again until the late 1960s. Despite the disruption to migration, and the destruction of so many whales, the Australian humpback populations slowly began to recover, although humpbacks are rarely sighted around New Zealand.

Two main changes in attitudes to humpback whales accompanied the slow rise in population numbers. Scientists had not lost their interest in the humpback whale, but they were forced to change the method and approach to the study of the whales from the days of established shore stations with associated scientific personnel. The steady flow of anatomical information from humpback dissections stopped, but observations and assessments of populations and behaviour continued when and where possible.

In 1967, only a few years after the IWC protection of humpback whales, a remarkable discovery relating to the song of the hump-back whale was made off the islands of Bermuda. While listening to the sounds made by humpback whales, scientist and musician Roger Payne recognised the patterns and rhythms of 'singing'. He heard what he described as 'alien oratorios, cantatas and recitatives'. There were calves in the vicinity, and Payne knew that they were immersed in these songs and that the sounds were an important part of humpback social life. He later described the realisation as one of the most significant moments of his life. The experience changed the way Payne saw whales. He began to see them as 'something more than animals'.[4]

Payne and others worked further on whale song. It was recorded and the recordings quickly became very popular. The impact of these recordings was sometimes profound. A retired whale gunner, who had killed many humpbacks once declared to scientist Dawbin that had he heard the humpback whale song earlier, he'd never have 'fired a shot at a whale'.[5]

The other main change was the worldwide growth of the late-twentieth-century conservation movement. In the 1960s and early 1970s, concern for the environment and its destruction by over-zealous development led to the formation and regeneration of a number of organisations. Individuals within these organisations developed strategies and ideas to pursue what they saw as the protection of the earth's environments and its inhabitants. Their scope was broad and often diffuse but they focused on the whale as a rallying symbol. The failure of the International Whaling Commission throughout the 1950s and 1960s to live up to its charter as outlined in the International Whaling Convention stimulated these groups to push for greater access to the commission. In 1965, two years before Payne's initial work on humpback whale song, the World Wildlife Fund (WWF) now known as the Worldwide Fund for Nature, first gained observer status at commission meetings. Gradually the number of groups with observer status grew and while these people could not speak at meetings they had access to delegates during breaks. Popular sentiment reinforced these political moves. Statements and campaigns of people and groups were aimed at increasing public awareness of the need to adopt conservation values more seriously and communicating these desires to politicians. The surge in the appeal of all whales led to an increased awareness of humpback whales and their sad history. People along the coasts began to see more humpbacks as the population increased and as casual attention was drawn more to keep an eye out for the whales.

As this occurred, surveys from the air and coastal vantage points along the coasts of Australia began to reveal that humpback whale numbers were increasing.

Reports in the early 1970s of Area IV humpback whales seen between the Albrohos Islands and the West Australian coast were interpreted by scientists such as John Bannister in Perth as indications that the population might be recovering. From 1976 he and others participated in a series of aerial surveys which confirmed the presence of the whales and as the surveys progressed, the recovery of the population. From 1976 to 1994, a series of aerial surveys has confirmed that the annual growth rate is about 10 per cent.[6]

In 1981 a small team was established in Sydney to watch and listen for the songs of humpback whales. The team make-up reflected the development in whale research and change in popular attitude. Scientists like William Dawbin, and Doug Cato, now developing his expertise as a whale song expert with the assistance of the Australian Navy, were joined by scientists from the Australian Museum and members of the rapidly growing conservation movement: Friends of the Earth, Project Jonah and Greenpeace. The searchers looked for whales from the high coast at Copacabana, north of Sydney and in a small naval vessel. No traces were found, but the group had earlier recorded whale song off Stradbroke Island, Queensland, in association with members of a Queensland University team. Whales were seen at Port Macquarie, but only fleetingly.

Off the coasts of Queensland an aerial survey was conducted by staff of the Queensland University. Organised scientific shore-based viewing of the Australian Area V humpback migration began in 1978, when a lookout was set up on Point Lookout, North Stradbroke Island by Queensland-based scientists Robert and Patricia Paterson. From this vantage point, 67 m above sea level, the Patersons and their associates began to see evidence of the humpback recovery. Professor Michael Bryden of Sydney and others used both shore-based and aerial surveys to continue the analysis and have watched as the Area V population which passes along the eastern Australian coast is recovering at its most efficient rate.

The observations of Paterson and Bryden and others have revealed that the humpback whale stock of the east Australian Area V migration group has increased at about 11 per cent per annum. In 1992 it was estimated at between 1650 and 2150 individuals. 'By comparison', wrote Paterson, 'the stock size at the termination of whaling in 1962 could have been as low as 100'.[7] Unfortunately, the numbers of the population which returns to the beautiful waters of Tonga is not growing as rapidly as populations off the coasts of west and east Australia. The exact cause of this slow recovery is not completely known despite the concern and work of scientists in New Zealand and Australia. Scientists like those of the New Zealand-based South Pacific Humpback Project are particularly concerned with the growth of the Area V humpback population stream which migrates past New Zealand and on up to Tonga. In June 2000 the true impact of Soviet hunting was revealed at the meetings of the Scientific Committee of the International Whaling Commission and it appears that the impact on this population was far more devastating than previously thought. It will take much longer for this population to recover from such slaughter.

In 1978, the Australian Government finally ceased all whaling from the Australian continent. Its reasons for the decision were varied and included the simple political need to respond to the prevailing mood of the time; it was advantageous for a government to be moving with popular opinion on whaling. It was also clear that a continuation of whaling was uneconomic. An inquiry was held, which carefully examined all the issues relating to whaling, including those of whale stock destruction. The most telling example of this practice in Australian waters was that of the humpback whale and the author of the Review was the experienced and committed R. G. Chittleborough. His argument was clear and well researched. The humpback whale had been destroyed beyond commercial advantage. Knowledge of the failings of the twentieth-century exploitation of this species had contributed to the cessation of Australian whaling.[8]

Whale watching

Hervey Bay was one of the many places along the coast where people began to notice the increase in whale numbers. In 1987, local fishermen and boat operators informally discussed the possibility of whale watching in the bay. Until these friendly meetings, whales had been noticed and perceived more as a nuisance than an asset or object of veneration. In fact many professional fishermen saw the humpbacks as a hazard to navigation and a hindrance to their occupation.

On one occasion, the crew of the fishing charter vessel *Fraser Princess* had an interesting encounter with a humpback whale. Twenty-two passengers were in the boat off Arch Cliffs, when someone noticed what they first thought to be a log. As Eddie May, one of the first to establish whale watching tours in Hervey Bay later explained, it was a female humpback whale entangled in a shark net, her

massive pectoral fins tight against her body and a thick line around her head and tail, bending the whale like a banana, still breathing, but unable to move. We had no idea what to do in this situation, but knew, unless we tried something, the whale would die. After a few futile attempts to get hold of the line, using of all things a casting rod and a gaff, we drove the vessel against the whale and threw the reef anchor over its body. With the anchor-winch we pulled it back and were able to cut the rope. We then started on the head and bit by bit we began removing the net. When we freed the large pectoral fins and the whale stretched them, we expected her to become aggressive perhaps or at least try to swim away. But no, she stayed in one position, gently moving the big fins backwards and forwards as if to stretch her muscles. When we finally came to the last bit of net around her tail and drove the *Fraser Princess* hard into the fluke, she actually assisted by lifting her tail to create a slide, along which the anchor would be guided!

The rescue took one and a half hours. There were then no standard procedures for such rescues, but the crew radioed Air Sea Rescue, which passed a message on to the Queensland National Parks and Wildlife Service (QNWS). Their staff chartered an aircraft to check on the whale and found it with its calf, quietly swimming. Throughout the rescue the calf remained with its mother, but at a safe distance from the boat.

'Everyone on board had a tremendous feeling of satisfaction', continues May, 'but being typical fishermen, they demanded we give them extra time for fishing. Later we were told that this was the first time a full adult humpback whale was rescued from a net.'[9]

Hervey Bay boat operator Rex Bacon, owner of the *Crab*, and others discussed the possibility of whale watching tours in the bay. In early September 1987, Brian Penny was the first to advertise whale watching trips. His vessel the *Tasman Venture* was soon joined by the *Crab*, *Princess II*, the *Islander* and the *Fraser Princess* as whale watching vessels.

In 1989, the Hervey Bay Marine Park was established and official guidelines to whale watching were issued. By 1990, 21 commercial whale watching permits had been issued. In 1995, eighteen operators offered whale watching trips into the bay. Now sixteen vessels regularly operate in Hervey Bay.

Now many whale watching tour operators are experienced and reliable observers and their observations are adding to the general understanding of humpback whales. These observations are in the context of a relationship between whale watching vessels and humpback whales and as such may be unique. Operators claim that this relationship is changing, with whales becoming less fearful of the operators. For example, during 1992 operators reported a change in the defensive behaviour of a cow as she protected her calf. Previously, a cow would keep herself between a boat and her calf, often swimming between the two as if to cut the curious calf away from approaching the boat. This new 'relaxed behaviour' continued the next year. Now the whales will stay closer to the vessels for longer. Despite passenger complements of up to 60, humpbacks will remain within 2 m of the vessel for up to an hour often swimming under and around the vessel.[10]

The change in attitude towards whales is no more evident than in the following quote from tour operator Eddie May:

> There was one other element to whale watching that took me by surprise: The idea of taking people to see these majestic creatures seemed a great way of earning a living, perhaps a bit of exploitation,

but in a humane and sustainable manner. Little did I realise that whale watching for me gradually changed from just 'earning a crust' to something intangible, almost a passion. It is rather difficult to describe one's feeling. To take thousands of passengers out to see them enjoying themselves is very satisfying, but then other emotions take over. You learn to appreciate that we are in the whale's environment, not the other way around. You become more protective and tell people not to throw rubbish overboard. And you become annoyed, when you see, that not everybody behaves as you feel they should. You develop a respect for the animals first and then nature as a whole.[11]

Soon after 1988, Trish and Wally Franklin decided to establish the Oceania Foundation, a private research organisation that has as its aims the investigation of whales and dolphins, the development of a climate of concern and respect for marine environments and the provision of education about the sea and its creatures.

With the sailing vessel *Svaanen*, the Franklins take tourists out into Hervey Bay on whale watching trips. They also record the whales they see and assess the immediate environment through activities such as regular water temperature and density measurements. The Franklins make careful observations of the movements and behaviour of the whales, activities which no doubt ensure their success as tourist operators, but which also add important information to the growing body of knowledge about humpback whales in Hervey Bay.

Over the years of the Franklins' operation, they have begun to recognise and name individual whales which return to the bay. The constant watching and familiarisation has convinced the Franklins— as it has other tour operators in the bay, that the humpback whales are increasingly comfortable with the tourist boats and that the combination of natural curiosity and familiarity has engendered a sense of security within the population of whales. This security has enabled a closer examination of the whales and builds a relationship between whales and tourists that grows with each season. The Franklins are convinced that the new generation of humpback whales, which has no memory of the hunting over 30 years before, is learning that the many tourist vessels in Hervey Bay and along the coasts of Australasia are not harmful.

Humpback whales have come very close to the *Svaanen* without exhibiting signs of stress. The whales will stay for up to 40 minutes, swimming under the vessel, spyhopping, and simply by their presence, charming the enthusiastic whale watchers on board. Once, two whales, called Bonnie and Clyde by the Franklins, stayed by the vessel and played, or perhaps performed a dance. The two, a male and female, stood vertically in the water, circled and spyhopped and sank slowly down, pectoral fins slightly extended, into the sea before remerging. Sometimes they slowly tipped and turned as they 'stood' by the vessel. The 'dance' was filmed by Wally Franklin.[12]

A similar whale watching/research group, the Earthwatch Institute, operates off the coast of Western Australia. With the 12 m catamaran *Whalesong*, Curt and Michele-Nicole Jenner make valuable observations of the humpback whale breeding grounds in the islands off the rugged Kimberley coast. During five years from 1992–96 the team made 1086 humpback photoidentifications and compiled 'case histories' on 45 individual humpback whales.

The humpback whales are protected by whale watching guidelines, which regulate to avoid potential harm to the animals or pod. In Hervey Bay, for example, boats are not to approach within 100 m of a whale, and to remain farther away if more than one vessel is in the vicinity of the whale. Skippers of whale watching vessels cannot approach a whale head on, or separate a cow from its calf. They are to travel at less than 4 knots and immediately the whale shows signs of distress, to move away.

Some scientists argue that the growing tourist industry is disruptive to the migration and the crowding of whales in places like Hervey Bay stresses the whales. Not all captains of tourist vessels comply with the regulations regarding distance from animals and some will chase and harass a whale in order to give passengers a view of the animal. In 1998 the captain of one vessel chased a humpback whale along the shores of Moreton Island and then out to sea, despite the obvious distress of the whale. The whale was swimming away quickly, surfacing regularly and completing half charging breaches at the vessel, before it swam out to sea.

Whale watching has grown quickly and now most ports on the migration routes, particularly those ports with fishing fleets, will offer some form of whale watching excursion during the migration. In addition to Hervey Bay and Byron Bay important humpback whale watching centres are Eden, Whitsunday Islands, Moreton Island, Ningaloo Marine Park, Shark Bay and Rottnest Island.

Strandings

Whale strandings, particularly mass strandings, are widely reported and cause great concern among an interested public. Many theories, none of them confirmed, are used to explain why cetaceans strand. It may be that the whales have lost a sense of direction because of parasites in the brain affecting their sense of location. Many strandings are the result of illness and often the stranding is simply a carcass washed onto the beach. As they grow and migrate, humpback whales become familiar with the shallows of the beaches and the reefs, rips and currents which may lead them into dangerous situations on the coast. Compared to other species, humpback strandings are rare.

One theory, put forward by Dr Margaret Klinowska of Cambridge University, is based on the possibility that whales migrate and navigate using the earth's magnetic field. Each locality has a distinct 'pattern' of field, which the whales may learn to recognise and therefore judge a sense of location. There is a daily fluctuation in this magnetic field, which may also change at times due to solar activity or to localised geomagnetic anomalies. These changes may confuse the whale's sense of judgement and lead it ashore.

As whale strandings began to evoke an emotional and popular response, groups formed to take action once whales were reported stranded. Often, bystanders become involved in the first rescue attempts. Established groups, both private and government, sometimes clashed over priority and control of the rescue. Interest groups were both anxious to assist and to establish their credentials as effective organisations and in doing so, attract public confidence and media attention. As guidelines and responsibilities were developed the tensions were reduced and became more coordinated. Now guidelines for action at a stranding, particularly for those first there are widely distributed and are available in many of the whale watching guides recently published.

Generally, these advise people first on the scene at a stranding to notify police or wildlife authorities. Rescuers attempt to clear the blowhole of the whale; to orient the whale along the beach, away from breaking waves; to rinse the eyes and blowhole clear of sand, but to avoid pouring water into the blowhole when it is open. Using wet sheets and buckets, they keep the whales' skin wet. As any animal can be stressed in unfamiliar and threatening situations, guidelines advise keeping large crowds away, and maintaining calm in dealing with the stranded whale.

A stranding: Peregian Beach, Queensland

Peregian Beach, on the east coast of Australia, lies in the centre of an exposed 15 km long beach running almost directly north-south. At Peregian the beach and sea floor drop gradually towards the sea.

On 16 August 1991, a 10.1 m humpback, probably on its southern migration, was seen swimming close to the shore. It was a clear sunny day, about 12°C, with the water temperature 19°C. The sea conditions were mild, with a localised but powerful rip running north along this section of beach. Just after noon, the whale was hit by two or three waves and pushed inshore, after which it became stranded. It lay along the beach, about 30 m seaward of the high tide mark, washed by the fringe of the waves but firmly stuck on the sand. At this stage the whale was moving vigorously, attempting to free itself from the sand.

Soon after the humpback stranded, people tried to push it back towards the sea. They alerted the crew of the Westpac surf rescue helicopter who 'raised the alarm'. Overall responsibility for managing responses to strandings in this area lay with the Fisheries Branch of the Department of Primary Industry. In this case, Trevor Long, of Gold Coast marine centre Sea World, was delegated the responsibility for the rescue attempt. Early on Friday afternoon, Chris Warner of Underwater World arrived and assessed the situation. He saw that the whale had only minor injuries, the result of a cookie cutter shark attack. Meanwhile cotton sheets had been placed over the whale to protect its skin, and a line of people stretched to the water's edge bringing buckets of water to pour over the animal in order to keep its temperature constant. The whale was nicknamed 'Peregian'.

By this time a large group of onlookers had assembled to watch the rescue. Media crews arrived, ensuring that this rescue attempt would achieve widespread coverage. The crowd numbers swelled as people became aware of the rescue attempt and crowd control began to be a problem for local rescue organisers. Barricades were set up. Queensland State Emergency Service staff raised tents and set up lights for the night operations and communications.

As the tide fell, the whale became a little more trapped in the sand. The next high tide was due at midnight but it was decided not to attempt pushing the animal out to sea at night for fear of injuring rescuers. As the tide rose, volunteers stayed with Peregian ensuring that it was not washed further ashore.

On Saturday morning, members of another interest group, ORRCA (Organisation for the Rescue and Research of Cetaceans in Australia) arrived and discussed operations with rescue organisers. Tensions arising from diffuse political and procedural interests were put aside in the interests of the rescue, but they highlighted the issues involved when different private and public organisations become involved with such a rescue.

At this time, the whale was still upright in half a metre of water, facing north-east towards the sea. With the growing crowds of onlookers and others trying to help, Peregian may have been stressed. About twenty people tipped buckets of seawater over its body but in their enthusiasm to help, some seawater was accidentally washed into the blowhole. Noise from crowds and generators for electricity may also have stressed the whale slightly, but it appeared to be calm. Occasionally it would raise its tail flukes and bring them down again, not violently but firmly. Its eyes were seen to follow some of the action around it.

Some rain fell on Saturday night. It had stopped by morning although the weather was overcast. At about 10.30 a.m. a bobcat was driven onto the beach, and as the tide rose, began to excavate a channel in front of the whale. The local council donated another bobcat and two excavators. Rescuers built two parallel walls, reinforced with sand bags on each side of the channel which by now extended beside the whale. A breach in the southernmost wall enabled seawater to flow in and around the whale as the tide rose.

At this stage the scene was remarkable. A crowd of between 5000 and 7000 stood behind the barricades. A group of rescuers, some in wetsuits, were around the whale as the four large machines worked to dig the channel. Offshore, the 20 m vessel *Sea World I* was waiting to pull the whale off the beach. Emotions were high, and although many commented on the unifying spirit of the effort, others later remarked that the high level of emotion hindered the rescue planning. As the rescue work continued, scenes of the crowds and work were broadcast on Australian and international television.

As the high tide approached, a rope was attached to a triangular harness. Two loops of material were placed around Peregian's pectoral fins and the line passed out to the *Sea World I*. At 1 p.m., the point of high tide, the whale was dragged and pushed out into the sea. To a chorus of cheers and whistles from the wetsuit-clad rescuers, Peregian gained confidence, slipped itself out of the harness and swam farther out to sea. The whale was not seen afterwards and it is considered to have been a successful operation.

Despite tensions between organised groups and the possible stress communicated to the whale by large and often emotional crowds, the widespread support and cooperation were considered to have been an important part of the rescue. The community support and intense media interest was an indication of the concern aroused by strandings. The Peregian Beach whale rescue represents the remarkable change in attitude to whales that occurred in the last half of the twentieth century.[13]

South from Cape Byron

The Area V humpbacks of eastern Australia leave Hervey Bay and swim south, then south-west to go around Cape Byron, the easternmost point of the Australian continent. The headland is marked by a lighthouse and associated buildings, one of which now houses the staff and exhibitions of the Byron Bay Whale Centre. This beautiful cape is an ideal location to see the migrations of the humpback whale. In July 1993, the first of regular whale watching weekends was organised. Signs on the long spit of land now explain the migrations to interested observers and suggest that on quiet mornings with still seas an observer can hear whales blow as they swim past. Throughout the season, trained observers sit on the headland patiently watching for the blows of the humpbacks as they pass. They record, and where possible photograph the whales, in doing so helping to build an increasingly detailed picture of the humpback migration.

The non-profit cooperative Byron Bay Whale Centre, dedicated to whale research and public education, was established in 1995. In a statement which explains the modern almost romanticised perception of whales, the literature of the Whale Centre notes that whales 'are a powerful symbol of nature; saving them has become symbolic of the global co-operative effort to protect all life and our planet's ecology'.[14]

To the many people now aware of the humpback migrations, the pace appears leisurely, particularly for the cows with new calves. These small pods linger in bays and river mouths, the cows teaching their young about behaviours required and continuing to foster the close bond between cow and calf. The 'roving disposition' so aptly named over 100 years ago by the whaler Charles Scammon re-emerges in this lingering, to the excitement of people for whom the sight of a humpback whale and calf rolling and blowing just off the coast or resting in harbours and river mouths is a wonderful experience.

This pattern of searching or roving up rivers or harbours is well known to researchers. From time to time, it may also be an escape from predators. In August 1930, as the Sydney Harbour Bridge neared completion, a humpback whale was seen as far up Sydney Harbour as Circular Quay. It was first seen near Rose Bay and chased by a media boat from the *Sydney Morning Herald* and by whale boats from Messenger Bros whalers, then based at Rose Bay.

The report in the *Sydney Morning Herald* described the pursuit:

> The whale led them over towards Mosman, and, after some time, into
> Circular Quay. From Bennelong Point it made across the Quay towards
> Dawes Point, and passengers on ferry steamers obtained an excellent
> view of it. One of the Messengers attempted a shot with a hand
> harpoon, but the monster lashed round with its tail, and shattered
> portion of the superstructure of the launch in which the hunter was
> poised, nearly throwing him into the water.

Those aboard the 'Herald launch' were enjoying the humorous side of this incident when the whale suddenly rose underneath their own frail craft, lifting it perceptibly. They were no longer amused.

> Workers on the harbour bridge had a material advantage over those
> on the water, in that they were able to follow the course taken by
> the whale whilst it was under the water. Their attempts to direct the
> hunters, however were unsuccessful and shortly afterwards the whale
> again made down the harbour.

The whale was chased by about twelve launches, but after swimming around Wolloomooloo Bay, it made for Rose Bay, and when night fell it had returned to Watsons Bay and it probably left the harbour soon after. Fishery expert D. G. Stead was quoted as saying that the whale had probably come into the harbour to escape 'killers'.

It was an historic whale as the *Herald* journalist pointed out. 'It achieved the honour of being the first whale to pass under the Harbour Bridge.'[15]

Whale watching at Eden

The southerly migration continues on both sides of the Australian continent and along the islands of New Zealand. As the whales pass coastal towns, they attract interest from the growing numbers of small vessels, the owners of which, in this short season, have turned to whale watching as an occupation. Some centres are more active than others.

At Eden, Twofold Bay, the whale watching industry had become a positive income earner for the region. Each October a whale festival is held and many tourists come to see the different species of whale that frequent the region, and to learn about the long whaling history of Twofold Bay. The skeleton of Old Tom the famous killer whale attracts many visitors to the Whaling Museum. Commercial whale watching began in the late 1980s and as with the whale watching businesses of Hervey Bay, these have grown with the increased interest in whales and whaling history.

In 1989, Ros and Gordon Butt began a whale watching operation. Their vessel the *Cat Balou*, still leaves on its frequent trips out to see the humpback and other whales from Snug Cove, the site of Twofold Bay's first whaling operation. As Ros and Gordon Butt became more experienced with identifying whales and watching and interpreting their behaviour, they noticed what they considered could be feeding behaviour. Local fishermen confirmed their growing realisation that whales were regularly feeding in the rich seas off Twofold Bay and the Butts sent photographs of this behaviour to scientists. In 1995 Greg Kaufman of the whale research group Pacific Whale Foundation confirmed that the whales, including humpback whales, were feeding.

Kaufman and the Butts saw immediately the tourist potential of such a realisation, and the benefits for both ecotourism and the whales. Kaufman was quoted as saying:

> I think the whales are using Eden as a roadhouse, dropping in and topping up on their way to and from the Antarctic . . . Ecotourism is the boom industry of the 90s and I don't think anything epitomises that more than the marine mammals. This is a resource you can sell over and over again without damaging it, without depleting it or having to replenish it . . . You're sitting on a gold mine here and I don't think anyone realises it.[16]

Researchers from the Pacific Whale Foundation return each season to observe and assess the whales off Eden. Their presence and support for the local community and the whales reinforces the strong message of concern and protection developing within the small community.

On the other side of the continent, the humpback whale population may disperse south-west before reaching the south of Western Australia. Some pass Rottnest Island off the coast of Western Australia, near Perth. Here, another popular whale watching industry has grown since 1989. Humpbacks congregate here for a short while from September to late November or December each year. Using tail fluke photographs and information provided by whale watching boats since 1989, whale biologist Chris Burton has shown that individual animals may stay in the area for as long as a week before continuing south. Most sightings are of single animals or pairs. The peak of the southerly migration here is usually in October, with cows and calves moving past from late October.

By December, the majority of humpback whales participating in the southern migration have left the land masses of Australia and New Zealand, and have entered the last phase of their journey, to the Southern Ocean and the Antarctic ice. Here too they will be revered by the few shiploads of tourists that come to Areas IV and V. For the Antarctic tourist a sight of a whale in the Southern Ocean is a remarkable event, one that confirms both the promise of the tourist travel brochure and the continuing worldwide respect for the great whales. The humpbacks of Area V, seen more often off the Balleny Islands and sometimes in the Ross Sea, are a continual reminder of the history of slaughter and the current protection of the Southern Ocean Sanctuary.

Southern Ocean and sanctuary

As they swim south, the humpback whales pass through the temperature changes of the Antarctic Convergence. Soon they will meet the first ice of the season and with it the first plankton blooms and krill swarms, and they will begin feeding. While the threats of pollution, shipping and environmental changes remain, they will no longer be attacked by whalers. As the whales of Area V pass 40°S they enter the Southern Ocean whale sanctuary; those of Area IV are completely protected by sanctuary agreements.

The humpback whales are protected as a species, but since the formal announcement of their status by the International Whaling Commission, they have been protected by other instruments. Once they reach the Southern Ocean, they are within the boundaries of the Southern Ocean Sanctuary, a region declared as a whale sanctuary by the IWC in 1994.

In 1992, at the 44th meeting of the IWC, France proposed a Southern Ocean Whale Sanctuary bordering on the Indian Ocean Sanctuary established in 1979. The proposal was to establish a sanctuary of indefinite duration, with a review of its impact after ten years. The proposal received strong opposition from whaling states, particularly Japan, which hunted for minke whales in the region. After much discussion the sanctuary was finally established in 1994, at the Mexico meeting of the IWC. The sanctuary area surrounds Antarctica with a northern border that extends north to 40°S except between 20°E and 130°E, where it is 55°S—contiguous with the Indian Ocean Sanctuary—and between 130°W and 160°W, where it is 60°S—

contiguous with the boundary established under the Convention on the Conservation of Antarctic Marine Living Resources.

In this vast and grandest of sanctuaries all whales are now protected, including the seven species of great whale, which are still classed as vulnerable by the International Union for the Conservation of Nature (IUCN). Together, the Indian Ocean Sanctuary and the Southern Ocean Sanctuary cover about 50 million km sq of ocean. Although there are no mechanisms to enforce or police these sanctuaries, their existence, and the enormous worldwide opposition to killing whales, now crystallised around a moratorium on commercial killing imposed by the IWC in 1982, remain as substantial deterrents to the killing of whales in the region. The presence of these sanctuaries poses a political challenge to the commercial viability of continued whaling, but not a legal obstacle. Japan, for instance, has lodged an objection to the commission and continues to kill 400 minke whales ostensibly for scientific research.

A collection of other international and national agreements protects humpback whales and all other whales in the Southern Ocean and along national coastlines. Protective legislation in New Zealand and Australia also extends through the Exclusive Economic Zone to 200 nautical miles from those nations' coastlines and includes claimed areas of Antarctica. The International Whaling Commission has been instrumental in developing the sanctuary concept and its efforts are supported by non-government bodies such as Greenpeace. The coverage is now international, rather than confined to national waters. After centuries, effective regulations cover the whale's migratory journey. For whales, the tragedy of the commons no longer applies. Efforts to maintain and extend these agreements continue and in June 2000, the governments of Australia and New Zealand, supported by many small island states, lobbied unsuccessfully for a South Pacific Whale Sanctuary, to cover the breeding grounds of humpback and other species which spend summer in the Southern Ocean Sanctuary. Despite their setback at this meeting of the IWC, the governments and supporters will continue to lobby for such a sanctuary.

Two legal regimes are part of this collection of protective agreements. The ideals and effects of both match those of the Southern Ocean Sanctuary. First the 1991 Environmental Protection Protocol to the Antarctic Treaty (Madrid Protocol) ratified by all signatory nations including Japan, by 1998, commits signatories to the 'comprehensive protection' of the Antarctic environment and of 'dependent and associated marine ecosystems' (protocol Article 2). In effect this means the Southern Ocean marine ecosystem. Further, the protocol makes specific reference to avoiding 'further jeopardy to endangered or threatened species' (Article 3). The humpback remains an endangered species.

Secondly, the Convention on the Conservation of Antarctic Marine Living Resources (CCAMLR) is charged with limiting exploitation of fish, squid and krill so as to conserve the marine ecosystem as a whole, and this goal is compatible with permitting the stocks of great whales to regenerate.

There are problems with the enforcement of these regulations as the growing piracy which surrounds the fishing for Patagonian toothfish in the Southern Ocean illustrates. But the regulations remain as more than guidelines and they are actively supported by a growing number of people and institutions throughout the world. The greatest support for the humpback whales remains with the people. Current scientific work ensures that some critical attention is directed at the humpback whales of Areas IV and V and that this attention is a form of watching brief, a means of continuing the public gaze upon the recovery of a much hunted species.

Current scientific research

The scientific research on humpback whales concentrates on the wider ecological relationships of the whales and their environments, the composition and strength of populations, based on observations, DNA studies and the migratory routes as observed in Antarctica, New Zealand and Australia and in Tonga. Studies of whale song continue, as does research using results from other humpback whale populations such those off Hawaii. Ways of identifying individual whales within populations have been developed. Each humpback whale fluke is unique and a laborious but growing program of photoidentification, first established in the mid-1970s, is continuing. Tourists are encouraged to send prints of clearly identifiable flukes to the relevant state authority. DNA studies, based on the DNA recovered from small samples of skin taken from a whale, provide a unique record for each individual sampled in this way. The long hours of observation and data collection continue in breeding grounds and in selected locations along the migratory routes. All this research helps to build the modern picture of the humpback whale. Perhaps ironically, the recent work with DNA indicates more separate and distinct humpback whale populations than previously thought. It may be that these populations do not interbreed, despite intermingling. Much remains to be discovered about these evocative creatures.

The research is carried out by government money (as expressed in Australia through institutions such as the Western Australian Museum and the parks and wildlife bodies of various states), private resources, the work of people like Trish and Wally Franklin and private research institutes such as the Pacific Whale Foundation.

A new relationship

From 1963 to the end of the twentieth century, the Australasian humpback whales have begun the slow but consistent growth towards population viability. They are now protected along the full circuit of their journey, and in Australia, New Zealand and Tonga, their seasonal passage is anticipated and celebrated by thousands of people, who watch, observe and in many cases draw inspiration from the animals. Local guidelines and regulations have set limits on distance and approach to the whales as they migrate past populated areas. A unique relationship is developing between interested people and populations of humpback whales increasingly comfortable with the presence of fascinated onlookers. As people learn more about these animals and their history, they more fully appreciate the fragility of their natural world and its environments and the necessity for an increased understanding of the responsibilities of humans within this world.

Full circle

I n 1804, the French natural historian Bernard Germaine Lacépède wrote:

> Enticed by the riches that would come from vanquishing whales, man disturbed the peace of their vast wilderness, violated their haven, wiped out all those unable to steal away to the inaccessible wasteland of icy polar seas . . . and so, the giant of giants fell prey to his weaponry. Since man shall never change, only when they cease to exist shall these enormous species cease to be the victims of his self interest. They flee before him, but it is no use; man's resourcefulness transports him to the ends of the earth. Death is their only refuge now.[1]

Thankfully, Lacépède's pessimistic outlook on the future of whales, based on the realities of early nineteenth-century whaling as much as on a bleak view of human nature, is not yet fulfilled. People have changed to the extent that whaling is now closely monitored and continually challenged. Large oceanic regions of the world are whale sanctuaries.

The humpback whales of Australasia have been protected since 1963. After being hunted to the point of commercial extinction populations are slowly growing. In 1996, the estimates for humpback population for Area IV were published as being between 3000 and 4000, and Area V 1400 and 1900. With an annual growth rate of about ten per cent, the population size in the year 2000 for Area IV would be 4000–5000 and Area V, 2000–2500.

Importantly, public perception of these animals has changed dramatically. They have moved from being regarded as a creature which exists primarily as a commercial unit, albeit with scientific and aesthetic value, to that of a being with almost spiritual power. Now, humpbacks and other whales are a focus for tourism and images of the successful human contacts with whales are promoted as powerful enticements to travel to locations along the migration routes. As the yearly migrations of humpbacks proceed past populated places on the coasts of Australasia and South-West Pacific islands they attract increasing attention from a public fascinated by their strength, persistence and mystery, and revolted by the past exploitation of their commercial usefulness.

Experienced operators of whale watching enterprises encourage an understanding of humpback whale behaviour that continues to build the public perception of humpback whales and to foster the wider issues of concern for the earth's environments. These understandings are not purely scientific, but they are usually well informed and based on lengthy periods of careful observation.

Many whale watching locations exist in old whaling sites and stations. These are becoming new economic and cultural centres. In some ways modern whale watchers are the heirs of traditional coastal whalers. Their work ensures an economic livelihood for the people who live and work nearby, and it provides a flow of information and ideas into scientific networks and public opinion.

Whaling has not ceased, and as recent DNA testing has indicated, humpback whales are occasionally victims of the continued hunt. The commercial drive to pursue whaling is strong and in late 1999 Japan and Norway, both nations with long whaling traditions, united in renewing the push to continue whaling. More so than ever before, their arguments have to be supported by scientific assessments. This is a direct result of the scientific contribution to conservation arguments throughout the twentieth century. These nations pursue their prey in the certain knowledge that their activities will be constantly challenged.

Ironically, some of our most important knowledge of humpback whales is derived from the long and sometimes complex relationship between scientists and whalers, which has resulted in close friendships as well as animosities. The history of research into humpback whales and their migration through the seas of Australasia, Antarctica and the South-West Pacific has been one of commitment, exploitation and revelation. Although incomplete, the body of information about humpback whales is a testament to the methods and processes of most cetacean scientists. Sometimes flawed by insufficient background research or even poor communication, the gathering of information, often using the private funds of individuals and small businesses, is one of the two great achievements of the human relationship with *Megaptera novaeangliae*.

The other is the relative success of the conservation movement. The movement to protect whales is now both broad and effective. While it is sometimes divided in approach and political motive its members draw strength and support from the emotional fascination with these mammals and from carefully considered scientific research and argument developed over long periods.

The major threat to humpback whales and their habitats is no longer from whaling, but from environmental change. Pollution of the seas, and particularly of the coastal routes of the humpbacks, is a continual and growing threat to their holding to the traditional migratory routes and breeding grounds. Increased levels of ultraviolet radiation from holes in the ozone layer may affect whales, their food, their successful migrations and survival.

Global warming may seriously affect feeding patterns, if retreating ice shelves and warmer seas impact on the enormous stocks of krill still in the Southern Ocean. Krill fishing is still seen as a potentially successful commercial venture despite recent failures to commercially harvest krill by Russian ships.

Much about the Australasian and South-West Pacific humpback whale populations remains to be researched. Increasingly scientists are examining the relationships between whales and their environment as a means to understand more completely the whales' life cycle and behaviour. Migration routes and patterns have not been completely mapped and understood. It may be that the depletion of the stock so severely reduced numbers that migration patterns changed. How much has this reduction affected the intermingling of stocks around the world? What is the effect of the increasing whale watching industry, which like whaling before it, ranges from feeding to birthing grounds. Can the whale sanctuaries be completely secured against pirate whalers?

The optimistic view of the humpback whale's future is that the world's populations are reasonably safe, that their capture and exploitation is forever forbidden and that the animals are protected by a fabric of bans, regulations and sanctuaries. Supporting these is a worldwide body of opinion, held by people from many different backgrounds and with different perceptions of society and economic development. All abhor whaling as cruel and useless. The pessimistic view is that although humpback whale populations are increasing, the increased human pressures—of tourism and pollution and climatic change—still pose major threats to the humpbacks' environments and survival.

Since the 1990s an albino male humpback has been seen off the coasts of Queensland. It has been nicknamed Migaloo, an Aboriginal word meaning 'white one'. Gradually those tourists and researchers who have seen it have become fascinated by its colours. They tell of its luminescence as it swims just beneath the surface. Others say the whale glows in the water, still more disbelieve it until they see it for themselves. Migaloo has become another symbol in the long history of people's dreams of whales and their migrations.[2]

The migration of the humpback whale has for the moment become a safer and more protected journey, one that encompasses thousands of kilometres and, from a human perspective, one that continues a passage from ignorance to knowledge, affection and respect. As whales continue this passage across our collective mind, they reaffirm a growing view of humans living in a world of shifting and fragile ecological balances, where resources are shared with a multiplicity of species. All are dependent on a secure ecological place and the effects of human change.

Notes

1 People and whales

1 Father Bourzes, 'A letter from Father Bourzes to Father Estienne Souciet, concerning the luminous appearance observable in the wake of ships in the Indian Seas etc.', *Philosophical Transactions*, XXVIII, 1713, 231–234.

2 W. Denison, *Varieties of vice-regal life*, Longman, London, 1870, 1, 409.

3 A. van Leeuwenhoek, 'A letter from Mr Anton van Leeuwenhoek containing his observations upon the seminal vessels, muscular fibres and blood of whales', *Philosophical Transactions*, XXVII, 1711–1712, 439–446.

4 H. Hawkins & R. Cook, 'Whaling at Eden with some killer yarns', *Lone Hand*, July 1908, 272.

5 S. Nolan, Treatise on whaling at Byron Bay, ms in Byron Public Library, 17.

6 A. Delano, *A narrative of voyages and travels in the northern and southern hemispheres comprising three voyages round the world; together with a voyage of survey and discovery in the Pacific Ocean and Oriental islands*, the author, Boston, 1817.

7 O. Brierly, Whales and whaling notes, MLMSSA546, 20.

8 T. Melville, Journal of voyages on *Britannia* and *Speedy*, 1791–1793, DMSQ36, 229.

9 ibid.

10 'The voyage of Octher made to the northeast parts beyond Norway, reported by himselfe unto Alfred the famous king of England, about the yere 890' in *Voyages*, R. Hakluyt, Dent, London, 1, 1967, 56–59.

11 Rev. W. B. Clarke to Mrs Godfrey, 25 November 1841, MLMSS 139/3, 66.

12 Quoted in J. Kenny, *Bennelong; first notable Aboriginal: a report from original sources*, Royal Australian Historical Society, Sydney, 1973, 17–18.

13 J. Morgan, 'Words about whales', *The Australasian*, 3 January 1931, and draft interview with William Dawbin, Dawbin Papers, ML.

14 O. Brierly, Whales and whaling notes, MLA546, 26.

15 Retold in Olaf Ruhen, *Harpoon in my hand*, Angus & Robertson, Sydney, 1966, 61–63.

16 Quoted in E. J. Slijper, *Whales*, 2nd edn, revised by R. Harrison, Cornell, New York, 1979, 13.

17 H. Oldenburg, 'Epistle dedicatory', *Philosophical Transactions*, 1, 1665–1666.

18 'Of the new American whale-fishing about the Bermudas', *Philosophical Transactions*, 1, 1665–1666, 11.

19 A. van Leeuwenhoek, 'A letter from Mr Anton van Leeuwenhoek containing his observations upon the seminal vessels, muscular fibres and blood of whales', *Philosophical Transactions*, XXVII, 1711–1712, 339–440.

20 ibid., 441.

21 ibid., 443, 445.

22 P. Dudley, 'An essay on the natural history of whales', *Philosophical Transactions*, 387, 1725, 258.

23 J. Hunter, 'Observations on the structure and economy of whales', *Philosophical Transactions*, LXXVII, 1787, 307–308.

24 Quoted in Sydney Harmer, *History of whaling extracted from Proceedings of the Linnean Society of London*, Session 142, 1929–1930, London, 1931, 58.

25 O. Brierly, Whales and whaling, MLA546, 20.

26 O. Brierly, 'Whales and whaling', *Athenaeum*, no. 1762, 3 August 1861, 160; 'Whales and whaling', *Athenaeum*, no. 1767, 7 September, 1861, 321, 323.

27 J. E. Gray, 'On the Cetacea which have been observed in the seas surrounding the British Isles', *Proceedings of the Zoological Society of London for the Year 1864*, 195.

28 J. Hector, 'On the whales and dolphins of the New Zealand seas', *Transactions and Proceedings of New Zealand Institute*, 7, 1872, 155–170; 'Notes on New Zealand whales', *Transactions and Proceedings of the New Zealand Institute*, 7, 1874, 251–267; op. cit., 1872, 157.

29 R. C. Andrews, *Whale hunting with gun and camera*, Appleton, New York, 1916, 17.

30 ibid., 20–21.

31 ibid., 21.

32 R. Payne, The music of whales, *Promenades*, New York Philharmonic Orchestra, New York, 1970, 10.

2 The life of humpback whales

1 R. C. Andrews, 'A remarkable case of external hind limbs in a humpback whale', *American Museum Novitates*, no. 9, June 1921.

2 A. Carter, 'Humpback', *New Zealand Geographic*, 30 April–June 1996, 45;

R. Connor & D. Petersen, *The lives of whales and dolphins*, American Museum of Natural History, New York, 1994, 79; R. Paterson, 'Unusual humpback whale sightings at Cape Moreton', *Memoirs of the Queensland Museum*, 35, 1, 1994, 224.

3 Quoted in Carter, 'Humpback', 32.

4 E. J. Slijper, *Whales*, 2nd edn, revised by R. Harrison, Cornell, New York, 1979, 91; A. Murdoch, *Sheer grit*, The Blue Cow Press, Nelson Bay, 1999, 76–77.

5 W. Dawbin, 'Biological interests at a whaling station', *Tuatara*, 1, 3, September 1948, 19.

6 E. J. Slijper, *Whales*, 97.

7 ibid., 195; M. Bryden, H. Marsh & P. Shaughnessy, *Dugongs, whales, dolphins and seals: a guide to the sea mammals of Australasia*, Allen & Unwin, Sydney, 1998, 27.

8 Peter Gill to author.

9 C. Scammon, *Marine mammals of the north-west coast of North America*, Carmony and Putnam, San Francisco and New York, 1874, 42.

3   Preparing for the journey

1 H. Omura, *Biological study on humpback whales in the Antarctic whaling Areas IV and V*, Scientific Reports Whales Research Institute, Tokyo, no. 8, 1953, 94. There have been numerous sightings of humpback whales in the far south. For example, in early 1996, during a whale survey on the *Aurora Australis*, scientists Debbie Theile, Peter Gill and others saw many humpbacks between 80°E and 110°E, an area where krill is abundant (Area V). Eighty years earlier, James Davis on the *Aurora*, then part of the Australasian Antarctic Expedition, 1911–14, saw humpback whales on several occasions, some in the company of 'Finners' and 'Killers' in loose pack ice and, on another day, in seas with icebergs. In January 1937, men of the research vessel *William Scoresby* marked 265 humpback whales within Area IV, between 85°E and 98°E and between 60°S and 65°S. In February 1936, 107 humpback whales were marked between 87°E and 99°E and between 60°S and 68°S. There are reliable sightings at latitudes near 68°S, some as far south as the 'Bay of Whales', an ice bay in the Ross Ice Shelf.

2 J. G. Forster, *A voyage around the world in his Britannic Majesty's sloop Resolution . . .*, printed by B. White, London, 1777, 509.

3 J. C. Ross, *A voyage of discovery and research in the southern and Antarctic regions*, 1, Murray, London, 1847, 265, 266.

4 J. N. Tønnessen & A. O. Johnsen, *The history of modern whaling*, Hurst and Australian National University, London and Canberra, 1982, 150.

5   H. R. Heyburn, 'William Lamond Allardyce, 1881–1930: pioneer Antarctic conservationist', *Polar Record*, 20, 124, 1980, 41.

6   E. Racovitza, 'Cetacès', *Resultats du voyage S. Y. Belgica en 1896–9*, 1–142.

7   J. A. Mörch, 'Improvements in whaling methods', *Scientific American*, XCIX, 1, 1 August 1908, 75; 'Manufacture of whale products', *Scientific American*, supp. no. 1722, January 1909, 15–16.

8   J. A. Mörch, 'On the natural history of whalebone whales', *Proceedings of the Zoological Society of London*, paper 30, 1911, 668–669.

9   M. Hinton, *Report on papers left by the late Major G. E. H. Barrett-Hamilton relating to the whales of South Georgia*, Crown Agent for Colonies, London, 1925, prefatory note.

10 S. Risting, 'Knölhaven', *Norsk Fiskeritidende*, 11 Hefte, 1912, 437–439, in M. Hinton, *Report on papers*, 180–193.

11 D. Lillie, 'Cetacea', *British Antarctic Terra Nova Expedition. Natural History Report on Zoology*, 1, 3, 1915, 85–124; O. Olsen, 'Hvaler og hvalfangst I Sydafrika', *Bergen Museums Aarbok*, 5, 1914–1915; W. Kükenthal, 'Untersuchungen an Walen', *Jenaische Zeitshchshrift Naturwissen*, 51, 1914; Collet, *Norges Pattedyr*, Christiana, 1912.

12 M. Hinton, *Report on papers*, 187.

13 Professor Collett, in M. Hinton, *Report on papers*, 91.

14 M. Hinton, *Report on papers*, 185.

15 Reports of the Stipendiary Magistrate for South Georgia to Colonial Secretary, 20 May 1912, in M. Hinton, *Report on papers*, 64.

16 M. Hinton, *Report on papers*, 64.

17 Lt Strong, in M. Hinton, *Report on papers*, 66, 67.

18 G. E. H. Barrett-Hamilton, in Hinton, *Report on papers*, 64.

19 F. Hurley, Diary, 1 November 1914–1925, April 1917, MLMSS389/2, 5/11/14.

20 M. Hinton, *Report on papers*, 57.

21 C. Larsen to Committee, *Report of the Interdepartmental Committee on Research and Development in the Dependencies of the Falkland Islands*, HMSO, London, 1920, 94–95.

22 Salvesen to Committee, *Report of the Interdepartmental Committee*, 85.

23 Harmer to Committee, *Report of the Interdepartmental Committee*, 71.

24 British Admiralty, 116, piece 2386, Public Records Office 5913, 50.

25 ibid.

26 H. Ferguson, *Harpoon*, Cape, London, 1932, 58.

27 Quoted in A. Grenfell Price, *The winning of Australian Antarctica: Mawson's BANZARE Voyages 1929–1931*, Angus & Robertson, Sydney, 1962, 108.

28 F. Hurley, 'Whale hunting with bomb and wireless', *Walkabout*, 6, 8, 1 June 1940, 7–16.

29 *Monthly Summary of the League of Nations*, September 1931, 234–235.

30 ibid., 235.

31 League of Nations, *Convention for the Regulation of Whaling*, Série de Publications de la Société des Nations, II, Questions Economiques et Financiés, 1931.II.B.20, October 1931, 2.

32 *Monthly Summary of the League of Nations*, September 1931, 235.

33 'Off on a whaling quest: journey of the *Ulysses* to Antarctic revives the glamour of fictional Moby Dick', *The Polar Times*, October 1938, 4.

34 L. H. Matthews, 'The humpback whale, Megaptera Nodosa', *Discovery Report*, XVII, 1937, 7–92, 9.

35 ibid., 87

36 J. C. Murphy, 'Slaughter threatens the end of whales', *The Polar Times*, March 1940, 3.

37 W. Dakin, 'Antarctic whaling', *Australian Quarterly*, 19 September 1947, 13.

38 Å. Jonsgård, J. T. Ruud & P. Øynes of the Norwegian Institute for Whale Research, 'Is it desirable and justified to extend the open season for humpback whaling in the Antarctic?', *The Norwegian Whaling Gazette*, 4, 1957, 160–177. Arguments centred around perceptions of the speed of stock recovery.

39 Division of Fisheries, Commonwealth Scientific and Industrial Research Organisation, *Australian humpback whales in 1955: prepared for the Scientific Committee of the International Commission on whaling*, CSIRO, 1955.

40 A. Yablokov, 'Validity of whaling data', *Nature*, 367, 13 January 1994, 108.

41 Peter Gill to author, July 2000.

Year	Number of Soviet fleets	Humpbacks taken	Reported to IWC
1957–58	1	2235	60
1958–59	1	4039	420
1959–60	2	12 945	720
1960–61	3	12 529	302
1961–62	4	5507	270
1962–63	4	2925	263
1963–64	4	368	0
1964–65	4	940	0
1965–66	4	1830	0
1966–67	3	729	0
1967–68	3	748	0

4 The northerly migration

1 M. Klinowski, in Bryden, *Dugongs, whales, dolphins and seals*, 126–127.
2 S. Gerard, *Strait of adventure*, Reed, Dunedin, 1938, 92–97.
3 Quoted in H. Walder, 'Whaling in Cook Strait', *The Australian Rod and Gun*, August 1950, 13–16.
4 Quoted in D. Grady, *The Perano whalers of Cook Strait, 1911–1964*, Reed, Wellington, 1982, 151.
5 Numbers of humpback whales taken from the Cook Strait and nearby waters are as follows:

Date	Quantities
1911–27	541 (approx.)
1928–46	1311
1947–63	1845

6 W. Dawbin, in D. Grady, *The Perano whalers*, 116; W. Dawbin to author.
7 'Lonehander' [Frank Bullen], 'A whaler's memories', *Auckland Herald*, 19 May 1928; 'Old whaling days', *Auckland Herald*, 30 August 1933.
8 D. Fagan, in *World Wide Magazine*, quoted in R. C. Andrews, *Whale hunting with gun and camera*, 6–7.
9 G. Walker, 'The sport of netting whales', *Life*, 1 November 1910, 95.
10 D. Lillie, 'Cetacea', 1915.
11 *Sydney Gazette*, 15 August 1828, 2.
12 O. Brierly, Journal, August 1844, MLA534, 33.
13 ibid., 30–31.
14 J. Morgan, draft ms in Dawbin Papers, ML; J. McKenzie, *The Twofold Bay story*, Eden Killer Whale Museum and Historical Society, 1991, 4.
15 O. Brierly, Diary, 1844, MLA534, 85.
16 *Bega Standard*, 20 August 1895.
17 *Sydney Mail*, 7 January 1903.
18 A. Dorrington, 'An Australian whaling station', *Lone Hand*, June 1907, 147.
19 *Eden Magnet*, 8 November 1911.
20 D. Stead, 'Tom the killer, and his friends', *Sydney Morning Herald*, 4 September 1938; 'The killers: whale's deadliest enemy', *Sydney Morning Herald*, 19 August 1938.
21 Ms in Dawbin Papers, ML.
22 ibid.
23 J. Morgan, 'The last of the killers', *Australasian*, 11 September. The skeleton of Old Tom was preserved and is now a prize exhibit and attraction in the Eden Killer Whale Museum.
24 W. Dakin, *Whaleman adventures: the true story of whaling in Australian*

waters and other southern seas related thereto, from the days of sail to modern times, Angus & Robertson, Sydney, 1934, Appendix VI.

25 ibid., 184.

26 ibid., 193.

27 ibid., 196.

28 Western Australia, *Interim report of the Select Committee of the Legislative Assembly appointed to inquire into the whaling industry*, presented on 4 March 1915, Government Printer, Perth, 1915.

29 Quoted in M. Colwell, *Whaling around Australia*, Rigby, Adelaide, 1969, 139.

30 D. Mawson in Colwell, *Whaling around Australia*, 143.

31 W. Dampier, *The Voyages of Captain William Dampier*, ed. John Masefield, Richards, London, 1906, 430.

32 'They've got a £2 mil. harvest', *Argus Supplement*, 25 July 1925, 2.

33 P. L. Brown, *Australia's coast of coral and pearl*, Rigby, Adelaide, 1974, 21.

34 R. G. Chittleborough, *Shouldn't our grandchildren know? An environmental life story*, Fremantle Arts Centre Press, Fremantle, 1992, 41.

35 Brown, *Australia's coast of coral and pearl*, 32.

36 D. Gates, 'Value of whale products falls: a review of the 1963 season marked by the cessation of humpback whaling', *Fisheries Newsletter*, 23, 2, February 1964, 16.

5   North to warmer seas

1 S. Nolan, *Treatise on whaling at Byron Bay*, 19.

2 T. Welsby, *Sport and pastime in Moreton Bay*, Simpson & Halligan, Brisbane, 1931.

3 G. Souter, 'Keen gunnery wins whales off our east coast', *Sydney Morning Herald*, 19 June 1954, 2; 'Whalers' kitchen is now complex industrial plant', *Sydney Morning Herald*, 22 June 1954, 2; G. Souter to author.

4 D. Burn, Norfolk Island Diary, MLB190-2, 27 December 1844, 115.

5 Nobbs, in J. Lewis-Hughes, *Whales! Launch the boats*, the author, Sydney, 1992, 4.

6 W. Denison, *Varieties of vice-regal life*, 421.

7 ibid., 420.

8 Rev. G. Nobbs to Admiral Moresby, 11 December 1868, in J. Lewis-Hughes, *Whales! Launch the boats*, 16–18.

9 Thomas Rossiter, Diary, 1877–1878, MLMSS3162, 30 October 1877.

10 J. Campbell, *Norfolk Island and its inhabitants*, Sydney, 1879, 96.

11 D. Barnes, Norfolk Island, MLB747, Chapter XI, 58–70.

12 V. Wheatley, 'Norfolk Island whaling is not for weaklings', *Pacific Islands Monthly*, 51, October 1949, 58.
13 B. Hilder, 'Whaling at Norfolk Island', *Walkabout*, 1 September 1958, 11.
14 ibid., 13.
15 W. Dawbin, 'Whaling and its impact on the people of the South Pacific', in P. Stanbury & L. Bushell (eds), *South Pacific Islands*, Macleay Museum, Sydney, 1984, 86.

6 The birthing and breeding grounds

1 R. Paterson, 'Unusual whale sightings at Cape Moreton', *Memoirs of the Queensland Museum*, 35, 1, June 1994, 224.
2 R. G. Chittleborough, 'Aerial observations on the humpback whale Megaptera Nodosa, with notes on other species', *Australian Journal of Marine and Freshwater Research*, 4, 2, November 1953, 225–226.
3 E. J. Slijper, *Whales*, 352; F. D. Ommaney, *Lost Leviathians*, Hutchison, London, 1971, 238.
4 L. Watson, in J. Costeau, *Whales*, trans. I. Mark Paris, Allen, London, 1988, 237.
5 D. Cato, 'Songs of the humpback whales: the Australian perspective', *Memoirs of the Queensland Museum*, 30, 2, July 1991, 284, 287.
6 W. Mariner, *An account of the natives of the Tonga Islands . . .* arranged by J. Martin, Murray, London, 1817, 311.
7 C. Scammon, *Marine mammals of the north-west coast of North America*, Carmony and Putnam, San Francisco and New York, 1874, 43.
8 F. Bullen published two versions of the Tongan whaling: 'Humpbacking in the Friendly Islands', *Colonial Good Words*, 189?, and *Cruise of the Cachalot*, Smith, Elder, London, 1898.
9 Bullen, *Colonial Good Words*, 628
10 ibid., 629.
11 ibid., 630.
12 ibid., 630.
13 Bullen, *Cruise of the Cachalot*, 262–265.
14 P. Ledyard, *Tonga: a tale of the Friendly Islands*, Appleton-Century-Crofts, New York, 1956, 146.
15 W. Dawbin, 'Whaling and its impact on the people of the South Pacific', in P. Stanbury & L. Bushell (eds), *South Pacific Islands*, Macleay Museum, Sydney, 1984, 88.
16 H. Vea & W. Straatmans, 'Preliminary report on a fisheries survey in Tonga', *The Journal of the Polynesian Society*, 63, 3–4, September–December 1954, 209.
17 W. Dawbin, *Whaling and its impact*, 88; W. Dawbin, Diary, 27 August 1957, ML.

18 W. Dawbin, Diary, 27 August 1957, ML.

19 R. Keller, *Report on the preliminary survey of humpback whales in Tongan waters July–October 1979*, International Whaling Commission, report 31, 1981, 205.

20 Described in O. Ruhen, *Harpoon in my hand*, 53–60.

21 J. Taylor, 'Whaling with the Tongans', *Christchurch Star*, 24 July 1979, 21.

22 R. Keller, 'Tonga and its whales', *WWF Monthly Report*, March 1982, Project 1485, 82.

23 ibid., 82, 84.

24 ibid., 82.

25 Figures quoted by D. Chapman, Status of Antarctic rorqual stocks, in *The whale problem: a status report*, W. Schevill (ed.), Harvard University Press, Cambridge Mass., 1974, 228. In the light of recently released statistics on the 'pirate' whaling of Soviet fleets, these figures are indicative only and require further revision.

26 D. Gates, 'Australian whaling since the war', *Fisheries Newsletter*, February 1963, 22–23.

27 Whale Industries Limited Annual Report, 1963, 2–3.

28 S. Nolan, *Treatise on whaling at Byron Bay*, 17.

29 R. G. Chittleborough, 'Australian humpback whaling', in *Whales and whaling*, Report of the independent inquiry conducted by the Hon. Sir Sydney Frost, Australian Government Publishing Service, Canberra, 1978, 1, Appendix 12, 276–287.

30 R. G. Chittleborough, 'Dynamics of two populations of the humpback whale, *Megaptera novaeangliae*, (Borowski)', *Australian Journal of Marine Freshwater Research*, 16, 1965, 33–128; W. Dawbin, 'The seasonal migratory cycle of humpback whales' in K. S. Norris (ed.), *Whales, dolphins and porpoises*, University of California Press, Berkely and Los Angeles, 1966, 145–170; W. Dawbin, 'Temporal segregation of humpback whales during migration in southern hemisphere waters', *Memoirs of the Queensland Museum*, 42, 1, June 1997, 105–138.

7   The southerly migration

1 M. Simmons & H. Marsh, 'Sightings of humpback whales in Great Barrier Reef waters', unpublished report, 12.

2 C. Larsen to Committee, *Report of the Interdepartmental Committee on Research and Development*, 1920, 94; J. Davidson to W. Dawbin, Dawbin Papers, ML.

3 *Byron Shire Echo*, 8 August 1997.

4 R. Payne, *In the company of whales* (video), Auckland, TVNZ Enterprises, 1992.

5 R. Eckersley, 'Scientists wait to hear the lost songs of the humpback whale', *Sydney Morning Herald* newsclipping, Dawbin Papers, ML; Peter Gill to author.

6 J. Bannister, *Western Australian humpback and right whales: an increasing success story*, Western Australian Museum, Perth, 1994, 23.

7 R. Paterson, P. Paterson & D. Cato, 'The status of humpback whales *Megaptera novaeangliae* in east Australia thirty years after whaling', *Biological Conservation*, 70, 1994, 141.

8 R. G. Chittleborough, 'Australian humpback whaling', in *Whales and whaling*, Report of the independent inquiry conducted by the Hon. Sir Sydney Frost, Australian Government Publishing Service, Canberra, 1978, Appendix 12, 276–287.

9 E. May, *We come in peace: humpback whales in Hervey Bay*, Eddie May, Hervey Bay, Qld, 1994, 35–36.

10 ibid., 18

11 ibid., 37; E. May to author.

12 D. McDonald (Dir.), *Angels of the sea* (video), Planet Earth Corporation, Sydney, 1999.

13 B. Fulton, *Humpback whale rescue: detailed stranding report*, Organisation for the Rescue and Research of Cetaceans in Australia, (ORRCA), Sydney, 14 October 1991; *Encounters with whales* (video), Ross Isaacs/Ocean Planet Images, Brisbane, 1992.

14 Ethics statement, Byron Bay Whale Research Centre, 1996(?).

15 'Big whale in Sydney Harbour', *Sydney Morning Herald*, 13 August 1930.

16 *Eden Magnet*, 5 October 1995, 12.

Full circle

1 Lacépède in J. Costeau, *Whales*, 13.

2 D. Paget, 'Seduced by the beauty of a migrating whale', *Sunday Telegraph*, 16 July 2000, 48.

Further reading

T here are many books and articles that provide information about humpback whales and other species of cetacean. The more recent or useful ones are listed here and within the endnotes.

J. L. Bannister, *Western Australian humpback and right whales: an increasing success story*, Western Australian Museum, Perth, 1994

J. L. Bannister, C. M. Kemper & R. M. Warnecke, *The action plan for Australian cetaceans*, Australian Nature Conservation Agency, Canberra, September 1996

M. Bryden, H. Marsh & P. Shaughnessy, *Dugongs, whales, dolphins and seals: a guide to the sea mammals of Australasia*, Allen & Unwin, Sydney, 1998

M. Cawardine, E. Hoyt, R. Fordyce & P. Gill, *Whales, dolphins and porpoises*, Reader's Digest, Sydney, 1998

J. Costeau, *Whales*, trans. I. Mark Paris, Allen, London, 1988

P. Gill & C. Burke, *Whale watching in Australian and New Zealand waters*, Australian Geographic, Sydney, 1999

G. Kaufman, B. Lagerquist, P. Forestell & M. Osmond, *Humpback whales of Australia*, Queensland Department of Environment and Heritage, Brisbane, 1993

J. N. Tønnessen & A. O. Johnsen, *The history of modern whaling*, Hurst and Australian National University, London and Canberra, 1982

Index

Index

[249]

DATE DUE

HIGHSMITH #45231